Power and Purpose

Power and Purpose

PAUL RAMSEY
and Contemporary Christian Political Theology

Adam Edward Hollowell

WILLIAM B. EERDMANS PUBLISHING COMPANY
GRAND RAPIDS, MICHIGAN / CAMBRIDGE, U.K.

Published 2015 by
Wm. B. Eerdmans Publishing Co.
2140 Oak Industrial Drive N.E., Grand Rapids, Michigan 49505 /
P.O. Box 163, Cambridge CB3 9PU U.K.

Printed in the United States of America

21 20 19 18 17 16 15 7 6 5 4 3 2 1

Library of Congress Cataloging-in-Publication Data

Hollowell, Adam Edward, 1981-
Power and purpose: Paul Ramsey and contemporary Christian political theology /
Adam Edward Hollowell.
pages cm
ISBN 978-0-8028-7188-6 (pbk.: alk. paper)
1. Ramsey, Paul. 2. Political theology.
3. Christianity and politics. I. Title.

BV4827.R36H65 2015
241'.62092 — dc23

2014032509

www.eerdmans.com

For Peggy, Vernon, Nita, and Al,
who lived with power and purpose

Contents

Acknowledgments

This project began nearly a decade ago as a doctoral dissertation in the School of Divinity at the University of Edinburgh. It would be difficult to overstate my debts to my dissertation supervisor, Oliver O'Donovan, for his gracious and patient instruction. It was an honor to learn from him. Michael Northcott and David Fergusson provided wisdom and encouragement throughout my research, and William Werpehowski offered invaluable criticism as my external examiner. Conversations with friends in Rainy Hall shaped my thinking during those years, especially Matthew Arbo, Graham Chernoff, Anderson Jeremiah, Chris Johnson, Chris Keith, Jon Lo, Elspeth Noble, Andrew and Jenny O'Neill, Chris Orton, Lydia Schumacher, Todd Stockdale, Andrew Tinker, and Blair Wilgus.

I visited the Duke University Graduate Program in Religion in spring 2008 and worked my way through the Paul Ramsey Papers. I am indebted to the staff of the Rubenstein Rare Book and Manuscript Library at Duke University, particularly Eleanor Mills and Zach Elder, for their patience and kindness. Stanley Hauerwas was characteristically generous as he helped me see the connections between Ramsey's work and his own. He is also responsible for putting me to work for Carole Baker, and they have both become treasured friends. Allen Verhey showed me what it means to be a charitable reader. His life set an unparalleled example for anyone who hopes to embrace both faith and learning.

I had the opportunity to present parts of this work to a variety of receptive audiences. I am grateful for invitations from the American Academy of Religion; the Graduate Program in Religion Theology and Ethics Colloquium, Duke University; Public Lectures in Theology and Ethics at the School of Divinity, Edinburgh; the Society of Christian Ethics; and the Society for the Study of Christian Ethics. Thanks for thoughtful conversation at these events are due to Guido de Graaff, Sean Larsen, Philip Lorish, Gilbert Meilaender, and Myles Werntz.

I returned to Durham to accept a position at Duke University Chapel in 2009. My writing has benefited directly, and indirectly, from conversations with colleagues, friends, and students from Duke and Durham, notably Gerly Ace, Kate Bowler, Luke Bretherton, Ben DeMarco, Peter Farmer, Jessica Howsam, Brett McCarty, Cameron Merrill, Greg Moore, Jeff Nelson, Will Parham, Kathleen Perry, Bruce Puckett, Andrew Rotolo, Christy Lohr Sapp, Andre Stokhuyzen, David Watson, Sam Wells, Janet Xiao, and Sam Zimmerman. Thanks go to Hannah Ward for providing helpful feedback on each chapter. I am deeply indebted to Reed McGinley-Stempel, who worked tirelessly to help me arrange the manuscript for publication and prepare the index.

Eerdmans has been a wonderful supporter of this project. Thanks are due to Jon Pott for his gracious response to the original manuscript. Editors Jenny Hoffman and Linda Bieze have offered invaluable help at every turn in the publishing process. I am grateful to the following journals, in which portions of this book were initially reviewed and published: *International Journal of Public Theology, Journal of Scriptural Reasoning, Journal of the Society of Christian Ethics,* and *Studies in Christian Ethics.*

Mark Storslee and Joshua Hordern deserve special recognition for their willingness to read draft after draft of my dissertation chapters. Jacob Goodson has encouraged this project for several years, and I am grateful for the insights into Ramsey's work that have come from our conversations. John Burk taught me to see that reimagining Ramsey's legacy also required reimagining Reinhold Niebuhr's legacy. It was a great joy to write an essay with him in the *International Journal of Public Theology,* and I am appreciative that he has allowed me to include that material in this book. Mark, Joshua, Jacob, and John are wonderful friends, and I could not have written this book without their insight, help, and encouragement.

Thank you to my mother, Anne, as well as my sister, Elizabeth, and her husband, Bryce. You have supported me for many years with enthusiasm, patience, and love. Thank you to my wife, Rachel, and our two children, Niles and Graham. You fill my life with joy and wonder.

Introduction

Not long ago, Paul Ramsey was the leading voice in Christian ethics in North America. His first book, *Basic Christian Ethics,* was the standard ethics textbook in seminaries and universities across the country, even outselling H. Richard Niebuhr's popular *Christ and Culture.*[1] Throughout the 1960s and 1970s, Ramsey wrote widely on pressing social issues, from sit-ins and Vietnam to reproductive technology and nuclear deterrence. He influenced several generations of Princeton University undergraduates as the Harrington Spear Paine Professor of Christian Ethics, and his graduate students are now among the most prominent voices in the field.[2] Even as Christian ethics changed, and the days of Reinhold Niebuhr's featured columns in *The New York Times* faded from view, Ramsey assumed the mantle of America's premier public theologian.

Today, Ramsey's intellectual legacy is in question. The well of secondary literature commenting on his work seems to have run dry. He is an afterthought to Christian ethics professors, who move swiftly from Niebuhr's "Protestant liberalism" to John Howard Yoder's and Stanley Hauerwas's "postliberalism." Most tellingly, emerging scholars who will lead the field in the coming decades have found no substantial need for

1. Paul Ramsey, *Basic Christian Ethics* (New York: Charles Scribner's Sons, 1950); H. Richard Niebuhr, *Christ and Culture* (New York: Harper and Row, 1951). For sales details, see the published book file for *Basic Christian Ethics,* Box 32, Paul Ramsey Papers, David M. Rubenstein Rare Book and Manuscript Library, Duke University.

2. Ramsey, ever precise, noted this in a speech given around the time of his retirement from Princeton: "A college generation is 4 years. From 1944 through 1982, I have had the privilege of teaching 9½ 4-year generations of Princeton students." Unpublished notes, Box 42, Ramsey Papers.

his work. Look up Ramsey in the index of most recent publications in Christian ethics, and you can expect to find a footnote or two acknowledging his importance — and little more. Frequently less. In the words of one contemporary thinker, Ramsey has "fallen off the radar screen of contemporary Christian ethics."[3]

Perhaps Ramsey was too attentive to the particular challenges of his day — for example, the moral legitimacy of the conflict in Vietnam, the now-defunct movement called "situation ethics," the mutually assured destruction (MAD) policy of the cold war — or perhaps he was too entangled with conversation partners who have themselves disappeared from the contemporary scene, for example, Anders Nygren, Joseph Fletcher, and William Frankena. Perhaps he was eclipsed, as were many others, by the turn to virtue theory and the resurgence of Neo-Augustinianism and Neo-Thomism in Christian ethics. Perhaps at heart he was simply a Kantian swayed by Enlightenment individualism, a Rawlsian swayed by political liberalism, or a white Southern moderate swayed by the comfort of order in a time of social revolution (all charges leveled against him). Whatever the reason, Ramsey's work is largely ignored today, and it is not at all clear that revisiting it will yield any significant return on the investment. (As anyone who has tried it knows, reading Ramsey requires quite an investment.)

Against this tide, I believe that Paul Ramsey is worth the investment, and that the potential yield of embracing his work is still considerable. If his political writings have any abiding value, and they do, it lies in his use of theological language to illuminate the structure of political agency and public goods. Amid his debates on particular moral issues, Ramsey searches for answers to questions at the heart of political theology. What is the essence of political authority? To what ends, and under what limitations, might force be justified? How might power be used prudently? These questions drive him deeper and deeper into theological reflections on the nature of the political realm, the contingency of moral judgments, and obligations of faithful obedience. In these deep waters we find his most lasting contributions to Christian ethics.

I am not the first to decry Ramsey's endangered legacy. What I offer here, however, is the unique suggestion that if his work is to remain lively, we must read him primarily as a political theologian. This was not his nat-

3. Charles Mathewes, dust-jacket endorsement of Kevin Carnahan, *Reinhold Niebuhr and Paul Ramsey: Idealist and Pragmatic Christians on Politics, Philosophy, Religion, and War* (Lanham, MD: Lexington Books, 2010).

ural disposition, nor has it been that of his commentators. Even early in his career, Ramsey understood himself as "an author who has been diverted from this task of urgent and central theoretical and theological importance for ethics by a felt need to write on *special problems* in Christian ethics."[4] Most commentators follow this lead, reading him as a political casuist with a preference for thorny moral quandaries over wider theological considerations.

This book charts a new course in scholarship on Ramsey by suggesting that his lasting impact lies not in his casuistry but in his political theology. Doing this requires rehabilitating his core theological insights and putting them in direct conversation with emerging voices in contemporary Christian ethics. In what follows I revisit well-known aspects of his work, such as his insistence on the political significance of God's covenant with creation, and I traverse new territory by exploring the role of judgment in his theology of repentance. I pay considerable attention to his description of practical reasoning and appreciation for the virtues, especially prudence. Most importantly, I highlight several resources that Ramsey offers to central debates in Christian ethics today. Where recent publications — including those by John Bowlin, Jennifer A. Herdt, Charles Mathewes, Eric Gregory, and Daniel M. Bell Jr. — largely ignore Ramsey's theology, I suggest several ways that his work remains lively.

Those with firsthand knowledge of Ramsey's irreplaceable spirit have written compelling accounts of his life, and I will not try to imitate those efforts here.[5] Instead, I begin by exploring his disappearance from contemporary Christian ethics. This requires a glimpse at the trajectory of secondary literature on his work, including a rationale for my proposal to read him as a theologian rather than a casuist. It also requires brief comment on his absence in Christian ethics today. By identifying several key

4. Paul Ramsey, *Nine Modern Moralists* (Englewood Cliffs, NJ: Prentice-Hall, 1962), p. 2; here and throughout, italics in quotations is in the original unless otherwise noted. Ramsey "saw the Christian moralist more as a travelling apostle than as a resident bishop," according to Oliver O'Donovan, "Obituary: Paul Ramsey (1913-1988)," *Studies in Christian Ethics* 1, no. 1 (1988): 86.

5. There is an excellent biography of Ramsey in the introduction to William Werpehowski and Stephen D. Crocco, eds., *The Essential Paul Ramsey: A Collection* (New Haven: Yale University Press, 1994), pp. vii-xxv. Both of the following volumes also offer chronological approaches to his work: David Attwood, *Paul Ramsey's Political Ethics* (Lanham, MD: Rowman and Littlefield, 1992); D. Stephen Long, *Tragedy, Tradition, Transformism: The Ethics of Paul Ramsey* (Boulder, CO: Westview Press, 1993).

thinkers who overlook Ramsey's contributions, I will lay the groundwork for the final chapters of the book, which indicate the importance of Ramsey's legacy for ongoing developments in the field.

Tracing Ramsey's Intellectual Legacy

In order to understand Ramsey's disappearance from contemporary Christian ethics, we first need to examine the development of secondary literature surrounding his work. These are still the early days of scholarship on Ramsey; after all, we have only recently passed the twenty-fifth anniversary of his death. Among the benefits of examining his work at this stage in the development of secondary literature is the release from the burden of adhering to an analysis of the elementary details of his life or the most immediately accessible concepts in his theological ethics. To put it another way, there is freedom in knowing that several introductory volumes on Ramsey have already been written.[6] These suffice to provide foundational accounts of his life and work, including his basic perspectives on political, medical, and sexual ethics. They include two *Festschriften,* which supply critical commentary on developments in his political ethics.[7] These collections paved the way for a rising tide of secondary literature in the late twentieth century that, as I have mentioned above, has largely washed back out to sea. As a consequence, readers hoping to understand the fundamental terms and concepts in Ramsey's just-war theory — for example, the centrality of principles of proportion and discrimination for *jus in bello,* critical modern thought on the morality of nuclear deterrence and war, and so on — will find no shortage of resources. Readers looking for connections between his theological concepts and the debates that occupy contemporary Christian political ethics will be disappointed. Ramsey receives scarcely more than a footnote in most recent treatments.

6. See Attwood, *Paul Ramsey's Political Ethics;* Long, *Tragedy, Tradition, Transformism;* Michael C. McKenzie, *Paul Ramsey's Ethics: The Power of 'Agape' in a Postmodern World* (Westport, CT: Praeger, 2001).

7. The first appeared during his lifetime and elicited a lengthy response from Ramsey in 1976. See James T. Johnson and David H. Smith, eds., *Love and Society: Essays in the Ethics of Paul Ramsey* (Missoula, MT: Scholars Press, 1974); Paul Ramsey, "Some Rejoinders," *Journal of Religious Ethics* 4, no. 2 (1976): 185-237. The second is a collection of essays commemorating his contributions to theological ethics. See James T. Johnson and Jeffrey Stout, eds., Special Issue, *Journal of Religious Ethics* 19, no. 2 (1991).

As I have observed, the overall approach in secondary literature is to treat Ramsey predominantly as a casuist. Within this frame there are two basic tendencies. The first is to organize and interpret Ramsey's work according to particular ethical questions or issues that occupied his mind.[8] Here interpreters nod to his theological "influences" before addressing his "contributions" to ethics. This presumes a sharp distinction between theology and ethics. More importantly, it suggests that Ramsey lacks any substantive theological "contributions."[9] While it is certainly helpful to examine his theological influences as a way of providing context and content for the interpretation of his casuistry, I want here to consider more explicitly what he can offer to theological reflection on political authority.

The second tendency has a sharper critical edge. Here commentators invalidate Ramsey's theological contributions by suggesting that he either neglects certain theological resources or submits unnecessarily to nontheological influences. This perspective is most apparent in early doctoral studies on Ramsey's ethics by a number of young Catholic scholars whose primary critique of him is, in one way or another, simply that he is not Catholic.[10] More aggressive is D. Stephen Long's suggestion that Ramsey's theological development is stunted by an early allegiance to philosophical idealism and the distorting influence of Reinhold Niebuhr.[11] Long presents

8. For example, Charles Curran sets out to "consider questions of political and medical ethics in dialogue with the writings of Paul Ramsey" (Charles E. Curran, *Politics, Medicine, and Christian Ethics* [Philadelphia: Fortress, 1973], p. 2). Other examples include Johnson and Smith, *Love and Society;* and the *Festschrift* dedicated to his medical ethics: Kenneth L. Vaux, Sara Vaux, and Mark Stenberg, eds., *Covenants of Life: Contemporary Medical Ethics in Light of the Thought of Paul Ramsey* (Dordrecht: Kluwer Academic Publishers, 2002).

9. Both McKenzie and Attwood employ Ramsey's theological foundations to illuminate finer points of his medical and political ethics in later chapters. See McKenzie, *Paul Ramsey's Ethics;* Attwood, *Paul Ramsey's Political Ethics.*

10. For two examples, see John Carville, "Love Transforming Justice in the Christian Ethics of Paul Ramsey," S.T.D. diss., Catholic University of America, Washington, DC, 1974; and Edwin F. O'Brien, "The Origin and Development of Moral Principles in the Writings of Paul Ramsey," S.T.D. diss., Pontificate University of St. Thomas, 1976, Box 54, Ramsey Papers. Ramsey was aware of several of these attempts and commented on them late in his career to an inquiring Ph.D. student writing her dissertation on his work. He wrote: "You may like to know that some dissertations on me done in Rome have seemed to me to be, by comparison, uninteresting, even pedantic (which, at least, I am not)" (Paul Ramsey to Deborah Streeter, July 7, 1978, Box 24, Ramsey Papers).

11. Long argues that Ramsey's theological development inherits a Niebuhrian realism that is "not indebted to Christian notions of sin, but to pagan notions of tragedy" (Long, *Tradition,* p. 40, n. 40). Daniel M. Bell Jr. also suggests that Ramsey's work "remains hobbled

Ramsey's ethics as shallow and ultimately nontheological, and he rejects the possibility of any lasting contributions in Ramsey's work to a theological interpretation of politics.

The present study seeks to avoid falling prey to either of these two tendencies. While I do examine Ramsey's engagements with Jean-Jacques Rousseau and Karl Barth, as well as the Niebuhr brothers, my aim here is not primarily to trace his influences but to show how he moves beyond these interlocutors to offer his own constructive theological insights. I also deliberately avoid limiting his theological developments to a lesser role as platform for his casuistry, be it political, medical, or sexual. Readers looking for a concluding chapter on the way his concepts of covenant or agape inform particular views on deterrence or counter-city warfare will be left wanting. So, too, will readers looking for a "crossover" chapter where I attempt to capture the underlying casuist techniques or interpretive themes uniting his political and medical (or sexual) writings. Instead, this study makes a conscious effort to hold his contributions to political theology up to their own light — without tying their significance to the casuistry of a particular issue or situation. It is a fresh approach to his work that I believe takes advantage of and moves beyond the body of secondary literature that is currently available. It also is, I believe, the best way to account for his importance to contemporary debates.

Ramsey and Contemporary Christian Ethics

If there is one defining emphasis in Christian moral thinking over the last few decades, it is the importance of virtue. The turn toward the virtues is largely attributed to the work of Alasdair MacIntyre, but significant early writings by Jean Porter and Oliver O'Donovan situate this turn within an explicitly Christian frame. It is significant that the latter two use Ramsey's work in making their case for the importance of virtue. For instance, Porter uses Ramsey to argue for the compatibility of rules and virtues in the discernment of right moral judgment.[12] O'Donovan's debts to Ramsey are

---

by Niebuhrian realism's theological deficiencies" (Bell, "The Way of God with the World: Hauerwas on War," in Charles R. Pinches, Kelly S. Johnson, and Charles M. Collier, eds., *Unsettling Arguments: A Festschrift on the Occasion of Stanley Hauerwas's 70th Birthday* [Eugene, OR: Wipf and Stock, 2010], p. 118).

12. See Jean Porter, *Moral Action and Christian Ethics* (Cambridge, UK: Cambridge University Press, 1995).

more diffuse, but he relies heavily on Ramsey's "The Case of the Curious Exception" in his account of virtue and practical reasoning in *Resurrection and Moral Order.*[13]

As we turn to more recent efforts in Christian ethics, however, the presence of Ramsey's work disappears. Neither Porter nor O'Donovan has made substantial use of Ramsey in over a decade, even as they continue to write extensively on political themes.[14] Jennifer A. Herdt's widely praised *Putting on Virtue* does not mention Ramsey or his approach to practical reasoning.[15] The most significant treatment of contingency and virtue in recent years, John Bowlin's *Contingency and Fortune in Aquinas' Ethics,* similarly omits any reference to Ramsey.[16] (I explore ways that Herdt and Bowlin might benefit from Ramsey's core insights on contingency in chapter 7 below.)

Ramsey does, at least, receive mention in a few accounts. Charles Mathewes appropriates a number of Ramseyan themes under the broad heading of Augustinianism, and to that end he is generally supportive of Ramsey's theological approach.[17] But he rarely engages Ramsey directly, and never, to my knowledge, does he make substantial use of his work. Instead, mention of Ramsey typically serves to reinforce a point Mathewes traces back to Augustine.[18] Daniel M. Bell Jr. takes from Ramsey the insight that it is more helpful to speak of the just-war *tradition* than of just-war doctrine or theory. This informs Bell's sharp distinction between "Just War Public Policy Checklist" and "Just War Christian Discipleship." Yet even the acknowledgment that Ramsey is "one of the principal architects of the

13. Oliver O'Donovan, *Resurrection and Moral Order: An Outline of Evangelical Ethics* (Grand Rapids: Eerdmans, 1994).

14. In apparent defiance of this trend is Oliver O'Donovan, "Karl Barth and Paul Ramsey's 'Uses of Power,'" in *Bonds of Imperfection* (Grand Rapids: Eerdmans, 2004), pp. 246-75. This essay, however, first appeared in *Journal of Religious Ethics* 19, no. 2 (1991): 1-30.

15. Jennifer A. Herdt, *Putting on Virtue: The Legacy of the Splendid Vices* (Chicago: University of Chicago Press, 2008).

16. John Bowlin, *Contingency and Fortune in Aquinas' Ethics* (Cambridge, UK: Cambridge University Press, 1999).

17. Ramsey is one of Mathewes's favorite mediators of Augustine. The latter says: "Our proposed Augustinian theology must be mediated by others, and so we begin from Paul Ramsey's statement: 'The mere fact that a man is a citizen elsewhere keeps him from being only a citizen here'" (Charles Mathewes, *A Theology of Public Life* [Cambridge, UK: Cambridge University Press, 2007], p. 164).

18. See, e.g., Charles Mathewes, *The Republic of Grace* (Grand Rapids: Eerdmans, 2010), p. 148.

recovery of just war late in the twentieth century" yields no significant engagement with his insights.[19] As we will see, this brief gesture to Ramsey's importance while, in practice, ignoring his work almost entirely is customary among contemporary ethicists.

The contemporary thinker who pays the most considerable attention to Ramsey is Princeton theologian Eric Gregory. Indeed, Gregory recognizes several aspects of Ramsey's project that are overlooked by others, for example, that he is a virtue thinker, that he seeks to correct a Niebuhrian account of love, and that intuitionism is insufficient as the ground of moral theory.[20] He admires the stringency of love in Ramsey's political writings, and he has a clear sense of Ramsey's improvements on Niebuhrian realism. Most importantly, unlike any other emerging voice in contemporary Christian ethics, Gregory imports central insights from Ramsey's work into his political project. Indeed, he is more of a "Ramseyan" than most.

Still, Gregory's focus remains largely on Ramsey's earliest book, *Basic Christian Ethics,* and its concentration on love. Significant elements of Ramsey's work fall through the cracks, including the relationship between his early agapism and developments in covenant theology, as well as his return to the doctrines of creation, Christology, and eschatology in his later work. These are important advances, and it is difficult to appreciate Ramsey's place among contemporary Augustinian voices without a broader account of his intellectual development. (I attempt just such an effort in chapter 8 below.)

Even taking account of Gregory's appreciation for his work, it should be evident at this point that contemporary Christian ethics has largely left Paul Ramsey behind. This is a great loss. The aim of this book is to show that Ramsey's work remains lively and can still yield considerable insight for current discussions in Christian political theology.

This Book's Design

This study pursues an understanding of how Ramsey's theological language describes, interprets, and accounts for the nature of political authority and

19. Daniel M. Bell Jr., *Just War as Christian Discipleship* (Grand Rapids: Brazos, 2009), pp. 71, 94-95.

20. Eric Gregory, *Politics and the Order of Love: An Augustinian Ethic of Democratic Citizenship* (Chicago: University of Chicago Press, 2008), pp. 179-80, 184.

the function that such descriptions have in defining and shaping concepts of the political good. Given this approach, the first chapter begins with what Ramsey calls the *Leitmotif* of his work: covenant.[21] In *Basic Christian Ethics,* he uses Rousseau's social contract philosophy as a heuristic device for exploring the political implications of Yahweh's covenant with Israel. A decade later, under the influence of Karl Barth, he offers a robust account of the relationship between covenant and the doctrine of creation in *Christian Ethics and the Sit-In.*[22] I examine his engagements with Rousseau and Barth, as well as the commitment to covenant theology. Opening with a discussion of his early work on covenant provides an accessible point of entry into his work and critical resources for subsequent chapters.

As Ramsey turns to concrete issues in political ethics in the 1960s, he is keen to keep his moral thinking rooted in firm theological convictions. Here he finds the concept of repentance to be a particularly helpful theological resource for understanding conflicts between moral limitations and responsibilities (often called the problem of "dirty hands"). Chapter 2 examines Ramsey's complicated theology of repentance, including his failed suggestion that politics is a realm of "deferred repentance" and his response to critics of his work during the Vietnam War. I suggest that he uses repentance to shed theological light on the nature of political agency, with special emphasis on the contingent and temporal status of all political judgment. This establishes contingency and temporality as central themes that will occupy much of the following discussion.

By the late 1970s, shifts in theological ethics and a relative absence of scriptural references in his political and medical writings (compared to *Basic Christian Ethics*) left Ramsey with the reputation of being an unscriptural thinker, or at least an insufficiently scriptural one. Chapter 3 explores two examples of what is today called "scriptural reasoning" in Ramsey's later political writings. In the first he suggests that the Genesis narratives of Noah and the Tower of Babel reveal significant truths about the promises and limitations of political authority. In the second he uses Luke 14:28-33 to argue that politics is "a kind of doing" that cannot escape the limitations of contingency and temporality. These two examples not only provide evidence of his refusal to abandon the scriptural roots of political theology; they also provide theological insights into political authority that can contribute to discussions in contemporary Christian ethics.

21. Vaux et al., *Covenants,* p. 256.

22. Paul Ramsey, *Christian Ethics and the Sit-In* (New York: Association Press, 1961).

Insights from Scripture occupy chapter 3; I defer broader observations for contemporary Christian ethics to the closing chapters.

In the second section I turn more directly to the theological components of Ramsey's moral theory. Chapter 4 explores his protection of the "magistrate's conscience" in *Who Speaks for the Church?*[23] It asks what his protective instinct reveals about his broader framework for political theology and moral theory. I suggest that Ramsey's frustration with the ecclesial pronouncements of the 1960s is closely linked to his wrestling with the movement called "situation ethics." Accordingly, I examine his objections to "act-agapism" in his book *Deeds and Rules,* as well as his emphasis on temporal and interpersonal "bonds" in Christian ethics.[24]

This conversation on moral agency sets the stage for chapters 5 and 6, which explore the role of deontology (rules of conduct) and teleology (the necessity of virtue) in Ramsey's later writings. The first aim is to provide a clear picture of how the temporal and interpersonal bonds in Christian ethics animate (and regulate) Christian participation in the political realm. To do this, we must leave behind the narrow debates concerning situation ethics and, more importantly, Ramsey's early theological account of repentance. Instead, chapter 5 examines his turn to tragedy as a regulating concept in his final book, *Speak Up for Just War or Pacifism,* and I offer a new analysis of Ramsey's debts to Reinhold Niebuhr, his unwavering commitment to the "Pauline prohibition," and the way these shape his peculiar political theology of tragedy.[25]

By the late 1960s, Ramsey felt that the arguments surrounding situation ethics left several questions unanswered concerning the place of rules within moral and practical reasoning. He took up the most important of these, the possibility of "justifiable violations" of moral rules, in "The Case of the Curious Exception."[26] In chapter 6, I suggest that his concerns about justifiable exceptions remain lively for two reasons. The first is that his theological emphasis on covenant remains a helpful resource for resisting the temptation toward "escape clauses" in moral deliberation that is still

23. Paul Ramsey, *Who Speaks for the Church? A Critique of the 1966 Geneva Conference on Church and Society* (Nashville: Abingdon, 1967).

24. Paul Ramsey, *Deeds and Rules in Christian Ethics* (New York: Charles Scribner's Sons, 1965; Lanham, MD: University Press of America, 1967).

25. Paul Ramsey, *Speak Up for Just War or Pacifism* (University Park: Pennsylvania State University Press, 1988).

26. Paul Ramsey, "The Case of the Curious Exception," in Gene H. Outka and Paul Ramsey, eds., *Norm and Context in Christian Ethics* (London: SCM, 1968), p. 67.

with us today. The second reason is my belief that Ramsey's account of practical reasoning helps illuminate the turn toward the virtues in contemporary Christian ethics. I defend this claim by demonstrating his influence over the early virtue theory of Jean Porter and Oliver O'Donovan.

The final section of the book aims to put Ramsey in conversation with contemporary thinkers such as Bowlin, Herdt, Mathewes, Gregory, and Bell. There can be no doubt, at this point, that formulating an appropriate response to a contingent world is central to Ramsey's political project. Furthermore, chapter 6 makes clear that he possesses deep sympathies with the contemporary turn to the virtues, even if he does not embrace that turn fully. Yet Ramsey provides no systematic theological account of contingency and its relationship to virtue. Here the contributions from Bowlin and Herdt enter the picture: both authors illuminate the role that contingency plays in the Christian life and offer robust accounts of "putting on" virtue. Chapter 7 suggests that Ramsey has much to learn from these two thinkers, but I also retrieve distinctive resources from earlier chapters to show how he can push the contemporary conversation forward.

Chapter 8 focuses on Ramsey and contemporary Augustinianism. Even as he adopts a Thomistic moral psychology, his political theology is thoroughly Augustinian. Yet, few of the contemporary authors who claim the Augustinian label have engaged substantially with Ramsey's work. In this chapter I explore Ramsey's place amid the contemporary return to Augustine by examining his use of *City of God* in *Speak Up for Just War or Pacifism,* and I trace his debts to H. Richard Niebuhr's *The Responsible Self.*[27] I suggest that his account of the power and purpose behind political judgment supplies a helpful corrective to both Mathewes and Gregory. And I show how his description of prudence as a vital part of the work of love pushes these thinkers toward a more robust account of the structure and limitations of political agency.

Chapter 9 builds on the emphasis on virtue and practical reasoning throughout the preceding chapters to articulate the importance of ecclesiology and discipleship for the cultivation of virtue. I particularly focus on Daniel Bell's account of Jesus as the justice of God and his attempt to bring justified war into the ecclesiological fold. I explore the development of Ramsey's Christology between *Basic Christian Ethics* and *Speak Up for Just War or Pacifism,* as well as his willingness to engage secular political theorists. I also praise Bell's emphasis on discipleship and show how Ram-

27. H. Richard Niebuhr, *The Responsible Self* (New York: Harper and Row, 1963).

sey's work maintains a similar concern for the integrity of Christian witness to the nation-state. In so doing, I highlight Ramsey's ability to rethink central theological concepts in his work and draw his readers' attention to fundamental questions in moral and political theology.

I hope that these introductory comments are adequate to acclimate the reader to the basic features of the forthcoming study. I believe that Ramsey's political writings offer a constructive set of themes for understanding how theological concepts define and shape the political good. They also offer unique insight into the theological significance of political authority and judgment that contemporary Christian ethics cannot afford to ignore.

PART I

Elements of Ramsey's Political Theology

CHAPTER ONE

Early Explorations in Covenant Theology

Covenant is the most ubiquitous frame of reference in Ramsey's theological ethics. It appears as early as the 1940s (in articles preceding *Basic Christian Ethics*) and as late as the 1980s (in a published letter responding to James Gustafson's interpretation of his work). Given its commanding presence, it is unsurprising that, late in his career, Ramsey refers to covenant as the *Leitmotif* of his work.[1] As one commentator notes, "Covenant is *the* biblical theme around which he chooses to organize his appropriation of biblical ethics."[2]

In his political writings the concept tends to come and go. It features heavily in *Basic Christian Ethics* and *Christian Ethics and the Sit-In*.[3] It recedes from his principal publications on war during the 1960s, which leads William Werpehowski to observe, "The virtual absence of talk of creation, covenant, and fellow humanity in Ramsey's political ethics is especially striking."[4] Yet covenant reappears as a central theme of his final book, *Speak Up for Just War or Pacifism,* and in the previously published appendix to that volume, "A Political Ethics Context for Strategic Thinking."[5]

1. Kenneth L. Vaux, Sara Vaux, and Mark Stenberg, eds., *Covenants of Life: Contemporary Medical Ethics in Light of the Thought of Paul Ramsey* (Dordrecht: Kluwer Academic Publishers, 2002), p. 256.

2. Jeffrey S. Siker, *Scripture and Ethics: Twentieth-Century Portraits* (New York and Oxford: Oxford University Press, 1997), p. 85.

3. Paul Ramsey, *Basic Christian Ethics* (New York: Charles Scribner's Sons, 1950); Paul Ramsey, *Christian Ethics and the Sit-In* (New York: Association Press, 1961).

4. William Werpehowski, *American Protestant Ethics and the Legacy of H. Richard Niebuhr* (Washington, DC: Georgetown University Press, 2002), p. 51. This claim assumes that *Christian Ethics and the Sit-In* is not among Ramsey's "political ethics."

5. Paul Ramsey, *Speak Up for Just War or Pacifism* (University Park: Pennsylvania State University Press, 1988); Ramsey, "A Political Ethics Context for Strategic Thinking," in Mor-

This chapter offers a point of entry into Ramsey's work by exploring his early writings on covenant, including his claim that covenant is the primary frame of reference for Christian considerations of political authority and judgment. Because he uses the term inconsistently, readers hoping for a systematic theological framework will be sorely disappointed. But that does not mean that Ramsey has little to say. In fact, he draws deeply from the wells of Scripture, political philosophy, and Christian doctrine as he explores the political implications of God's covenantal relationship with creation. These efforts occupy two of his earliest political writings: *Basic Christian Ethics,* where he uses Jean-Jacques Rousseau's social contract as a heuristic device for identifying the political implications of Israel's covenant with Yahweh; and *Christian Ethics and the Sit-In,* where he leans heavily on Karl Barth's covenant/creation framework to lay the groundwork for his later political ethics. Lessons from these engagements with Rousseau and Barth run throughout his later political writings, and they will be crucial resources for the arguments that follow in this book. The best place to begin, then, is with the politics of the covenant.

The Covenant/Contract Analogy in *Basic Christian Ethics*

Basic Christian Ethics was at one time the primary textbook for college and seminary courses on Christian ethics. The Religious Book Club adopted it in 1950 as their September club selection, which contributed significantly to its high sales. They called it "a weighty and enduring treatment of the subject, one of the year's great books."[6] By the end of the following year it continued to outsell even H. Richard Niebuhr's popular *Christ and Culture.*[7]

Ramsey had originally intended to write a shorter volume. On August 1, 1949, he received a letter from the publisher guaranteeing publication of the manuscript and echoing the "excellent report" from their reader, who, Ramsey later learned, was Reinhold Niebuhr. Despite his praise, however, Niebuhr suggested that the manuscript required additional chapters to

---

ton A. Kaplan, ed., *Strategic Thinking and Its Moral Implications* (Chicago: University of Chicago Center for Policy Study, 1973), pp. 101-47.

6. "Basic Christian Ethics," *Religious Book Club Bulletin* 23, no. 9 (1950): 1-2, Box 32, Paul Ramsey Papers, David M. Rubenstein Rare Book and Manuscript Library, Duke University.

7. H. Richard Niebuhr, *Christ and Culture* (New York: Harper and Row, 1951). For sales details, see the published book file for *Basic Christian Ethics,* Box 32, Ramsey Papers.

address two concerns: first, that the book "does not deal with that side of ethics which is concerned with 'institutions' or the organized social arrangements of mankind"; second, that "[Ramsey] does not elucidate how the 'love' ethic of the Scriptures and of Christian life is related to the rational norms of justice and the equity by which the life of the world is ordered and its institutions organized."[8]

Ramsey initially resisted the idea of lengthening the manuscript, suggesting instead that he be given the option of revision within five years.[9] But eventually he supplied three additional chapters to the publisher, "This Human Nature," "Christian Love in Search of a Social Policy," and "The Religious Foundation for Community Life." As we shall see, later in his career Ramsey came to value the last of these additional chapters as containing the most reliable material of the volume. He often referred back to it, as he did in one particularly testy letter responding to an inquiry from a Ph.D. student. Ramsey snapped, "first, the Biblical material concerning God's acts in times past, and, second, the final chapter of BCE, were not accidents."[10] In fact, without the publisher's insistence that he follow Niebuhr's recommendations, the final chapter would not have appeared at all.

It was professor Charles W. Hendel at Yale University who taught Ramsey to read philosophical and biblical texts side by side.[11] A few years later, when Ramsey was assigned to teach "Bible" at Princeton shortly after joining the faculty there, he carried this practice with him. He employed the analogy between covenant and contract as a key theme in his under-

8. William Savage to Paul Ramsey, August 1, 1949, Box 32, Ramsey Papers. The review was blind for Ramsey at the time. He revealed in later correspondence that it was "Reine Niebuhr" (Paul Ramsey to Gilbert Meilaender, Sept. 18, 1981, Box 17, Ramsey Papers). See also D. Stephen Long, *Tragedy, Tradition, Transformism: The Ethics of Paul Ramsey* (Boulder, CO: Westview Press, 1993), p. 35.

9. Paul Ramsey to William Savage, March 7, 1948, Box 32, Ramsey Papers.

10. Paul Ramsey to David Schmidt, Jan. 8, 1982, Box 25, Ramsey Papers. Ramsey expressed regrets about "Christian Love in Search of a Social Policy," observing to Gilbert Meilaender that the chapter "was a mistake — or at least didn't do what the third final chapter added — about covenant" (Ramsey to Meilaender, Sept. 18, 1981, Box 17, Ramsey Papers).

11. Hendel was head of the philosophy department, and Ramsey took two courses with him in the early 1940s. Much of the analysis in *Basic Christian Ethics* follows the structure and content of his notes from those courses, as well as Charles W. Hendel, "The Meaning of Obligation," in Clifford Barrett, *Contemporary Idealism in America* (New York: Macmillan, 1932), pp. 237-96. Boxes 42, 43, and 44 of the Ramsey Papers contain notes from his courses at Yale as well as lecture notes from his early years at Princeton.

graduate teaching. As early as 1949, he suggests that engaging with "early modern social philosophers" will produce "greatly increased understanding of the biblical notion of covenant."[12] His early political writings use this tactic, and he often sounds like a college professor as he advances his argument. (E.g, "On hearing the word 'covenant,' we are likely to think of some civil contract between parties equal before the law and more or less equal in other respects, or else we think of the idea of 'social contract' employed by early modern political theory.")[13]

Rousseau initially appears in Ramsey's doctoral thesis on philosophical idealism, which marshals concepts from *The Social Contract* and *The Discourses* to make various observations about Bernard Bosanquet's philosophical idealism (Josiah Royce, too, though to a lesser extent). Chief among those observations is Ramsey's belief that Bosanquet had been overly swayed by Rousseau, as well as Kant, in the belief that duty is strictly self-imposed. For Ramsey, the self cannot be the root of moral obligation precisely because "a proper generic definition of obligation is the 'will of God.'"[14]

In *Basic Christian Ethics,* Rousseau emerges again as a uniquely helpful resource. Against Millar Burrows's *An Outline of Biblical Theology,* Ramsey observes a fundamental divide in social contract theories "according to whether two contracts were assumed or only one."[15] Single-contract theories establish "absolute sovereignty" because they require no further agreement for the foundation of political authority. Double-contract the-

12. Paul Ramsey, "Elements of a Biblical Political Theory," *The Journal of Religion* 29, no. 4 (1949): 262; see also Ramsey, *Basic Christian Ethics,* p. 368.

13. Ramsey, "Elements," p. 259. See also Paul Ramsey, "A Theory of Democracy: Idealistic or Christian?" *Ethics* 56, no. 4 (1946): 251-66; Paul Ramsey, *Deeds and Rules in Christian Ethics* (New York: Charles Scribner's Sons, 1965; Lanham, MD: University Press of America, 1967).

14. Paul Ramsey, "The Nature of Man in the Philosophy of Josiah Royce and Bernard Bosanquet," Ph.D. diss., Yale University, 1943, Box 53, Ramsey Papers, p. 203. This is why, as he writes in 1946, "Genesis understands sin as sin *before God* and therefore apprehends it with intensity as an ultimate infraction. . . . Rousseau understands sin as sin *over man*" (Ramsey, "A Theory of Democracy," p. 256). Stephen Long's reading of Ramsey's early work fails to account adequately for places, such as these, where Ramsey subjects both Rousseau and "absolute idealism" to fundamentally theological critiques. See, e.g., Long, *Tradition, Tragedy, Transformism,* p. 43.

15. Ramsey, *Basic Christian Ethics (BCE),* p. 368. Hereafter, page references to this work appear in parentheses within the text. See also Millar Burrows, *An Outline of Biblical Theology* (Philadelphia: Westminster, 1946).

ories, by contrast, first establish "limited sovereignty" and then negotiate a second contract for political authority on the basis of inalienable human rights (pp. 368-69). The problem with Burrows's account is not only that "he does not distinguish clearly enough" between these two theories, but that he also fails to appreciate the implications of the distinction when considering them alongside Israel's covenant (p. 368). Ramsey is adamant that the covenant cannot be similar to a double-contract theory, because the parallel would suggest both that Yahweh possesses only limited sovereignty and that Israel retains certain inalienable rights in the relationship.

This disagreement with Burrows leads Ramsey to develop an analogy between Rousseau's social contract and Israel's covenant with Yahweh. He argues: "Without ceasing to be fully aware of the danger of misleading analogies, it is still true to say that . . . Israel's covenant was more like a single covenant establishing absolute sovereignty" (p. 370). I want to highlight three parallels in the covenant/contract analogy: the emphasis on absolute sovereignty; the formation of the political community; and the significance of consent. This will afford a critical perspective on Ramsey's early use of covenant as a theological foundation for political ethics.

First, Ramsey is principally attracted to the analogy for its ability to highlight the absolute sovereignty of Yahweh. Rousseau's social contract assigns an unqualified sovereignty to the general will that is "simple and single, and it cannot be divided without being destroyed."[16] Ramsey observes a similarly transcendent and indivisible political authority in "the sovereign God [who] cannot be represented except by himself" (p. 380). Of course, alongside his enthusiasm for this first aspect of the analogy, Ramsey acknowledges a significant dissimilarity that plagues it. Whereas the social contract brings into existence the general will (and therein a sovereign political authority), the story of Israel reveals a preexisting political authority calling the Hebrew people into covenantal relationship. Israel is able to recognize the sovereign that precedes them precisely because Yahweh "had already decisively spoken and revealed his purpose to them in delivering them from Egypt."[17] Therefore, a significant difference arises "mainly from the fact that Rousseau constructs a sovereign while Israel

16. Jean Jacques Rousseau, *The Social Contract and Other Later Political Writings*, ed. and trans. Victor Gourevitch, Cambridge Texts in the History of Political Thought (Cambridge, UK: Cambridge University Press, 1997), p. 111.

17. Ramsey, Unpublished Notes, Box 43, Ramsey Papers.

(*BCE,* p. 378). By calling attention to both the similarity Ramsey uses the social contract as a heuristic device to solute (and eternal) sovereignty of God.

The second parallel lies in the fact that both the social contract and Israel's covenant yield collective political bodies. Rousseau sets out to protect individual freedoms that are threatened by the state of nature and natural, physical inequalities. The result is a contract that produces "a moral and collective body made up of as many members as the assembly has voices, and which receives by this same act its unity, its common *self,* its life and its will."[18] Ramsey likens this to the way Yahweh's creative action "served as a kind of charter or national constitution" for the Hebrew people (*BCE,* p. 367). He says, "[I]n covenanting with Israel [Yahweh] *made* her a nation" (p. 372). The analogy highlights the fact that it was "the covenant with Yahweh by which the community came into existence."[19]

Here again we confront dissimilarities. One of the two aspects that Rousseau identifies in natural humanity in *The Discourses* is self-interest. Civil society secures individual freedoms precisely because it is rooted in self-interest (and with self-interest, property).[20] The problem is that a political community founded on self-interest cannot sustain itself forever. Thus *The Social Contract* describes a perpetually degenerate general will: "The body politic, just like the body of a man, begins to die as soon as it is born and carries within itself the causes of its destruction."[21] Ramsey contrasts this with the Israel's eschatological destiny, which is sealed by God's perpetual renewal of the covenant. He points to chapter 24 of Isaiah, saying, "Israel's unusual share in the relationship is described as 'breaking the everlasting covenant,' breaking the unbreakable!" (*BCE,* p. 371).[22]

18. Rousseau, *The Social Contract,* p. 50. W. Blake Odgers describes the construction: "As soon as individuals have entered into a 'social contract' . . . they become a political community, a body politic" ("A Defence of Rousseau's Theory of the Social Contract," *Journal of the Society of Comparative Legislation* 16, no. 2 [1916]: 328).

19. Ramsey, Unpublished Notes, Box 42, Ramsey Papers.

20. Jean Jacques Rousseau, *The Discourses and Other Early Political Writings,* ed. and trans. Victor Gourevitch, Cambridge Texts in the History of Political Thought (Cambridge, UK: Cambridge University Press, 1997), p. 127. The other is pity. See also p. 161, where Rousseau says: "The first man who, having enclosed a piece of ground, to whom it occurred to him to say *this is mine,* and found people sufficiently simple to believe him, was the true founder of civil society."

21. Rousseau, *The Social Contract,* p. 109.

22. As one author has written recently, "Certainly, the relationship between God and Israel is defined in part by a conditional element. Israel is expected to serve him by obey-

While Israel's responsibility is to be faithfully obedient, the covenant is never reliant on her obedience. It is eternally upheld by the promise of Yahweh to "maintain intact the covenant he *commands*" (pp. 370-71). Thus the covenant/contract analogy serves to highlight both the formation of Israel as a political community and the unique character and assurance of its eschatological destiny.

The final parallel concerns the significance of consent and obligation in the establishment of contract and covenant. I mentioned earlier that Ramsey's early engagements with Rousseau in his doctoral research drove him to reject the self as the ground of moral obligation. In "The Nature of Man" he criticized Bosanquet and Royce for their proximity to Rousseau, as well as for their failure to account for the will of God in concepts of obligation.[23] Yahweh's initiation of the covenant supplies Israel with "a nature as a religious nation which can no more be broken than you can break his covenant with the day and his covenant with the night so that day and night no longer come at their appointed times (Jer. 33:20, 21)!" (*BCE,* p. 372). This reinforces the divine will as the source of moral obligation and the radical obedience expected of Israel. But Ramsey was also aware of the fact that Israel's covenant with Yahweh included the expectation of "ratification" or faithful embrace of the covenant which God "commanded" (p. 381). When speaking of Israel's obedience to covenant, he says, "the people Israel are not only chosen by God, but they also 'choose' Him for their God, and voluntarily enter into the covenant with Him, freely undertaking to obey His laws."[24] Despite his misgivings about Rousseau's source of obligation, he takes notice of the importance of consent in the social

---

ing his commandments and living pious lives. But the unconditional element remains the bedrock of the relationship; God never ceases to love the Israelites even if they fail to live up to their obligations and are punished" (Robert Eisen, *The Peace and Violence of Judaism* [Oxford: Oxford University Press, 2011], p. 20).

23. In 1946 he writes that "mere consent does not suffice to determine the nature of political obligation. Since consent itself may be sinful, it is obliged to be right; it ought to agree only to what is just" (Ramsey, "A Theory of Democracy," p. 259). If Ramsey is attracted to the parallel need for "ratification" or consent in covenant and contract, he remains equally eager to avoid adopting Rousseau's account of moral obligation rooted in the self. See also *BCE,* p. 303.

24. Unpublished Notes, Box 42, Ramsey Papers. Rousseau, for his part, posits that morality is wholly absent in precontractual human relations. W. T. Jones notes: "In a word, political morality depends on the consent of the citizens, and the consent of the citizens depends on there being a general will" (Jones, "Rousseau's General Will and the Problem of Consent," *Journal of the History of Philosophy* 25, no. 1 [1987]: 106).

contract, as well as its (limited) similarities with God's command for Israel to respond faithfully to the formation of the covenant.

The failure of the covenant/contract analogy to capture the relationship between consent and obligation drives Ramsey, at last, away from Rousseau. He suggests that for a closer parallel we must look elsewhere, yet not to "John Locke's limitation of sovereignty but to Jean Bodin and Hugo Grotius" (*BCE,* p. 381).[25] Bodin appreciates that there might be some *recognized* authority to give law without consent. His political authority "rules by a kind of implicit 'consent,' but consent is not necessary to his law." This approximates the transcendence of Yahweh over the covenant and the idea that "Israel . . . was under obligation *to God,* who himself was not made sovereign by contract but by his own strong hand" (p. 382). On Ramsey's terms, Bodin's appreciation for the ability of political authority to demand obligation without consent more clearly resembles Israel's sovereign than Rousseau's general will built on self-interest.

Grotius suggests that because the political subjects "are not thereby demonstrably superior to the person so constituted," it is unintelligible for individuals to transfer the right of governance to a sovereign and simultaneously to retain that right to themselves (p. 383).[26] Ramsey says: "The people keep possession of themselves and their personal liberty, but their civil liberty and 'the perpetual right of governing them, as they are a people,' these are alienated" (p. 384). This transference of the "rights *of a governing kind*" places upon the sovereign the responsibility not to abandon the collective body or to "turn them over to the governance of another" (p. 384). The security of the relationship rests not on continued consent but on the protection of the sovereign. Ramsey believes this more adequately reflects the Old Testament notion that once Israel responded to being chosen by Yahweh, not even disobedience could terminate the covenant. It was paradoxically understood as "breaking the unbreakable!" (p. 371).

This late turn to Bodin and Grotius reveals the extent to which Ramsey's whole covenant/contract analogy is rather of two minds. If these two thinkers are more helpful, why neglect them for such a long engagement

25. To go in the direction of Locke would be to blur, as Burrows does, the difference between single- and double-contract theories.

26. Grotius argues that "in the formation of a civil society or in its subjection to a ruler or rulers, a promise is made . . . to abide by whatever the majority, or those entrusted with power, should decide" (Hugo Grotius, "The Right of War and Peace," in Oliver O'Donovan and Joan Lockwood O'Donovan, eds., *From Irenaeus to Grotius: A Sourcebook in Christian Political Thought* [Grand Rapids: Eerdmans, 1999], p. 794).

with Rousseau? Throughout the section Ramsey moves simultaneously toward and away from Rousseau: he is drawn to the social contract's ability to highlight features of Israel's covenant, and yet he must constantly push away from the philosophical emphasis on self-interest. Thus he frequently reminds readers that he is "in the midst of wide analogy" and "fully aware of the danger of misleading analogies" (pp. 379, 370). Even with these warnings, however, the section does not quite accomplish what Ramsey hoped it would. In some of his later writings, his frustration led him to disavow Rousseau altogether.

From Israel to the "Human Community"

I recall this extended covenant/contract analogy not simply to highlight its inadequacies but to demonstrate Ramsey's early reliance on covenant theology. Notice the features of Israel's covenant that emerge as central to his analysis in *Basic Christian Ethics.* First, Israel only finds its political existence in relationship to the absolute and eternal sovereignty of God. Only in light of this sovereignty can we make any sense of their composition as a collective body, as a political people, who await the eschatological promises of God's covenant. Further, Israel's political agency rests entirely on God's prior action on their behalf. They do not "consent" to God's sovereignty, for the very existence of their life in community presumes and displays that sovereignty. Yet faithful obedience — "ratification" of God's work — is their proper response. These are the building blocks of Ramsey's covenant theology, and they ground his view of sovereignty, political agency, and moral obligation throughout his career. What he has failed to do, at this early point, is make a compelling case for Israel's political covenant as the ground for a broader public theology.

Ramsey opens the discussion of covenant and social contract by observing that "in the Bible God appears as a covenant-making, covenant-restoring, and covenant-fulfilling God; Israel, as people of the covenant and a covenant-breaking people" (p. 367). Shortly thereafter, he adds that covenant is "the foundation of human life in community" (p. 367). This transition — from the community of Israel to the human community — takes place on a number of occasions in the final chapter of *Basic Christian Ethics.* He notes that a study of Israel's covenant enables us to attend to the political "relevance or irrelevance" of the sovereignty of God (p. 384). It also "gives man whereon to stand in opposing the present shape of the world" (p. 387). Most explicitly, he says, "Political decision also should be guided by the righteousness of God we know through the covenant, especially the restoration of the covenant in Jesus Christ. . . . As long as God's covenant endures, human community cannot rightly be grounded in anything else" (p. 388). Each of these moves demonstrates his belief that the political significance of Israel's covenant applies, in Christ, to all political communities.

But Ramsey supplies no theological rationale for this transition. He fails to spell out how Yahweh's relationship with Israel relates to the human community as a whole, and he lacks adequate doctrines of creation, Christology, and eschatology on which to rest these claims.[27] The covenant/contract analogy distracts him from providing the adequate structural (i.e., theological) support that is necessary for an account of political obligation rooted in covenant. As we shall see, Ramsey realizes these deficiencies and seeks to correct them in later work.

More immediately, the influence of Karl Barth in the 1950s leads him to make a sharp turn away from the usefulness of social contract theory in political theology. He comes to see the tradition that Rousseau represents as ultimately a distraction, and one that promotes "a mistaken view of God's creation in man."[28] In later work he seizes upon the doctrine of creation and attacks Rousseau, noting that "the idea of *covenant*-bond stands between or beyond the idea of *contract*" because "the creation in him is in order to covenant."[29] These later developments are most clear in his

27. The closest he comes to connecting creation and covenant in *Basic Christian Ethics* is to cite approvingly Paul Minear's claim that "in creating the world, God made a covenant with it" and add that, "in covenanting with Israel, he *made* her a nation" (*BCE,* p. 372). In other words, "the nationalistic promise is not given without other words: 'in thee shall all the families of the earth be blessed'" (Ramsey, Unpublished Notes, Box 42, Ramsey Papers).

28. Ramsey, *Christian Ethics and the Sit-In,* 31. While Ramsey moves away from Rousseau, he never gives up on the idea that covenant is the ground of all political relationships. In an interview conducted in his office in 1986 he observes, "How in all the relations of life do we respond responsibly to one another and to God? We are a people covenantally related together, in a nation. We resolve to be together as a people through time." Vaux et al., eds., *Covenants,* p. 256.

29. Ramsey, *Christian Ethics and the Sit-In,* pp. 36, 31. In the late 1970s he wrote to an inquiring doctoral student: "I would never locate our 'creation for covenant' in our wills alone; then I would be a contractarian. . . . [W]e are born into political communities that are extant, unless you believe these really come about by contract." Paul Ramsey to Deborah Streeter, July 7, 1978, Box 24, Ramsey Papers.

appropriation of Barth's doctrine of creation in *Christian Ethics and the Sit-In.* Ramsey finds in Barth a theological foundation capable of sustaining a constructive political ethic rooted in covenant. I now turn to his more developed accounts of creation and covenant.

Creation and Covenant

Referring to the gradual release of volumes of Karl Barth's *Church Dogmatics* throughout the 1950s and 1960s, Ramsey writes late in his career: "I read every volume of Barth as those were issued in English translation, as soon as they came out! This was my summer's reading!"[30] The most important of those volumes for his theology of covenant was *Church Dogmatics* III/1, *The Doctrine of Creation* (published in English in 1958).[31] While he gestures toward the importance of Barth in *Basic Christian Ethics,* it is not until the 1961 publication of his second book, *Christian Ethics and the Sit-In,* that he begins to incorporate Barth's systematic perspective into his political theology.

In the second half of this chapter I want to analyze Ramsey's use of *Church Dogmatics* III/1 for his account of the central role of covenant in Christian political ethics. What will be immediately apparent to readers familiar with Barth's theology is that he does not use III/1 in a way that Barth likely would have approved, nor in a way that is compatible with the "special ethics" of *CD* III/4.[32] One of the central challenges of interpreting *Christian Ethics and the Sit-In* is parsing the way that he draws on III/1 while moving in a non-Barthian direction.[33] The substance of this claim will become clear in the forthcoming pages.

30. Paul Ramsey to David Attwood, December 8, 1984, Oliver O'Donovan personal collection.

31. Karl Barth, *The Doctrine of Creation,* vol. III/1 of *Church Dogmatics,* ed. G. W. Bromiley and T. F. Torrance; trans. J. W. Edwards, O. Bussey, and Harold Knight (Edinburgh: T&T Clark, 1958).

32. Karl Barth, *The Doctrine of Creation,* vol. III/4 of *Church Dogmatics,* ed. G. W. Bromiley and T. F. Torrance; trans. A. T. Mackay, T. H. L. Parker, H. Knight, H. A. Kennedy, and J. Marks (Edinburgh: T&T Clark, 1961).

33. David Attwood notes, "Barth's concern is a wide and general one, and Ramsey borrowed his language in order to use it in social and political ethics in a way that Barth never did, and indeed would have resisted" (Attwood, *Paul Ramsey's Political Ethics* (Lanham, MD: Rowman and Littlefield, 1992), p. 22. See also Robin W. Lovin, "Covenantal Relationships and Political Legitimacy," *The Journal of Religion* 60, no. 1 (1980): 2.

Given the tendentious nature of Ramsey's reading of Barth, I orient the discussion around two central questions. The first is a narrower one: What is Ramsey doing when he adopts and adapts this theology of covenant and creation from *Dogmatics* III/1? To answer this question, I consider the essential features of Barth's formula that creation is the "external basis" of covenant, and covenant is the "internal basis" of creation. This launches an examination of the ways Ramsey alters Barth's systematic account to rework the covenant/creation motif as a foundation for political morality. The second question is broader, and it sets the stage for several themes central to the remainder of the book. Stretching beyond Ramsey's explicit appropriation of Barth, how do these early explorations in covenant theology affect broader themes of political authority, moral agency, and the uses of power in his later political writing?

Before moving explicitly to the content of Barth's doctrine of creation, however, I want to offer a brief initial description of the scholarly and commercial reception of *Christian Ethics and the Sit-In* in the early 1960s. There is a tendency to overlook its importance among Ramsey's political writings, and paying attention to some of the details of its publication will help frame my attention to his adaptation of Barth. Perhaps more interestingly, however, it will help to paint a picture of Ramsey as a young scholar hoping to build on the foundational theological work that he had accomplished in *Basic Christian Ethics.*

Christian Ethics and the Sit-In

In 1961, Association Press distributed numerous copies of *Christian Ethics and the Sit-In* to reviewers in an attempt to piggyback on the previous success of *Basic Christian Ethics.* Several months after its release, however, James Best wrote to notify Ramsey that they had sold only 150 copies and that "review-wise it has not yet been a spectacular success."[34] Although they sold over a thousand copies by year's end, the second year of publication saw the distribution of only 184 copies. Ramsey barely made enough in total royalties to cover his $500 advance, and he ended up buying 100 of the remaining 1,000 books left in stock at the close of 1964.[35] By contrast, *War and the Christian*

34. James Best to Paul Ramsey, July 11, 1961, Box 33, Ramsey Papers.

35. For these figures, see the published book file on *Christian Ethics and the Sit-In,* Box 33, Ramsey Papers.

Conscience (also released in 1961) had by the end of that year already outsold all of the other books in the series on Christianity and politics from Duke University Press in which it appeared.[36]

Ramsey wrote *Christian Ethics and the Sit-In* with high hopes for its success. He suggested the book for promotion by the Religious Book Club (rather than *War and the Christian Conscience*) because he felt that the former was "not such heavy reading."[37] Even when sales continued to falter, he requested that a revised and enlarged edition be released with a substantial amount of new material and rearranged chapters. He felt that it was important to provide "further extension of the conceptual analysis that was begun to be set forth in that book."[38] The publishers offered a sympathetic but swift refusal, noting that the number of first-edition copies remaining in stock would be sufficient to sustain the current rate of sales for several years.[39] Nine months later, *Christian Ethics and the Sit-In* was out of print.

The book's woeful lack of commercial success did not dampen Ramsey's appreciation for its contents. In the early 1980s, he appealed to Karl Barth as the one who provided "the major leap forward" in his thinking about theological ethics.[40] That "leap" came in *Christian Ethics and the Sit-In* by way of the formula in *Dogmatics* III/1, in which covenant is the internal basis of creation, and creation is the external basis of covenant. I now turn to address the role of that motif in Barth's doctrine of creation.

Karl Barth's Doctrine of Creation in *Church Dogmatics* III/1

Barth arranges his discussion around exegesis of the creation stories of Genesis 1–2:4b and Genesis 2:4b-25. He addresses the former under the heading "Creation as the External Basis of the Covenant."[41] Here "exter-

36. The publishers congratulated Ramsey, saying, "[*War and the Christian Conscience*] is selling very well. . . . I think you should be pleased, as we are, regarding the favorable attention it has received throughout the country." See John Hallowell to Paul Ramsey, April 5, 1962, Box 33, Ramsey Papers. See also Paul Ramsey, *War and the Christian Conscience: How Shall Modern War Be Conducted Justly?* (Durham: Duke University Press, 1961).

37. Paul Ramsey to James Reitmulder, Jan. 23, 1961, Box 1, Ramsey Papers.

38. Paul Ramsey to Stanley Stuber, Jan. 30, 1964, Box 1, Ramsey Papers.

39. Robert Elfers to Paul Ramsey, Feb. 18, 1964, Box 1, Ramsey Papers.

40. Paul Ramsey, "A Letter to James Gustafson," *Journal of Religious Ethics* 13 (1985): 74.

41. Barth, *The Doctrine of Creation*, III/1, p. 94. Hereafter, page references to this work appear in parentheses within the text.

nal basis" expresses the view that the creative action of the triune God forms the cosmos and the earth, preparing a place that makes possible the relationship between God and humankind (pp. 207-8). External basis represents the structural framework and the physical substance that enable both human-human and human-divine relationships (including the reconciling work of Christ). As such, his doctrine of creation allows for no "external presupposition" of creation; beyond creation there is only Trinity (p. 43).

Barth addresses the second creation story under the heading "The Covenant as the Internal Basis of Creation" (p. 228). "Internal basis" expresses the view that covenant is the purpose or driving force of creation because the covenant-love of the divine Creator precedes, sustains, and eclipses the history of creation. He says:

> The fact that covenant is the goal of creation is not something which is added later to the reality of the creature, as though the history of creation might equally have been succeeded by any other history. It already characterises creation itself and as such, and therefore the being and existence of the creature. The covenant whose history had still to commence was the covenant which, as the goal appointed for creation and the creature, made creation necessary and possible, and determined and limited the creature. (p. 231)

Thus the internal character of creation — its nature and limitations, the ends placed before human society, and the essence underlying humanity — is drawn from the covenant.

Barth draws on Reformed covenant theology when he speaks of the history of the covenant as the covenant *of grace.* He rarely refers to the covenant in history, or the history of covenant, without calling it the covenant of grace — or simply *the* covenant. For Barth, history itself is embodied in the history of Israel such that she lives out what creation ascribes to humanity — that is, covenant (pp. 238-39). He describes "the history of the covenant of grace instituted by God between Himself and man; the sequence of the events in which God concludes and executes this covenant with man, carrying it to its goal" (p. 59). The covenant of grace thus takes place *in* history and *in* time because the historical and temporal creation is the (external) sphere in which God has chosen to save God's people (p. 66).

Three further observations concerning the external basis/internal basis motif will ease the transition into a discussion of Ramsey's appropriation of the formula. First, Barth sustains an emphasis on the creature and creaturely well-being. Despite the narrative of disobedience in the opening chapters of Genesis, he is adamant that the creature is "destined, prepared and equipped to be a partner of this covenant" (p. 97). There are no aspects of the created existence — in his words, "no attributes, no conditions of existence, no substantial or accidental predicates of any kind" — that are not formed for covenant with God in creation (p. 96; see also p. 230).

Second, Barth constantly reminds readers that the covenant driving creation also draws it toward its eschatological end (p. 97).[42] There is no teleology for the creature outside of covenant with God; what unites Israel's history with that of the cosmos is their shared eschatological end. There is a deep connection between what *was* at the beginning of creation and what *awaits* creation at its end. He does not mitigate the tension characteristic of time in created history, but he does affirm God's love as what sustains creation from start to finish (p. 317).[43]

My third observation is slightly longer. While Barth demonstrates the inseparability of covenant and creation, he also maintains that they are not identical:

> Creation is not itself the covenant. The existence and being of the one loved are not identical with the fact that it is loved. . . . Nor is creation the inner basis of the covenant. . . . The inner basis of the covenant is simply the free love of God, or more precisely the eternal covenant which God has decreed in Himself as the covenant of the Father with His Son as the Lord and Bearer of human nature. . . . (p. 97; see also p. 44)

There is an important distinction between creation and covenant that resembles the difference between the existence of the creature and the fact that the creature is loved. The creation-covenant formula thus *cannot be reversed* to read that covenant is the external basis of creation, and creation is the internal basis of covenant. This is a reminder that existence and well-being are not identical and that the well-being of God's creatures is

42. Creation places covenant not only at the beginning of all things but also at the end of all things. Covenant itself is the goal of creation. See also p. 42.

43. Around this time H. Richard Niebuhr makes a similar claim in "The Idea of Covenant and American Democracy," *Church History* 23, no. 2 (1954): 130-32. Barth, unlike Niebuhr, repeatedly affirms that the goal of covenant is explicitly connected to Jesus Christ. See *The Doctrine of Creation,* III/1, p. 232.

constituted by "simply the free love of God." To be created *for* covenant is one thing, to be *in* covenant is another.

I will have to suspend further comment on Barth's doctrine of creation for now. This summary of his external basis/internal basis understanding of creation and covenant should be sufficient to consider the differences between his doctrine and Ramsey's early political theology. As such, I will now reflect on the ways Ramsey adopts and adapts this understanding of creation and covenant.

Ramsey's Adaptation of the Creation/Covenant Formula

After reading *Dogmatics* III/1 in 1958, Ramsey delivered the Clarence D. Ashley Lectures on Law and Theology at New York University School of Law. In those lectures he says:

> If man is created for Exodus, it should not be surprising if there is present among the utterances of his created nature an echo of his call into covenant. . . . As Karl Barth might put the point that has to be made: natural justice or the requirements made known to us through fundamental inclination or disinclination are the external or natural basis, the precondition, and the possibility of Exodus into covenant; while covenant-righteousness is the internal basis, the true meaning and the final purpose of whatever utterances of essential human nature may be produced in man's intellect as he seeks to know the good.[44]

This is Ramsey's first mention of the formula, though it was not published until 1962 in *Nine Modern Moralists*. His more substantial engagement came, however, in *Christian Ethics and the Sit-In* (1961).[45]

I have mentioned above that Ramsey does not use *Dogmatics* III/1 in a way that Barth would have likely approved, nor in a way that is compatible with the special ethics of *Dogmatics* III/4.[46] For this reason, William

44. Ramsey, *Nine Modern Moralists* (Englewood Cliffs, NJ: Prentice-Hall, 1962), p. 244.

45. William Werpehowski rightly observes the fact that *Christian Ethics and the Sit-In*, despite the later publication date, addresses problems that emerged in several chapters in *Nine Modern Moralists*. See "Christian Love and Covenant Faithfulness," *Journal of Religious Ethics* 19, no. 2 (1991): 128-29.

46. Of course, *CD* III/4 was not available in English in 1958. My point is not that Ramsey should have used III/4, merely that his use of III/1 goes in a different direction.

Werpehowski notes that he has "his own purposes" in the appropriation of Barth.[47] David Attwood adds that his "application of the idea was not in the direction Barth intended."[48] While these observations are certainly accurate, Ramsey also never presumes that his position will remain wholly within the Barthian framework. Rather, as an unpublished piece in the Paul Ramsey Papers indicates, he felt that too many Reformed thinkers are afraid to "wrestle with [Barth] for insight" in the realm of ethics, having deepened their "knowledge into God which his theology yields."[49]

In *Christian Ethics and the Sit-In,* his wrestle with Barth produces the assertion that "an analysis of 'natural' justice on the basis of covenant-creation is imperative *even for a Barthian theological ethics.*" This stems from his unhappiness with the perception that "guidance for the political order" can easily be derived from "church law" or "the human law developed within the community of believers." He seeks an account of how "creation-covenant may provide criteria for this movement of secular law from worse to better," and he charges theological ethics with the task of establishing these criteria.[50]

Here, of course, in the appeal to creation and covenant for the movement of the social order from worse to better, is the Ramseyan transformist ethic closely aligned with H. Richard Niebuhr's fifth type, that of Christ-transforming-culture. To that I add that his call for closer attention to the structures of the moral life is also a common theme in his interpretation of Barth. In *Nine Modern Moralists,* Ramsey is concerned that "there may be a danger that some who follow Barth's lead will fail to elaborate fully a doctrine of man or to articulate an ethic which results from the proclamation of the gospel."[51] As late as the 1980s, in "Liturgy and Ethics," he still maintains that "Barth will have nothing to do with legal righteousness, but anyone who supposes that this means that the

47. William Werpehowski, *American Protestant Ethics and the Legacy of H. Richard Niebuhr* (Washington, DC: Georgetown University Press, 2002), p. 38. Werpehowski also rightly notes that "Ramsey was willing to speak generally of his adoption of 'Barth's formula,' but he failed in the course of his special ethics to refer his readers to it" ("Christian Love and Covenant Faithfulness," p. 127).

48. Attwood, *Ramsey's Political Ethics,* p. 19.

49. Paul Ramsey, "Review of *Right to Life,*" undated, Box 25, Ramsey Papers.

50. Ramsey, *Christian Ethics and the Sit-In,* p. 23.

51. Ramsey, *Nine Modern Moralists,* p. 36. He expresses concerns that Barth's rejection of independent anthropological claims (i.e., nonchristological accounts of human nature) will mistakenly abandon anthropology altogether (and therein deprive ethics of key philosophical and theological resources).

Christian life is structureless simply has not read him."[52] These insights stem from his reading of *Dogmatics* III/1, and he takes Barth's doctrine of creation as a source for identifying moral structures that constitute and shape our public lives.

Already in the quotation highlighted above from *Nine Modern Moralists,* Ramsey speaks of "natural justice" as something to be derived from a theology of creation and covenant.[53] In *Christian Ethics and the Sit-In,* he again develops an account of natural justice (in a distinctly non-Barthian fashion), as well as one of political order. Together they mark the two most significant features of his adaptations of the creation/covenant formula. I will address both concepts, beginning with natural justice.

The roots of justice for Ramsey lie in the positive function of covenant working in creation to determine norms of equity and desert in nature and in political institutions. Justice brings humanity together in right relationships and equitable arrangements, thereby creating the conditions for the possibility of charitable and loving action. It bears "the external marks of man's destiny for steadfast covenant love. It provides only the external possibility of covenant."[54] This means that the work of covenant as the internal basis of creation produces an element of justice in the natural created order.

As the external basis of covenant, natural justice is also the external basis of the work of Christian love. The unity of charity and justice is rooted in creation and found in "the goal toward which we are being redeemed," that is, in Christ (p. 49).[55] Ramsey uses Micah 6 to explain justice as the positive moral function of covenant:

> The state and its law as an ordinance of creation, natural justice, human and legal rights, and social institutions generally, so far as these

52. Paul Ramsey, "Liturgy and Ethics," *Journal of Religious Ethics* 7, no. 2 (1979): 144.

53. Ramsey, *Nine Modern Moralists,* p. 244.

54. Ramsey, *Christian Ethics and the Sit-In,* pp. 25-26. Hereafter, page references to this work appear in parentheses within the text.

55. Charles Harris comments: "Ramsey argues that in order for men to exist in any higher relationship with one another — e.g., that of charity — there must be certain conditions which are the 'external' basis of the higher relationships. Among these conditions is the institution of natural justice in which each man is given his exact due and regarded as an equal in an abstract sense with every other man before the law" (Charles E. Harris, "Love as the Basic Moral Principle in Paul Ramsey's Ethics," *Journal of Religious Ethics* 4, no. 2 [1976]: 245-46).

> have a positive purpose under the creative, governing, and preserving purposes of God — all are the external basis making possible the actualization of the promise of covenant; while covenant or fellow humanity is the internal basis and meaning of every right, true justice, or law. This enables us to see why the requirements of charity, or of steadfast covenant-love, and the requirements of justice, or of natural right, are ultimately inseverable. Each conditions the other, and we are told that what is required of us is only to do justice [the justice that provides an in-principled expression of divine charity or gives external basis for or promise of, or prepares in the desert a highway for God's mercy] and to love mercy [the mercy that determinately fashions our human justice] and to walk humbly in covenant with God. (pp. 25-26)

Ramsey uses the external basis/internal basis formula to establish natural justice as the work of covenant love in creation. In this way the meaning of justice is "resting upon the foundation of the created order" and, at the same time, "the promise and pledge or the possibility of covenant-love" (pp. 99, 30).

If natural justice is the positive function of covenant love working in creation, political order serves the negative function of restraining sin. Ramsey asserts that "repeatedly broken covenants" cause disorder, which "can destroy . . . the presuppositions and external basis of covenant" (p. 51). Therefore, "the Christian understanding of the fallen creation and its *always already* broken covenants gives the justification for a regard for order as well as for justice" (pp. xiii-xiv). The responsibility of the state to supply political order in a world of repeatedly broken covenants is to make possible "man's life in community" (p. 50). Thus, it is not merely natural justice, but "the political order with its justice and its law . . . [which] are the external basis, the promise, the possibility and capability for covenant-community" (p. 18).[56] Because the state is "a body composed of covenant relations," it is responsible for maintaining the external possibility of those relations through political order (p. 50).

56. He does not establish the more formal distinction between *lex, ordo,* and *iustitia* until his book *The Just War.* There he asserts that *lex* and *ordo* represent two aspects of order itself, the legal order and the order of power (Ramsey, *The Just War: Force and Political Responsibility* [New York: Charles Scribner's Sons, 1968; reprint, Lanham, MD: Rowman and Littlefield, 1983], pp. 11-12).

Covenant, Creation, and Political Agency

Even given Barth's likely displeasure with Ramsey's appropriation of III/1, we can observe a number of ways that Ramsey uses the creation/covenant motif to propel his political theology forward.[57] Notice that his early emphasis on the link between creation, Christology, and eschatology finds stronger footing within Barth's framework. He warns against abstracting from the world and losing "the capacity to be undergoing change by creation-covenant in which and toward which we live and by the ultimate reality of the church and the Spirit of Christ" (p. 61).[58] That capacity rests on the Barthian distinction (and tension) between what we are (creatures in a good but fallen creation) and what we are to become (creatures in eschatological covenant with God) (p. 59).

This distinction also informs a revised account of political obligation. Early in this chapter I mentioned Rousseau's attempts to root moral obligation in the self. Ramsey expressed dissatisfaction with this account, arguing instead that only the divine will can establish the moral good toward which we move. Barth's eschatology provides him with the theological resources to describe the tension between obligation and agency (consent in Rousseau), as well as the space between what we are and what we are to become. Ramsey says: "[T]he saving distinction ought to be kept clear . . . between creation and covenant, between the cohesions of any actual human community and the fact that we are and therefore are to become one in Christ" (p. 59).[59] It is a "saving" distinction precisely because it describes the eschatological tension of our lives and our ultimate end in covenant with God in Christ. It safeguards the sovereignty of God and therein the distinction between divine love and creaturely faithfulness. At the same time it upholds the significance of the political good and the weight of moral obligation by pointing to the fact that we are not yet at the goal for which we are destined.

Notice also how sharply Ramsey's claim that political and ethi-

57. I am not suggesting that Ramsey's political themes are wholly faithful to Barth's line of reasoning in III/1. Instead, I am pointing to the way that the external basis/internal basis motif remains recognizably Barthian in origin, even as Ramsey appropriates it to various ends in his political theology.

58. As Timothy P. Jackson says, "Behind Ramsey's axiology lies his eschatology" (Jackson, *The Priority of Love: Christian Charity and Social Justice* [Princeton, NJ: Princeton University Press, 2003], p. 107).

59. It is the distinction between "a formal condition of relationship from its realization" (Werpehowski, *American Protestant Ethics,* p. 41).

cal judgments take place in history resembles Barth's assertion that all covenants are historical covenants. This is most frequently expressed in Ramsey's repetition of the idea that it is, after all, "in this world, and not some other, [that] covenant must be enacted" (p. 102). His account of humanity is such that "God who created me . . . at the same time gave me a nature in the form of fellow humanity in the historical time and space of my existence in covenant" (pp. 37-38). Although he drops Barth's phrase "covenant of grace," he sustains the deep Barthian relationship among covenant, history, and time. As we shall see, the emphasis on the temporal character of human political relationships is an enduring theme in Ramsey's political theology.

Finally — and most important — Ramsey generalizes the external/internal motif to include a range of concepts, not simply creation and covenant. This relies heavily on Barth's insistence that covenant and creation are connected, yet not identical. As I observed earlier, to be created for covenant is one thing; to be in covenant is another. Ramsey uses this configuration widely in his political theology, even when he does not refer explicitly to a doctrine of creation or a theology of covenant. Early, in *Christian Ethics and the Sit-In,* he says that "the justice we know is still not the same thing as love — just as nature is not grace or grace nature, and creation is not covenant nor covenant the same as creation" (p. 127). In later writings we encounter other concepts that reflect the same internal/external structure.[60] Let me illuminate the most important of them here.

Just three years after *Christian Ethics and the Sit-In* came out, Ramsey published his most comprehensive statement of political theory: "The Uses of Power."[61] In 1968 he placed it as the headlining essay of *The Just War.* There he declares:

> The proposition that the use of power, and possibly the use of force, belongs to the *esse* of politics (its *act of being*) and is inseparable from the *bene esse* of politics (its *proper act of being,* or its act of being *proper* politics) is denied by two views of the state, or of political community.

60. E.g., "The ordinance, law, or covenant of marriage is the internal basis and meaning or purpose of created human sexuality" (*Christian Ethics and the Sit-In,* p. 22). "I affirm that there is some virtue in man's ordinary moral decisions, and . . . I also affirm that no moral judgment is sufficient by nature alone, without in one way or another the saving and transforming power of the *agape* of Christ" (*Nine Modern Moralists,* p. 4).

61. Paul Ramsey, "The Uses of Power," *Perkins Journal* 18, no. 1 (1964): 13-24; this essay appears in Ramsey, *The Just War,* pp. 3-18.

Later he adds:

> Power, which is of the *esse* of political agency, may be a conditional value only; but order and justice, which are ever in tension yet in interrelation, both are values that comprise the well-being, the *bene esse,* of political affairs and the common good which is the goal of political action.[62]

Notice how the *esse/bene esse* structure follows the external/internal motif.[63] Power is not a good in itself; it finds its place as the external basis for order and justice, which comprise the internal "well-being" of the common good. One common misinterpretation of Ramsey's work is the suggestion that he views the exercise of force as the essence of political agency.[64] But power has a technical (and provisional) function in this account, a "conditional value only." Power is not the *bene esse* of politics; that belongs to the "terminal goals" of order and justice. Yet power is the medium by which the political agent moves the community with purpose toward the good. Thus does Ramsey insist that "a political action is always an exercise of power and an exercise of purpose. Power without purpose and purpose without power are both equally nonpolitical."[65] The purposive exercise of power is the currency of movement toward political goods of order and justice.

62. Ramsey, *The Just War,* pp. 5, 11.

63. I would also suggest that Ramsey's core claim — there is a political *act of being* that is distinct from yet inseparable from politics' *proper act of being* — recycles the structure of Barth's distinction between what it is to be human (created) and what it is to be properly human (i.e., to be in covenant with God). I mentioned earlier that Barth's attention to eschatology provides Ramsey with the theological resources to describe our capacity for moral transformation. It rests on the distinction (and tension) between what we are (creatures in a good but fallen creation) and what we are to become (creatures in eschatological covenant with God). That same structure is here driving his emphasis on the technical (and provisional) function of power as that which connects the *esse* and *bene esse* of the political realm. At the same time it draws attention to the good end to which creation (and therein the political realm) is ultimately destined: the unity of charity, order, and justice. Again, the point is not that Barth would agree with this appropriation of his work, but simply that Ramsey makes wide use of this conceptual apparatus.

64. See, for instance, Stephen Long's claim: "Yet for Ramsey, unlike Aquinas and Augustine, the presence of evil — force, coercion, violence — becomes the essence of politics" (Long, *Tragedy,* p. 44). Ramsey would reject the claim that all force and violence are inherently evil, and perhaps request a more nuanced reading of this claim: "The use of power, and possibly the use of force, is of the *esse* of politics" (Ramsey, *The Just War,* p. 5).

65. Ramsey, *The Just War,* pp. 29, 8.

If it is not already clear, let me say it again: Barth would surely reject Ramsey's claims in *Nine Modern Moralists* and *The Just War* — and how! There is quite a difference, for instance, between the *esse* of the creature in Barth's doctrine of creation and the *esse* of politics in Ramsey's political theology. There is also a difference between what it is for a human to be a human and what it is for a state to be a state, or, in Ramsey's preferred terms, a magistrate to be a magistrate. I dispute no one who calls attention to such subtleties. In fact, one of the "two views of the state" that Ramsey rejects in the above quotation is Barth's political ethics in *Church Dogmatics* III/4![66] My point is simply this: once Ramsey appropriates Barth's external/internal construction on the themes of covenant and creation, he organizes a whole range of concepts through this structural motif.

As I have suggested earlier, Ramsey's interactions with Barth propel his political theology forward by providing a range of theological and structural foundations. I have granted that many of those movements forward are also movements away from Barth's moral and political theology. The roots of justice for Ramsey lie in the positive function of covenant working in creation to determine norms of equity and desert in nature and in political institutions. Oliver O'Donovan describes this position by noting that living well "must be described in terms consistent with simply 'living.'"[67] *Christian Ethics and the Sit-In* establishes precisely this concept by arguing that governing rightly must be consistent with simply governing. Ramsey extends this thinking in *Nine Modern Moralists* and *The Just War.* He seizes on Barth's doctrine of creation and uses it to articulate this interpretation of purpose and political agency.

66. I have observed above that it is noteworthy that Ramsey used *Church Dogmatics* III/1 to reinforce his political theology rather than III/4. "Uses of Power" uncovers the reason for that turn by revealing several criticisms of the special ethics of III/4. Obviously, I am not claiming that Ramsey, in *Christian Ethics and the Sit-In,* prefers III/1 to III/4. The English translation of III/4 did not appear until after 1961. My point here is more generally that the influence of III/1 continued to shape and drive his political ethics even as his later work voiced criticisms of III/4. For more on this, see the very important essay: Oliver O'Donovan, "Karl Barth and Ramsey's 'Uses of Power,'" in Oliver O'Donovan and Joan Lockwood O'Donovan, eds., *Bonds of Imperfection* (Grand Rapids: Eerdmans, 2004), pp. 246-75.

67. O'Donovan, "Karl Barth and Ramsey's 'Uses of Power,'" in *Bonds of Imperfection,* p. 259.

Covenant Foundations

Even as covenant comes and goes in Ramsey's political writings, these early engagements with Rousseau and Barth laid the groundwork for all subsequent work. They root his political thinking in a concept of covenant undergirded by doctrines of creation, eschatology, and Christology. They structure his public theology around commitments to justice, order, and agape. They solidify his commitment to covenant as the primary frame of reference for Christian considerations of political authority and judgment.

The promises and failures of the covenant/contract analogy unearth important claims in Ramsey's covenant theology: the absolute and eternal sovereignty of God is the ground of all political power and authority; our collective political existence only takes shape in relationship to this sovereignty and in light of our eschatological destiny; our political agency rests entirely on God's prior action on our behalf. The "leap forward" through Barth's doctrine of covenant and creation provides Ramsey with resources for an account of moral obligation rooted in divine will. Even in the political realm, we wait with eschatological hope and, in the meantime, pursue political goods of justice, order, and love. In other words, these early explorations in covenant theology establish the basic theological foundations of his vision of political life. Ramsey charges the state both with ensuring that the political community continues to exist and with the pursuit of covenant-defined aims toward which the political community is ultimately ordered.

The tension of these two features of political life — the *esse* and the *bene esse* — represents and reflects the tension of historical time between creation and the *eschaton.* How to organize political life in that time is the defining question of Ramsey's political work. Of course, while covenant is the earliest of his theological motifs, it is not the only one that captures his imagination. His subtle appropriation of repentance — a theme largely untouched in his writings from the 1950s — holds an important place in *War and the Christian Conscience.* The usefulness of repentance as a political concept, as well as its impact on the development of Ramsey's political thought, occupies the next chapter.

CHAPTER TWO

Repentance and Political Agency

In *Democracy and Tradition,* Jeffrey Stout introduces the problem of "dirty hands" as a way of examining the habits of accountability that govern political judgments.[1] The term captures a persistent philosophical conflict codified in an important essay by Michael Walzer in the early 1970s.[2] It suggests that political leaders will face situations that require the violation of traditionally inviolable moral norms in an effort to preserve some higher political good. In Stout's language, it pits determinate political obligations (preservation of the state, protection of the innocent, etc.) against limits on the legitimate use of means available to fulfill such obligations (just-war principles of proportion and discrimination, the inexcusability of torture, etc.). Stout rightly observes that the problem of dirty hands holds in focus one of our most deeply rooted anxieties about the political realm: the question of whether committing moral atrocities is an inescapable aspect of political office. He also notes that these anxieties reflect the deep connection between the moral life of a community and the accountability of those in political office.[3]

Both Stout and Walzer draw on a tradition of thinking in American public theology that wrestles with political conflicts between moral limitations and responsibilities. As Ramsey began to approach this tradition more seriously in the early 1960s, he was keen to keep his contributions

1. Jeffrey Stout, *Democracy and Tradition* (Princeton, NJ: Princeton University Press, 2004).

2. Michael Walzer, "Political Action: The Problem of Dirty Hands," *Philosophy and Public Affairs* 2, no. 2 (Winter 1973): 160-80.

3. Stout, *Democracy and Tradition,* p. 200.

to the discussion rooted in firm theological convictions.[4] He attempted various descriptions of this problem throughout his career, and, as we shall see in a later chapter, his last word on the subject relied heavily on a concept of tragedy. Yet, by thinking out of the logic of the "War Articles" exchanged between Reinhold and H. Richard Niebuhr, Ramsey initially framed his theological approach to the problem of dirty hands in the language of repentance. The aim of this chapter is to investigate why Ramsey was drawn to repentance as a theological lens for thorny political situations, and what his use of the concept reveals about his overarching framework for political theology. Perhaps more importantly, I will also attempt to show why he abandoned the concept in later work. As a general rule, Ramsey was less interested in providing a systematic theological account of politics than he was in grabbing hold of whatever theological point of reference might be useful for rejecting strictly secular accounts of the political realm. This is truer of his use of repentance as a political concept than any other.

Right Political Action and the Inviolability of the Pauline Prohibition

Several of Ramsey's most important writings on political realism and justified war wrestle with the public significance of theological claims and the problem of dirty hands. Although he does not use this term specifically, he refuses, from the start, any suggestion that the political realm can be morally interpreted through power politics (i.e., might makes right) or technical performance of the kind that never demands prudence, only calculation. He also pledges allegiance to the political significance of the "Pauline prohibition" never to do evil that good may come (Rom. 3:8).[5]

4. D. Stephen Long and Stanley Hauerwas have noted that the principal shift between the overtly political elements of *Basic Christian Ethics* and *War and the Christian Conscience* is one between the justice of going to war and "*how* the Christian uses violence" (D. Stephen Long and Stanley Hauerwas, foreword to Paul Ramsey, *Basic Christian Ethics* [Louisville: Westminster John Knox Press; reprint, 1993], p. xxi).

5. "And why not say (as some people slander us by saying that we say), 'Let us do evil so that good may come'? Their condemnation is deserved!" (Rom. 3:8; NRSV). For a concise discussion of the wider theological impulses behind Pauline ethics, see chapter 1 of Richard B. Hays, *The Moral Vision of the New Testament: A Contemporary Introduction to New Testament Ethics* (San Francisco: HarperSanFrancisco, 1996).

Rather, he pursues a genuinely theological account of the political realm that supplies a moral vision for faithful obedience and, at the same time, remains sensitive to the realities and limitations of political existence.

In both *War and the Christian Conscience* and *The Just War,* Ramsey navigates the problem of dirty hands with reference to three central commitments. The first is his belief in the possibility of faithful Christian obedience, even within the political realm. As Michael McKenzie notes, Ramsey "sees no *necessary* conflict between the demands of 'agape' on the individual Christian and the demands of politics in the public realm."[6] This means that the central responsibility of those in political office is to "guide the thrust of political action into ways that are right."[7] It also locates the just-war tradition within "the interior of the ethics of Christian love."[8] To deny these conclusions would be to deny the possibility of redemption (and sanctification) in the political realm. For Ramsey, stepping into political office cannot simply involve an intentional embrace of wrongdoing or an inevitable submission to evil practices. He fights to preserve an account of faithful obedience in the form of constructive and purposive political action.

His second commitment is to an understanding of the "structural difference between personal moral agency and political agency."[9] He inherits the tendency to divide moral issues along this line from Reinhold Niebuhr. While Ramsey did not embrace Niebuhr's belief that "group relations can never be as ethical as those which characterize individual relations," he did speak of the need for ethicists to attend to what "specifically differentiates the political good from the good in general."[10] As Stout notes, "Ramsey identified himself closely with the 'realism' of Reinhold Niebuhr and consistently tried to make his writings acutely sensitive to the responsibilities and concerns of the powerful."[11] These limitations and obligations formed

6. Michael C. McKenzie, *Paul Ramsey's Ethics: The Power of 'Agape' in a Postmodern World* (Westport: Praeger, 2001), p. 115.

7. Paul Ramsey, *War and the Christian Conscience: How Shall Modern War Be Conducted Justly?* (Durham: Duke University Press, 1961), p. 12.

8. Paul Ramsey, *The Just War: Force and Political Responsibility* (New York: Charles Scribner's Sons, 1968; reprint, Lanham: Rowman and Littlefield, 1983), p. 142.

9. Ramsey, *War and the Christian Conscience,* p. 9.

10. Reinhold Niebuhr, *Moral Man and Immoral Society* (New York: Charles Scribner's Sons, 1932), p. 83; Ramsey, *The Just War,* p. 9.

11. Jeffrey Stout, "Ramsey and Others on Nuclear Ethics," *Journal of Religious Ethics* 19, no. 2 (1991): 213.

the unique context that Ramsey thought constituted the difference between personal and public morality.

Despite these influences from Niebuhr, Ramsey felt a strong need to temper his understanding of a public/private distinction with a third commitment. He imposes onto the Niebuhrian distinction a strict allegiance to fixed moral concepts (e.g., "murder . . . means the same whether this is done by individuals or states").[12] As Stout notes, he was "deeply uneasy about Niebuhr's writings on the use of force, precisely because of their scant attention to the morality of means."[13] Stephen Long examines the relationship between Ramsey and Niebuhr at length in *Tragedy, Tradition, Transformism,* where he notes that "Ramsey views the prudential ethics of Niebuhrian realists as leading reflection on the Christian moral life into the 'wasteland of utility.' "[14] Ramsey attempts to repair this by upholding the inviolable status of moral norms, even in political emergencies.

Stout nicely captures the source of Ramsey's allegiance to these fixed norms:

> Niebuhr was not a utilitarian, but he did seem to imply that any means might be justified in waging war against an especially dangerous and odious foe. From Ramsey's point of view, this placed in jeopardy a central scriptural tenet, the Pauline prohibition of doing evil that good may come (Romans 3:8). Ramsey therefore set himself the task, in all of his writings on war and statecraft, to salvage the absolutist theme without sacrificing the prudent spirit and pastoral sensibility of Niebuhrian realism.[15]

The Pauline prohibition limited Ramsey's willingness to identify politics as a realm hopelessly abandoned to conflicting pursuits of lesser evils. Thus he notes that the just-war theory "defines right doing that good may come of it, not wrong doing quixotically alleged to be warranted solely by consequences expected to follow."[16] The corollary to his belief that right action is

12. Ramsey, *War and the Christian Conscience,* pp. 11-12.

13. Stout, "Ramsey and Others," p. 213.

14. D. Stephen Long, *Tragedy, Tradition, Transformism: The Ethics of Paul Ramsey* (Boulder, CO: Westview Press, 1993), p. 68.

15. Stout, "Ramsey and Others," p. 213. For instance, Ramsey insists that "it can never be right to do wrong for the sake of some real or supposed good" (Ramsey, *The Just War,* p. 142).

16. Paul Ramsey, "Politics as Science, Not Prophecy," *Worldview* 11, no. 1 (1968): 21.

possible in the realm of politics is an adherence to the prohibition of doing evil that good may come.

One challenge to readers investigating these concepts in his work is that he does not always execute the discussions with great clarity or ease. Ramsey may often be the most insightful thinker on a topic, but he is rarely the most accessible. For instance, in *War and the Christian Conscience,* he focuses his attention on the issue of dirty hands through the use of a difficult term, "deferred repentance."[17] It sounds here as though political officials are being given license to do whatever they please, at least for a time. (One can hardly imagine the John the Baptist of Matthew 3 adding any qualifiers to the command "Repent!" much less one that suggests postponement of the commanded act.) For this reason, Stout calls the troubled phrase "the most visible sign of strain in Ramsey's attempt to remain faithful to Niebuhr's realism while affirming the Pauline prohibition."[18] Perhaps most significantly, calling attention to his use of repentance as a theological category in his early writings fits uncomfortably with the fact that the lasting memory for many of his colleagues from the 1960s and 1970s is his refusal to repent of his judgments on the justice of the Vietnam War.

Ramsey's suggestion that repentance can be deferred is certainly challenging, and out of the failures of this phrase, and other criticisms, his later work seeks to reformulate these core ideas with stronger adherence to the Pauline prohibition and a clearer definition of the concept of tragedy. Yet, while he abandons the phrase, he does not abandon repentance as an important political motif. Furthermore, I believe that we forgo considerable benefit from Ramsey's insights — as well as an opportunity to work toward a clearer picture of how political judgment may be understood through the theological lens of repentance — if we move too quickly past the arguments of *War and the Christian Conscience.* In fact, I would suggest that what Ramsey attempts, admittedly unsuccessfully, in his comments on deferred repentance takes us to the core of his political theology, and it raises unavoidable questions for those seeking, as he did, a genuinely theological political theology. The remainder of this chapter explores that possibility.

He rejects the view that "killing in war is intrinsically wrong, but this immorality may nevertheless be done if the acts of war are calculated to lead to a lesser available evil among the consequences" (p. 20).

17. Ramsey, *War and the Christian Conscience,* pp. 11-14, 311.

18. Stout, "Ramsey and Others," p. 215.

Deferred Repentance?

The 1960s were Ramsey's most prolific years as a political thinker. In 1961, he published both *Christian Ethics and the Sit-In* and *War and the Christian Conscience.*[19] Amid the reliably Ramseyan themes of these two volumes — concepts of covenant and agape, explorations of justice, law, and virtue — lies the obscure suggestion that politics is a realm of "deferred repentance."[20] I mentioned above that he searches for a way to defend against a rigid distinction between public and private morality by insisting that "no case can be made for the view that what is wrong for a man may be right for a government." At the same time, he is sensitive to the fact that the remedying of certain political behaviors may require more time than certain individual behaviors. Thus, "whatever is immoral an individual, in his private capacity, should cease doing at once."[21] By contrast, political morality may not be so immediately within reach. That is to say, political officials may not be able to set right all of the political wrongs before them with the expediency of an individual ceasing a personal action or habit.

Two examples will help clarify what he means by this description. The first has to do with the magistrate's inability to rectify immediately the moral evil of disproportionate weaponry. He writes:

> There should be statesmen who themselves are quite clear as to the immorality of obliteration warfare (as well as to the wrong of deterring evil by readiness to do the same thing) who are still willing to engage in negotiation directed to the end of limiting war to justifiable means and ends through a period of time in which they may have to defer their nation's repentance.[22]

19. Ramsey, *War and the Christian Conscience; Christian Ethics and the Sit-In* (New York: Association Press, 1961). See the published book files in Box 33, Paul Ramsey Papers, David M. Rubenstein Rare Book and Manuscript Library, Duke University.

20. Ramsey, *War and the Christian Conscience,* p. 12; *Christian Ethics and the Sit-In,* p. 116.

21. Ramsey, *War and the Christian Conscience,* p. 12. As early as 1958, in the Clarence D. Ashley Lectures on Law and Theology, Ramsey notes that "God places the requirement of righteousness in some sense upon the whole nation as well as upon individuals in their private affairs." See *Nine Modern Moralists* (Englewood Cliffs, NJ: Prentice-Hall, 1962), p. 250. The last two chapters of this volume are taken from the Ashley Lectures.

22. Ramsey, *War and the Christian Conscience,* p. 12. David Attwood aptly captures this tension in Ramsey's account by saying that "the morality of politics is not to be set apart

The catch, of course, is that the security that safeguards continued negotiations is to some degree assured by the deterrent effect of the immoral weapons. When Ramsey speaks of the distinctive context of political endeavors, he also speaks of the magistrate who "remains convinced that politics is his vocation."[23] To withdraw from office at each moment of deterrent-ensured freedom would be to abandon altogether the pursuit of right policy and proportionate weaponry. Yet the political official also cannot compromise the verdict that the deterrent effects of disproportionate weaponry are plainly and unavoidably immoral. Deferred repentance describes that period of time purchased by immoral weapons but harnessed for the removal of those weapons.

The second example comes by way of his discussions of race relations in *Christian Ethics and the Sit-In.* Speaking of the U.S. government's moral responsibilities to apartheid South Africa, he says:

> [Politics] is an area of deferred repentance — but not forever. If there has been no propitious moment yet in recent history for the United States to take action . . . that moment may soon come when . . . our country can no longer defer making effective repentance for its complicity in injustice. Then we will face questions as to the use of strong and definite economic pressures with the purpose of radically assisting in the transformation of the whole structure of race relations in a country abroad. . . . [T]he fact is that . . . we are inexorably involved in supporting economically the domestic policies of the present South African government.[24]

In this case he roots the idea of deferred repentance in the search for the politically prudent moment for effective moral action. He knows that each passing moment is another instance of the government's ongoing complicity with actions of South African political leaders. Yet he also appreciates that such complicity will not be easily or quietly erased. Deferred repentance is an attempt to grant political officials the freedom to seek the most prudent and properly effective action rather than simply the most immediate.

---

from the morality of any other subject, but neither is the morality of politics identical to private morality" (Attwood, *Paul Ramsey's Political Ethics* [Lanham, MD: Rowman and Littlefield, 1992], p. 52).

23. Ramsey, *War and the Christian Conscience,* p. 11.

24. Ramsey, *Christian Ethics and the Sit-In,* p. 116.

These examples make clear that Ramsey's aim is to encourage purposive pursuit of moral gains in the limited context of the political realm. His account rests on the moral inviolability of just-war principles to the extent that "even the politics of deferred repentance is made quite impossible, where there is nothing in violation of fundamental principle to repent of, and to negotiate out of the realm of possibility."[25] Notice, further, that negotiation itself does not constitute political repentance. The change of course that repentance requires must involve the rectifying of immoral policies and practices. Nonetheless, purposive negotiation can be a hallmark of the rightly acting magistrate, and deferred repentance describes the time granted to those in office for the proper work of political authority.

Criticisms of Deferred Repentance

As I mentioned above, the troubling aspects of this account stem most obviously from the fact that the phrase sounds neither politically constructive nor morally steadfast. In David Little's contribution to *Love and Society: Essays in the Ethics of Paul Ramsey,* he writes that deferred repentance suspends the principle of discrimination in the means of warfare in order to ensure specific discriminate political ends. That is to say, it waives the moral criteria governing actions in war. Little says triumphantly: "We have here, from Ramsey's own pen, an example of its being *in some sense* reasonable or tolerable for a magistrate to make a decision by disregarding, temporarily, the application of the principle of discrimination to the *means* of action in favor of considering its application to the *ends* of action!" He argues that Ramsey's magistrate "should be fully conscious of the grave moral evil implicit in the course of action he permits," though he "ought not in any way to minimize the gravity of the matter, but . . . simply ought to postpone doing something to rectify it."[26]

Ramsey responds to Little's criticisms two years later in an essay titled "Some Rejoinders." He squarely rejects the suggestion that deferred repentance has to do with intending or licensing indiscriminate political means. It cannot mean "that statesmen ought simply to sin bravely and

25. Ramsey, *War and the Christian Conscience,* p. 13.

26. David Little, "The Structure of Justification in the Political Ethics of Paul Ramsey," in James T. Johnson and David H. Smith, eds., *Love and Society: Essays in the Ethics of Paul Ramsey* (Missoula, MT: Scholars Press, 1974), p. 156.

ever more bravely repent."[27] Instead of licensing magistrates to waive the principle of discrimination, deferred repentance involves the pursuit of discriminate means (and ends) in a political realm where the rectifying of immoral policy may not be immediately available (or prudent). He describes this pursuit by speaking of a magistrate "negotiating [something] out of the realm of possibility . . . and living with unjust war policies while effecting the reformation of such policies."[28]

Ramsey also argues that Little's reading obscures his description of the posture of the magistrate caught between an unbreakable principle of discrimination and a broken political order built on and sustained by indiscriminate weaponry. He exaggerates this point, arguing that "a [just-war] statesman is not likely to suppose that meantime he can be excused for engaging in a few tit-for-tat city exchanges." Thus he speaks of deferred repentance as "the use of the time granted by deterrence to 'ransom the time' by a creative political reconstruction of deterrence systems."[29] This marks the difference between working to rectify immoral means in spite of those means and waiving the moral norms governing political action.

Shortly after the publication of *War and the Christian Conscience* in 1961, Ramsey received a letter protesting the idea of deferred repentance from John Hick, then of Princeton Theological Seminary. Their exchange is particularly useful for understanding the meaning of the term and his approach to the significance of repentance as a political concept. Hick takes issue with what he calls "the sinister notion of deferred repentance," saying that it "sounds suspiciously as though it simply means not doing what one sees to be right, or doing what one sees to be wrong."[30] Ramsey's response is illuminating:

27. Paul Ramsey, "Some Rejoinders," *Journal of Religious Ethics* 4, no. 2 (1976): 210. Little's suggestion that deferred repentance uses indiscriminate means in pursuit of discriminate ends cannot square with Ramsey's belief that certain and determinate universal political ends (i.e., perpetual peace, the abolition of war, etc.) are impossible this side of the *eschaton.* One feature of our creaturely existence is that "the *highest* we can actually aim at is the limited use of limited force; and God knows that is utopian enough" (Ramsey, *War and the Christian Conscience,* p. 128.

28. Ramsey, "Some Rejoinders," p. 209. Ramsey saw a shining example of such action in the announcement by U.S. Secretary of Defense Robert McNamara in June 1962 that the United States would no longer prepare to target civilian populations with nuclear weapons in the event of an attack (see Ramsey, *The Just War,* pp. 211-13; see also Stout, "Ramsey and Others," pp. 215-16.

29. Ramsey, "Some Rejoinders," p. 211.

30. John Hick to Paul Ramsey, June 27, 1961, Box 11, Ramsey Papers.

> [Deferred repentance] is not sinister, but is rather of relating moral principles to political action acknowledged to be "the art of the possible" in such fashion as to prevent this "art of the possible" from becoming a realm of either technical performance or power politics wholly unrelated to morality. "Deferred repentance" means primarily, not doing what one sees to be wrong (though this may in some sense still be true) but doing from among the possible collective acts the one that is most right among the possibles and the one best calculated to make more of what is right a possibility for future political choice. It is, therefore, to do the *politically* right, the best *possible* good.[31]

He calls attention to the belief that the political good cannot simply be one of resignation to evil. That would be to relinquish the possibility of Christian love and faithfulness at work even in the political realm. This is driven by a concern that the logic of choosing between "lesser evils" will erode into a kind of excuse-giving rather than moral justification. His insistence that deferred repentance involves the selection of the "most right among the possibles" indicates that even if the "least possible evil" and the "greatest possible good" could be used to describe the same political act, the interpretive difference is of great theological significance. He says this another way in an interview late in his career: "The least unavoidable evil simply is the greatest possible good; no tears, please."[32]

Ramsey's response to these criticisms helps demonstrate that in deferred repentance he seeks an interpretation of political action that identifies and encourages a constructive sense of moral purpose even in the limited context of the political realm. But he also fails to articulate a wider theological account of repentance on which these claims rest. The troubled nature of the phrase stems in part from its obscure theological roots and lack of connection to a more traditional understanding of the role of repentance in the Christian life. Here we will benefit greatly by moving from Ramsey's unique and limited account of deferred repentance to a set of

31. Paul Ramsey to John Hick, July 13, 1961, Box 11, Ramsey Papers. Ramsey adds: "Unless you are going to say that there is no difference between the morality of private and of responsible action (I say there is no difference in the principle that pertains), there is need for some equivalent concept of 'deferred repentance.'"

32. He says later that the phrase "I choose the lesser evil" is "more like an excuse than a justification" (Kenneth L. Vaux, Sara Vaux, and Mark Stenberg, eds., *Covenants of Life: Contemporary Medical Ethics in Light of the Thought of Paul Ramsey* [Dordrecht: Kluwer Academic Publishers, 2002], p. 165).

wider observations about his theology of repentance and the significance of political judgment.

Repentance as Political Action

In 1943 Ramsey submitted an essay entitled "Sin, Repentance, and History" to the editor of *Christianity and Crisis,* Reinhold Niebuhr, who supplied it with a new title, "The Manger, the Cross, and the Resurrection."[33] In it Ramsey makes an important distinction between two forms of repentance. He says: "Repentance in which we suffer remorse for an action the evil character of which has thrust itself or has somehow been hauled into our consciousness, is clearly different from that repentance which is appropriate for our deeper, unconscious sin" (p. 3). He calls the first of these "repentance for unrighteousness" and the second "repentance for righteousness" (p. 3).

Contrition is the appropriate character of repentance for unrighteousness because of the delayed nature of the act. He says: "Sorrow or remorseful repentance for things we have done in the past, the sinfulness of which we now see, is something which must always be *subsequent* to the sin itself" (p. 3). He reintroduces this concept the following year in "Natural Law and the Nature of Man," saying, "One becomes aware of having sinned against what he knew before the act and knows after the act to be the moral law; and remorseful repentance leading to self-improvement are then in order."[34] That is, repentance of this kind can only take shape when looking back on what we recognize as wrongdoing.

What he terms repentance for righteousness, however, is more elusive. He observes: "Repentance for our unconscious sin, make no mistake about it, is repentance for our righteousness. It is superfluous to say 'for our supposed righteousness,' because before God all human righteousness is 'supposed' until God has acted and judged" ("The Manger," p. 3). The concept does not imply that we should repent of that righteousness which is imputed through the judgment and grace of God, but rather that we recognize even in our current pursuit of faithful action the broken character of human agency. He notes: "We also sin, not knowing what we do,

33. Paul Ramsey, "The Manger, the Cross, and the Resurrection," *Christianity and Crisis* 3, no. 4 (1943): 2-5. Hereafter, page references to this essay appear in parentheses in the text. See also D. Stephen Long, *Tragedy, Tradition, Transformism,* p. 95.

34. Paul Ramsey, "Natural Law and the Nature of Man," *Christendom* 9, no. 3 (1944): 373.

whenever we act at all; even when, as by a metaphor we say, *we* do good" (p. 3). That now unchanging aspect of fallen creation, even in the pursuit of good, requires repentance.

The question that emerges from this is how we are to repent self-consciously for "unconscious sin." Ramsey lingers on the issue because of his anxiety over the crippling effect of perpetually "trying to be sickly sorrowful for what we are now doing" (p. 3). He is wary of overly emotive responses to sin. The roots of this approach lie in his theological wrestle with the fact that "we cannot remorsefully repent and put away from us *all* our sins, because this would mean ceasing to do what we are *now doing*" (p. 3). The unavoidable simultaneity of action and repentance (for "righteousness," following his earlier distinction) renders contrition a secondary, crippling, and somewhat inappropriate response.

At this point his theological commentary moves in a distinctly political direction. The principal example of one who understands that contrition is not the only response to sin is the Christian soldier who "repentantly fights the just war" but "is not one who is always blubbering over his gunpowder!" (p. 4). Ramsey describes this approach to sin and righteousness, saying, "More fundamental than sorrow for our past sins is a repentant faith which *in acting* nevertheless *waits* for the Lord to complete by His Divine Providence the goodness of our finite actions, and which still trusts Him when in His Divine Judgment our action is thwarted and rejected" (p. 4).[35] He italicizes "in acting" to highlight the importance of "judgment about what is good," however "infected by our sinful righteousness" that judgment may be (p. 4).

In war this means that one principal form of repentance can be a decisive act of political judgment. That is not to say that human agents transcend their "infected" character. Rather, it recognizes that God's transcendence places our political judgments under a greater judgment and therein sustains them as moral acts. In Ramsey's words, "An ethics grounded in justification in Christ has no . . . urgent need to avoid making judgments

35. He repeats this claim the following year with reference to Martin Luther. Ramsey says: "Such repentance is that to which Luther referred when he wrote, in the first of his ninety-five theses, 'Our Lord and Master Jesus Christ in saying, "Repent ye, etc." intended that the whole life of believers should be penitence.' This repentance is the orientation of the self away from itself *while* acting, away from both its righteousness and its unrighteousness, from both its idolatries and its idolatrous correction of idolatry, from its goodness and its guilt" (Ramsey, "Natural Law," p. 374).

of right and wrong in politics."[36] This makes clear the way in which his reflections on repentance provide a theological platform for a constructive ethic characterized by purposive judgments on what is good and right.

Ramsey's Understanding of Repentance in the Context of the Vietnam War

Several decades after these early theological writings, many critics faulted Ramsey for his delayed recognition of the unjust U.S. military action in Vietnam. Only later did he admit the error of his judgments: "I freely grant that in the fury and fog of the verbal wars I failed to keep my agenda for reasoning morally about insurgency and counterinsurgency warfare entirely distinct from my own conviction that we were in Vietnam honorably."[37] He admits this again in a letter to Glen Stassen in 1978, saying, "I judged the war to be proportionate long after I should have changed my mind."

He was under pressure both to repent of his own judgments on the war and to incorporate a more substantial place for contrition for the ills of war in his political theory. The problem was that he saw no necessary connection between those two demands. Thus, even as he acknowledges to Stassen the wrongness of his judgments, he refuses to compromise the truthfulness of the moral norms governing war. He writes: "If I now went back and changed the political and military theory in order to accomplish repentance, I would be a very poor ethicist indeed."[38] In order, then, to understand how he approaches and employs the theme of repentance within the context of the Vietnam conflict, as well as to understand his response to calls from his critics for contrition, I turn to two significant pieces of correspondence from the 1960s and 70s.

A Letter to James Childress

An extensive letter to James Childress at the Kennedy Institute in 1977 elaborates Ramsey's refusal to allow the emotion of regret to overshadow

36. Ramsey, *War and the Christian Conscience,* p. 13.

37. See Ramsey's comments in Richard John Neuhaus, ed., *Speaking to the World: Four Protestant Perspectives* (Washington, DC: Ethics and Public Policy Center, 1983), p. 21.

38. Paul Ramsey to Glen Stassen, Feb. 14, 1978, Box 26, Ramsey Papers.

an insistence on the moral norms of justifiable war. Ramsey discusses the call from others for an account of contrition in his political ethics:

> Perhaps I have not searched for the precise word or words to use for the still-remaining inward reverberations of agape in justified participation in war, because mine has been too much an "ethics of action." Under that head, I would call your attention to more than a moral trace that remains in the structure of acts of war for me, namely, the cruciality of the distinction between direct intention and indirect collateral killing. . . . That still seems more crucial than "compunction" or "regret."[39]

By pointing to the "moral trace" involved in his account of political action, Ramsey assumes that regret must be made possible by prior standards with which to judge right from wrong. For instance, the distinction of note here is one separating direct intention (murder) from indirect killing. He had long contended that "murder is never ordinate; but unfortunately a good deal of killing may be."[40] His point to Childress is simply that if we are to feel regret in war rightly, then we must have a sense of which actions should certainly evoke that sentiment, for example, murder, and which remain morally ambiguous — for example, killing.

The danger of calling for regret or repentance without proper attention to moral principles is that it can quickly become an instrument of self-justification. This is precisely his concern with calls for regret or contrition as the principal substance of a political ethic. It invites self-deception and the erosion of moral principles governing acts of judgment. To Childress he decries this error and says that the omission of contrition as a feature of his political thought "is to be explained (not excused) by the silliness of repenting for something that one judges to be an actual duty even while engaging in its performance, calling down on all heads alike God's 'justification.'" In light of the previous discussion of the two forms of repentance we can see clearly the target of his claim. Sorrow and regret are counterproductive to *current* moral action — their theological function is subsequent to the act. They also offer no justification for an otherwise immoral act. Ramsey says this to Childress in political terms: "Repentance or sorrow doesn't do anything to excuse [a war]." That is why, again, the

39. Paul Ramsey to James Childress, Jan. 21, 1977, Box 5, Ramsey Papers.

40. Ramsey, *The Just War,* p. 348.

"Christian soldier does not blubber over his gunpowder — or the religious equivalent of that."[41]

Ramsey rightly sees that this calls for an additional question in the discussion with Childress. If Christians pursue political action through constructive judgments of right and wrong, how are they also to account for and limit the hubris behind those judgments? Michael McKenzie helps to capture his response to challenges of this kind, noting that Ramsey's just war-theory "was never meant to imply the presence of *real* justice on one side, its absence on the other. It does imply, however, that distinctions can still be made regarding competing and *relative* claims for justice."[42] The just-war theory should only ever involve relative judgments of right and wrong; this was the impetus behind his belief that it "is better called the theory of *justified* war!"[43]

In the letter to Childress, Ramsey pushes away from "objective" claims to justice by trying "to get away from the 'juridical model,' of declaration as a sentence from an impartial court." Nonetheless he maintains:

> Still, one does the ostensibly just thing without subjective guilt. So there not only can but must be relative judgments of justice ad bellum, without the claim to encompass objective justice. Here I would say the overarching Christian perspectives of sin, tragedy, God's overruling, forgiveness, historical vocation, etc., have their profound significance — but not that of vacating the room and need for jus ad bellum.[44]

In response to the call for a more robust account of political repentance, he refuses to compromise the moral necessity of ostensible judgments. If repentance is not to become an instrument of self-justification, if it is not to lose its "profound significance," it must not be used as a tool for vacating the proper function of political judgment.

This is why illuminating the "structure of acts of war" is more crucial

41. Ramsey to Childress. The imagery of a soldier blubbering over gunpowder is one of Ramsey's favorite ways of making his point. See also Ramsey, "The Manger," p. 4; *Basic Christian Ethics,* p. 188.

42. McKenzie, *Paul Ramsey's Ethics,* p. 114. In the original publication of "A Political Ethics Context for Strategic Thinking," he speaks of "the relative justice of all kingdoms, empires and nations" (Morton A. Kaplan, ed., *Strategic Thinking and Its Moral Implications* [Chicago: University of Chicago Center for Policy Study, 1973], p. 102).

43. Ramsey, *The Just War,* p. 4.

44. Ramsey to Childress.

to Ramsey than pushing notions of compunction or guilt. This is also why he speaks in *War and the Christian Conscience* of principles of righteousness "by which wrong gains some meaning."[45] Moral norms simply play a more fundamental role in the determination of right political action — to allow contrition or regret to diminish the significance of right judgment would be to mischaracterize the moral task before us.

A Letter to Kent Knutson, Editor of Dialog

In early 1967, Ramsey's essay "How Shall the Vietnam War Be Justified?" was published in *Dialog* with a revised title: "Is Vietnam a Just War?"[46] Not only did the editor's alteration of the original title offend Ramsey's appreciation for the distinction between ostensible and objective justice (and therein just war and justified war), but several of his critics were incensed by the essay itself. Robert Hoyer and Gordon J. Dahl responded with strongly critical essays in the next issue of *Dialog,* entitled, respectively, "Sad Self-Justification" and "Repentance Rather than Rationalization."[47] Ramsey then wrote a letter on May 10, 1967, to Kent Knutson, editor of *Dialog,* responding to Hoyer and Dahl. It was published later that year under the heading "Two Extremes: Ramsey Replies to His Critics."[48]

Both essays criticize his refusal to condemn U.S. participation in Vietnam. Hoyer observes: "The sadness lies in the fact that [Ramsey has] left no room for Christian ambivalence and doubt, no room for repentance."[49] In response, Ramsey offers a distinction similar to the one between ostensible justice and objective justice:

45. In 1961 he expresses this by saying that the magistrate "does what he can and may and must, without regarding himself as lord of the future or, on the other hand, as covered with guilt by accident or unforeseen consequences" (Ramsey, *War and the Christian Conscience,* p. 201).

46. Paul Ramsey, "Is Vietnam a Just War?" *Dialog* 6, no. 1 (1967): 19-29. See also McKenzie, *Paul Ramsey's Ethics,* p. 124.

47. Robert Hoyer, "Sad Self-Justification," *Dialog* 6, no. 2 (1967): 142-44; Gordon J. Dahl, "Repentance Rather than Rationalization," *Dialog* 6, no. 2 (1967): 144-45.

48. Paul Ramsey to Kent Knutson, May 10, 1967, Box 14, Ramsey Papers; Paul Ramsey, "Two Extremes: Ramsey Replies to His Critics," *Dialog* 6, no. 3 (1967): 218-19. Here I will cite the original version of the editorial letter, found in the Ramsey Papers.

49. Hoyer, "Sad Self-Justification," p. 142.

> I do not regard a line of ethical or political reasoning which justifies an action over its alternatives as thereby "justifying" human agents or persons before God, rightwising their standing or making them righteous. For Hoyer, justification has the effect of levelling all distinctions between the just and the unjust, and the relatively more or less just; and this I do not think was the meaning of God's causing his rain to fall upon them both or His sun to shine upon each alike.[50]

Hoyer misunderstands this impulse to protect the role of relative judgments in the Vietnam conflict. As McKenzie notes, "Hoyer has confused the horizontal with the vertical. Or better, he has left no room for the horizontal."[51] Ramsey aims to maintain the radical transcendence of "vertical" relationships between humanity and God without erasing the significance of "horizontal" relationships governed by the relative justice of human judgments. (I will say more about his use of horizontal/vertical language in chapter 3.) His point is that while ostensible judgments surely do not justify an individual before God, neither does the universal need for forgiveness "level" all earthly distinctions.

Hoyer also overlooks the fact that without moral distinctions there is no basis for choosing one action over another. Ramsey says:

> One really cannot suck everything into "justification," "faith," "repentance"; or level everything before these grand moments in the Christian life. Not least of the telling arguments against this is that then there would be no reason why even Lutherans worry so much about what they should do. Even in luminous moments of faith, they are still concerned to know what to do.[52]

50. Ramsey to Knutson.

51. McKenzie, *Paul Ramsey's Ethics,* p. 127. What McKenzie observes of Ramsey's doctrine of sin also applies here to his theology of repentance: "the 'natural' or 'secular' person is not as bad off as many Christian moralists believe; likewise, the Christian moralist may not be as well off as he or she thinks. This leveling out should result in respect for many of the political decisions which are handed down by politicians and less certitude on the part of those Christians who see the gospel infallibility addressing every social issue" (p. 13).

52. Ramsey to Knutson. Elsewhere, quoting an unnamed speaker at Perkins School of Theology, he approvingly observes, "One cannot stand before God and there be nothing else to be done in moral and social life" (Paul Ramsey, "Tradition and Reflection in Christian Life," *Perkins Journal* 35, no. 2 [1982]: 46).

The problem with a theological interpretation of political action that abandons moral distinctions is that some cultural alternative quickly fills the void. In the example of the Vietnam War, Ramsey is acutely aware that an American ethic will take the place of a Christian ethic. Thus he warns:

> If we do not prolong Christian moral judgments into life and show that life-situations are corrigible to Christian ethical analysis, and that even Lutherans have justifiable ways of telling what they should or should not do, then the consequence will not be shapeless behavior in which one act is like any other before God. The result will rather be that Christian life and thought will be shaped by the "evil military necessity/pacifist" syndrome. Something from the American way of life will tell us what to do![53]

Setting aside his jabs at Lutherans, these two comments exhibit his anxiety concerning the consequences of Hoyer's logic. A theology of repentance of that kind threatens to eliminate any possibility of a constructive moral and political good.

His response to Dahl, though shorter, is essentially the same. He says, "You could not call for 'repentance rather than rationalization' unless by some alternative form of rationalization you first established what it is we politically should repent of."[54] He insists on the fundamental priority of moral norms to any functional notion of political repentance. He also rejects any appeal to repentance as a way of avoiding difficult political determinations of right and wrong.

The following year, in "Politics as Science, Not Prophecy," Ramsey observes:

> Theologically speaking, we grasp something of God's *overruling* of man's ruling and self-ruling. To use this notion in our analysis of *present* experience, however, to introduce it into our analysis of the prospective shape of things to come or (hopefully) to be given to experience ahead is always a category mistake.[55]

The category mistake made by Hoyer and Dahl is one of "levelling" all moral judgments under the weight of the "grand moments" of the Chris-

53. Ramsey to Knutson.

54. Ramsey, "Two Extremes," p. 219.

55. Ramsey, "Politics as Science," p. 18.

tian life. What becomes most clear in his response is the attempt to avoid that mistake by appreciating the proper tension between a need for human judgments and the transcendence of divine judgment. Repentance is made possible by the prior identification of moral norms and takes shape in the pursuit of constructive political action.

Repentance and Political Judgment

These wider theological observations help clarify the earlier inquiry into what Ramsey means when he calls politics a realm of deferred repentance. It is not a release from responsibility for what is morally right or an attempt to license evil as a means to some good end. It is his commentary on the purposive pursuit of right action within the systemic limitations of the political realm. However misleading the phrase may be, it is essentially a call for magistrates "to do the *politically* right, the best *possible* good."[56]

More important than rescuing this troubled phrase, however, is what these interpretive gains reveal about Ramsey's contributions to a theological understanding of repentance and political judgment. In light of Ramsey's later arguments, we are now in a position to integrate these various discussions of repentance and make several observations about his contributions to political theology on this theme. First, notice the emphasis on political judgment. This tends to appear in the form of deference to those in positions of political authority; nonetheless, he directs our attention toward the structure of the political act rather than the transcendence of the agent. In his response to David Little, Ramsey speaks in favor of "not so much the levelling of kings and emperors as the elevation of the private consciences of free men in political initiatives and resistance."[57] The "elevation" brought about by this emphasis on judgment is one that promotes discrimination between political alternatives on any level of authority.

This is because the principal theological distinction here is between divine judgment and human judgments. There is a recurring interplay between what is human (limited judgments, ostensible justice, knowledge of repentance for unrighteousness, and so on) and what is divine (eternal judgment, objective justice, knowledge of repentance for righteousness, and so on). Ramsey repeatedly insists on the significance of the distinction

56. Ramsey to Hick.

57. Ramsey, "Some Rejoinders," p. 187.

precisely because he wants both to avoid the presumption that human judgments neatly reflect divine judgment and to grant to those limited judgments their due regard in created existence. He attributes great moral import to particular political judgments of justice and injustice while simultaneously contextualizing those judgments in a theological account of divine transcendence. We witnessed a very similar interpretation of Israel's participation in Yahweh's unbreakable covenant in the previous chapter.

Ramsey also uses repentance to emphasize the fact that the political realm is inescapably temporal. That is to say, it is characterized and governed by its movement through time. As noted above, one of his purposes for introducing the concept of deferred repentance is an attempt to account for matters of timing, patience, and expediency involved in prudential determinations of right political action. This builds on his (H. Richard) Niebuhrian sensitivity to the fact that repentance in the political realm may require patience or calculated inactivity. His distinction between repentance for righteousness and repentance for unrighteousness is also an attempt to understand what it means for each moment of the Christian life to be one of repentance.

Lastly, the concept serves as a theological entry point into a discussion of the way that all political judgments are necessarily contingent. That is to say, political endeavors are never entirely under (or out of) our control. This is evident in Ramsey's description of politics as "the science of the possible" in *War and the Christian Conscience,* as well as his insistence to John Hick that magistrates pursue "the most right among the possibles."[58] It also becomes clear in his demand to Hoyer and Dahl that the indispensability of contingent and relative judgments of justice and injustice must be held in proper theological perspective. This attention to contingency as a feature of all political endeavors produces, perhaps counterintuitively, a heightened sensitivity to the importance of political judgments. I will have much more to say about the temporality and contingency of political judgments in the following chapter.

The principal aim of *War and the Christian Conscience* is to explore the tradition of just-war thinking and explicate the moral norms governing political policies and practices. But Ramsey's attention is always squarely on the *structure* of political authority and agency. As Joseph Allen notes, he understands his task as an advocate of political realism to be "primarily an effort to perceive those characteristics always and everywhere present in

58. Ramsey, *War and the Christian Conscience,* p. 11; Ramsey to Hick.

politics, including possibilities for good and for evil."[59] While repentance plays a relatively minor role in his more systematic political arguments, I assign to it a significant interpretive function to the extent that it helps us see clearly his logic of political agency, appreciation for structural limits on political authority, and emphasis on the theological significance of purposive political judgments. He uses repentance to demonstrate the reliance of all such judgments on a prior theological account of God's judgment. He also highlights certain unavoidable features of political agency, given the contingency and temporality of created existence.

As Ramsey turns to concrete issues in political ethics in the 1960s, he is keen to keep his moral thinking rooted in firm theological convictions. In *War and the Christian Conscience,* he finds the concept of repentance to be a particularly helpful theological resource for understanding conflicts between moral limitations and responsibilities, as well as highlighting central features of political agency. These themes run throughout his work, though rarely with the same theological point of reference. In fact, later in his career Ramsey attempted to resuscitate his reputation as a scriptural thinker by exploring similar themes through a biblical lens. The last step of this initial section on Ramsey's search for political theology is to examine his use of Scripture to shore up these enduring insights on authority and judgment. This takes us to his scriptural reasoning in *The Just War* and *Speak Up for Just War or Pacifism.*

59. Joseph L. Allen, "The Discriminating Realism of Paul Ramsey," *Worldview* 12, no. 12 (1969): 14.

CHAPTER THREE

Late Scriptural Reasoning on War and Statecraft

Nowhere else does Ramsey ground his arguments in Scripture as firmly as he does in *Basic Christian Ethics.* As he was fond of saying, he was assigned to teach introductory courses in "Bible" during his early years at Princeton University, and the composition of those lectures involved more study of Scripture than he had done during the whole of his seminary education. The arguments of that first book are scriptural through and through. As Stanley Hauerwas and Stephen Long note in their foreword to the Library of Theological Ethics edition of *Basic Christian Ethics,* "Ramsey's use of biblical, theological, and philosophical material for ethical reflection was unparalleled at the midpoint of the twentieth century."[1]

By the late 1970s and early 1980s, however, shifts in theological ethics and a relative absence of scriptural references in his pointedly political and medical writings left Ramsey with the reputation of being an unscriptural thinker — or at least an insufficiently scriptural one. Whether spurred by these criticisms or not, Ramsey's use of Scripture jumps significantly in his final book, *Speak Up for Just War or Pacifism.* Furthermore, the roots of a more heavily scriptural account of Christian political thought run at least to the closing chapter of *The Just War.* I am not particularly interested in defending Ramsey's use of Scripture in Christian ethics against other theological ethicists; I am inclined to agree with Jeffrey Siker's suggestion that "perhaps at times [Ramsey] shares company with Augustine, who engaged in poor exegesis but good Chris-

1. Stanley Hauerwas and D. Stephen Long, foreword to Paul Ramsey, *Basic Christian Ethics* (reprint, Louisville: Westminster John Knox Press, 1993), p. xiii.

tian ethics."[2] But I am distinctly interested in the role Scripture plays in his later political writings and what this reveals about his mature political theology. I am interested in what today is often called "scriptural reasoning," both how Ramsey does it and what we learn from him as he does.

In this chapter I want to examine two instances of Ramsey's later scriptural reasoning: one is a reading of two narratives from Genesis, and the other is a reading of the parable of the builder and the king from Luke 14:28-33. Each one offers a unique window into his later theological thought, and I believe they are important instances of his refusal to compromise the theological roots of his political ethics. To say it another way, I believe that these two examples not only provide a sharp rebuttal to those who accuse Ramsey of abandoning or obscuring his theological commitments when he wrote about political morality, but they also provide lasting theological insights that can contribute to discussions in contemporary Christian ethics. I will save these broader conclusions for the final chapters of this book. For the moment, our task is to examine his return to Scripture in his later political writings.

Genesis Narratives and Political Power

In the early 1970s, Ramsey seeks an account of moral and political reasoning that is capable of responding to the U.S. government's expanding stockpile of nuclear weapons and its policy of Mutual Assured Destruction.[3] Of his writings from that period, the most significant is "A Political Ethics Context for Strategic Thinking," which originally appeared in a volume entitled *Strategic Thinking and Its Moral Implications.*[4] The piece is an attempt, as James Turner Johnson notes, to explore "the ground shared by himself and the secular strategists with whom he would communicate."[5] In the first half of the essay he accepts the assignment of saying "something

2. Jeffrey S. Siker, *Scripture and Ethics: Twentieth-Century Portraits* (New York: Oxford University Press, 1997), p. 96.

3. See Paul Ramsey, "The MAD Nuclear Policy," *Worldview* 15, no. 11 (1972): 16.

4. Paul Ramsey, "A Political Ethics Context for Strategic Thinking," in Morton A. Kaplan, ed., *Strategic Thinking and Its Moral Implications* (Chicago: University of Chicago Center for Policy Study, 1973), pp. 101-47.

5. James Turner Johnson, "Morality and Force in Statecraft: Paul Ramsey and the Just War Tradition," in David H. Smith and James Turner Johnson, eds., *Love and Society: Essays in the Ethics of Paul Ramsey* (Missoula, MT: Scholars Press, 1974), p. 110.

theological" about strategic thinking.[6] In the second half he presents a number of conclusions from his life's work on "the morality of war and deterrence."[7] It was clearly an important essay to Ramsey, and at the end of his career he reprinted a revised version as an appendix to *Speak Up for Just War or Pacifism.*[8]

Two features of this essay are particularly important. One is his reading of H. Richard Niebuhr's *The Responsible Self,* which Ramsey uses to articulate the importance of responsibility for Christian political ethics.[9] (I will delay comment on this until chapter 8 below, where I outline Ramsey's place among the Augustinians in contemporary Christian ethics.) The second feature is most pressing for this discussion: Ramsey's reading of two Genesis narratives (the tower of Babel and the covenant with Noah) as points of entry into a discussion of political realism.

Ramsey's approach to the text is heavily shaped by his reading of the second volume of Helmut Thielicke's *Theological Ethics.*[10] Thielicke developed a Lutheran approach to political ethics in Hamburg, Germany, during the 1960s and 1970s, while Ramsey was working on similar themes at Princeton. By that point Ramsey's disappointment in the moral reasoning of *Church Dogmatics* III/4 had soured his early commitments to Barth's covenant framework for ethics. (I outlined this progression in chapter 1.) In the 1970s, therefore, Ramsey found himself aligned much more closely with Lutheran interpretations from Thielicke, among others, who perceive the state as an "order of necessity." Chief among the insights he takes from Thielicke is the belief that the "myths of Genesis" provide

6. Paul Ramsey, *Speak Up for Just War or Pacifism* (University Park: Pennsylvania State University Press, 1988), p. 183.

7. Ramsey, *Speak Up,* p. 195. The original version contains an intermediary section addressing Philip Green's *Deadly Logic: The Theory of Nuclear Deterrence* (Columbus: Ohio State University Press, 1966).

8. Stanley Hauerwas once wrote the following to Ramsey: "The thing I really liked, however, is 'A Political Ethics Context for Strategic Thinking' and especially the first section. The use of Babel and Niebuhr are just extraordinarily well done. Moreover it makes clear the theological presuppositions that lie behind your political ethics." Stanley Hauerwas to Paul Ramsey, September 27, 1973, Box 11, Paul Ramsey Papers, Special Collections and Manuscripts, Perkins-Bostock Library, Duke University [hereafter Ramsey Papers].

9. H. Richard Niebuhr, *The Responsible Self* (New York: Harper and Row, 1963). See also H. Richard Niebuhr, "The Idea of Covenant and American Democracy," *Church History* 23, no. 2 (1954): 126-35.

10. Helmut Thielicke, *Theological Ethics,* vol. 2: *Politics,* ed. William H. Lazareth (London: Adam and Charles Black, 1964; reprint, 1969).

"one of the world's best commentaries on government."[11] Never one to think that Christian Scripture must speak only to Christians, Ramsey assumed that the biblical narratives could offer a point of entry into political realism even for secular thinkers who did not share a Jewish or Christian theological framework.[12]

In the original publication of "A Political Ethics Context for Strategic Thinking" (1973), he proposes "a rapid sketch of insights into and perspectives on mankind's existence in political communities to be gained from looking at ourselves through the synoptic 'pre-historic' culture myths in the first book of the Hebrew Bible named 'In the Beginning' (*Genesis,* the Greeks called it)."[13] In "Force and Political Responsibility," the first major essay that he wrote on political ethics after *The Just War,* Ramsey offers a similar reflection on the usefulness of the narratives. It is worth quoting at length for what it reveals about his approach.

> In speaking of these stories, I may sound like a literalist. I claim rather to be a mythologist, who happens to believe that there is more light and truth concerning the political task of mankind to be found in these myths than in any number of theorems about politics consecutively arranged, or in any amount of "systems analysis" or decision-making with or without the assistance of computers. The claim is doubtless true of other great cultural myths as well; but these are ours. . . . Instead of taking these stories to be either literally or mythically true, you are welcomed to regard them as legends and fantasies. I suggest only that you join me in the thought-experiment of asking what would be the contours of man's political task on the underside of these myths *if* they were true of the human condition. I ask you to think *as if* you with all men are present at political creation, at the Fall, at Babel, and with Noah after the

11. Thielicke, *Theological Ethics,* p. 47.

12. He cites Thielicke's reading of Genesis in numerous settings. For instance, in 1973 he assigns "Force and Political Responsibility" as "homework" to a group of military chaplains and uses the Genesis narratives as a starting point for describing the context of political action (Paul Ramsey, "Military Service as a Moral System," *Military Chaplain's Review* 2, no. 1 [January 1973]: 8). In 1979 he wrote to Michael Walzer in praise of *Just and Unjust Wars,* recommending that Walzer's position "bears strong resemblance" to Thielicke's. Paul Ramsey to Michael Walzer, June 12, 1979, Box 29, Ramsey Papers.

13. Ramsey, "A Political Ethics Context for Strategic Thinking," p. 101. As early as 1962, Ramsey observed that the story of the Tower of Babel can "teach us a great deal about man's political life" (Paul Ramsey, "Turn Toward Just War," *Worldview* 5, nos. 7-8 [1962]: 8).

> evil propensities of men's hearts in that generation deservedly ended in the first destruction — and the end of that end was government. What then would government mean?[14]

This is a remarkable request from someone who is so often accused of obscuring or avoiding his theological commitments in public conversations. The reference to the biblical myths as "ours" will seem outdated to today's readers, but his belief that any reader was welcome to join the conversation is no less inviting. Ramsey implores his audience to think with him, to *reason* with him through Scripture as he investigates the place and purpose of government in our life together.

First, the covenant of Noah (Gen. 9):

> God blessed Noah and his sons, and said to them, "Be fruitful and multiply, and fill the earth. The fear and dread of you shall rest on every animal of the earth, and on every bird of the air, on everything that creeps on the ground, and on all the fish of the sea; into your hand they are delivered. Every moving thing that lives shall be food for you; and just as I gave you the green plants, I give you everything. Only, you shall not eat flesh with its life, that is, its blood. For your own lifeblood I will surely require a reckoning: from every animal I will require it and from human beings, each one for the blood of another, I will require a reckoning for human life.
>
> Whoever sheds the blood of a human,
> by a human shall that person's blood be shed;
> for in his own image
> God made humankind.
> And you, be fruitful and multiply, abound on the earth and
> multiply in it."
>
> Then God said to Noah and to his sons with him, "As for me, I am establishing my covenant with you and your descendants after you, and with every living creature that is with you, the birds, the domestic animals, and every animal of the earth with you, as many as came out of the ark. I establish my covenant with you, that never again shall all

14. Paul Ramsey, "Force and Political Responsibility," in Ernest W. Lefever, ed., *Ethics and World Politics: Four Perspectives* (Baltimore: Johns Hopkins University Press, 1972), pp. 45-46.

> flesh be cut off by the waters of a flood, and never again shall there be a flood to destroy the earth." God said, "This is the sign of the covenant that I make between me and you and every living creature that is with you, for all future generations: I have set my bow in the clouds, and it shall be a sign of the covenant between me and the earth. When I bring clouds over the earth and the bow is seen in the clouds, I will remember my covenant that is between me and you and every living creature of all flesh; and the waters shall never again become a flood to destroy all flesh. When the bow is in the clouds, I will see it and remember the everlasting covenant between God and every living creature of all flesh that is on the earth." God said to Noah, "This is the sign of the covenant that I have established between me and all flesh that is on the earth." (Gen. 9:1-17; NRSV)

From this story Ramsey suggests the realization that government is the good gift of God for the preservation of the fallen world. The covenant installs "a power" that "holds in place the imaginations of men's hearts."[15] To this end it commissions political authority by these words: "Whoever sheds the blood of a human, by a human shall that person's blood be shed; for in his own image God made humankind" (Gen. 9:6). But this "condemnation" of the shedding of blood is accompanied by the fact that the covenant graciously "holds the waters of God's wrath in place" (p. 185). The covenant that authorizes the use of force also includes the promise that God's judgment will never again take the destructive form it took in the flood. This, in Ramsey's view, is what frees us to pursue justice in a fallen world. The intermixing of limitation and empowerment in the covenant is crucial. He learned this from Thielicke, who says, "The world between the fall and the judgment is not only empowered to set up states, it is *condemned* to do so."[16] The covenant of Noah thus exhibits the link between limitation and preservation, restraint and gift, empowerment and condemnation, that marks the "nature, mission, and means" of government in a fallen world (p. 185). Ramsey offers two additional phrases — "power vs. power" and "the law of move and countermove" — to describe the character of political engagements in this period of time between the fall and the last judgment. He argues that "the Noachian covenant means that . . . power must be lim-

15. Ramsey, *Speak Up,* p. 185. Hereafter, page references to this work appear in parentheses within the text.

16. Thielicke, *Theological Ethics,* p. 441.

ited by further power, else it is bound to become arbitrary and unlimited" (p. 186). The upshot of this is a rejection of any analysis of political action adhering to a philosophy of might is right. He writes in unpublished notes on Thielicke that such an approach "is a decision against the Noahic order of the world . . . against the principle of order from which the state derives and on which all authority and law depend."[17] In this way he appeals to the covenant as evidence, even for secular readers, that government is best understood through dynamics of anticipation, response, and responsibility rather than simply the unbridled exercise of power.

Second, the story of the Tower of Babel:

> Now the whole earth had one language and the same words. And as they migrated from the east, they came upon a plain in the land of Shinar and settled there. And they said to one another, "Come, let us make bricks, and burn them thoroughly." And they had brick for stone, and bitumen for mortar. Then they said, "Come, let us build ourselves a city, and a tower with its top in the heavens, and let us make a name for ourselves; otherwise we shall be scattered abroad upon the face of the whole earth." The Lord came down to see the city and the tower, which mortals had built. And the Lord said, "Look, they are one people, and they have all one language; and this is only the beginning of what they will do; nothing that they propose to do will now be impossible for them. Come, let us go down, and confuse their language there, so that they will not understand one another's speech." So the Lord scattered them abroad from there over the face of all the earth, and they left off building the city. Therefore it was called Babel, because there the Lord confused the language of all the earth; and from there the Lord scattered them abroad over the face of all the earth. (Gen. 11:1-9; NRSV)

According to Ramsey, this story reveals the reality that human striving is always and everywhere subject to divine authority and overruling. He repeats H. Richard Niebuhr's notion that "each man and nation has 'a view of the universal', but none has 'the universal view'" (*Speak Up,* p. 184). Politically speaking, "there is confusion of tongues, confusion of justices" (p. 184). Because our political lives continue to operate under the divine judgment witnessed at Babel, contingency of knowledge and limitation of certainty are fixed elements of the context of political action. Michael

17. Unpublished Notes, Box 45, Ramsey Papers.

McKenzie nicely captures the function of this narrative when he says that "the story of humanity is consistently one of submerged pretensions . . . divine judgment is always the result of such *hubris.*"[18] To put it another way, the story of Babel displays Ramsey's understanding of what it means to be political agents living in the earthly city.

Charles Curran criticizes this use of the Genesis narratives by arguing that it subverts the impact of the advent of Christ on political ethics: "The political life of man in this world goes on under the sign of Babel, and nothing this triumphalistic secular age can do will undo that verdict. Jesus Christ has come into the world and sent his Spirit upon us, but political activity goes on much as before under its own sign."[19] Curran is right to recognize that Ramsey reads these Old Testament stories as revealing enduring truths about the context of political action that remain unchanged by the advent of Christ. Yet, the fact that Christ has changed everything does not mean everything has changed. Curran confuses the difference between a Christian political ethic wholly determined by the earthly city and one faithful to the heavenly city in the midst of the earthly one. Ramsey never suggests that these narratives contain the *final* word that Christians have to say about the political realm.[20] (As David Smith notes, in Ramsey's political ethics "the irrelevance of love . . . is the one thing that can never be assumed.")[21] He simply suggests that they reveal significant truths about inherent features of political authority: a mixing of limitation and empowerment, the necessity of power and responsibility, the difficulty of identifying true justice. In correspondence Ramsey once insisted that the limitations of just war are "to be Christologically reflected upon in the service of life in a fallen world (not derived

18. Michael C. McKenzie, *Paul Ramsey's Ethics: The Power of 'Agape' in a Postmodern World* (Westport, CT: Praeger, 2001), p. 8.

19. Charles E. Curran, *Politics, Medicine and Christian Ethics* (Philadelphia: Fortress, 1973), p. 14. As McKenzie notes, "Curran sees Ramsey as letting the 'Earthly City' go too much its own way, with too little allowance for justice and love to shape its parameters. . . . Curran sees Ramsey as walling off the two cities from one another, following Augustine too closely in his pessimism" (McKenzie, *Paul Ramsey's Ethics,* p. 8).

20. Rather, as James Childress notes, "For Ramsey, then, in contrast to Barth, the Fall and God's governance of man *post lapsum* and pre-resurrection are 'decisively important for Christian political theory'" (James F. Childress, *Civil Disobedience and Political Obligation* [New Haven, CT: Yale University Press, 1971], p. 95).

21. David H. Smith, "Paul Ramsey, Love and Killing," in James T. Johnson and David H. Smith, eds., *Love and Society: Essays in the Ethics of Paul Ramsey* (Missoula, MT: Scholars Press, 1974), p. 7.

from the Fall)."[22] In other words, he was convinced that a careful thinker could not help but make a distinction between ethics determined by Christ in a fallen world and ethics determined by the Fall. In both approaches, sin is decisively important for ethics, but only one is a *Christian* ethic. Against Curran, nothing in this reading of Genesis seems to me to contradict Ramsey's pursuit of a genuinely *Christian* ethic.

Curran also voices concerns that "there are no balancing remarks about a more positive role of the state."[23] This overlooks Ramsey's adoption of the Lutheran view, via Thielicke, that "enforcement and power are an *alien* work of [God's] mercy" (*Speak Up,* p. 185). Government as a preservative ordinance is a positive role of the state stemming from (and ordained by) God's mercy. More importantly, this also overlooks the fact that Ramsey goes farther than does Thielicke in his vision for the positive role of the state. David Attwood makes this clear when he says that "there is a world of difference between the typically positive way in which Ramsey speaks of the state's concern to preserve justice and order, and the way in which Thielicke speaks negatively of the state as an emergency institution."[24] While Thielicke speaks of "the demand for the limitation of power," he lacks the tension between limitation, obligation, and justification so ubiquitous in Ramsey's writings.[25] His prescriptive norms of the just-war theory contain within them moral obligation that assumes a constructive social function to the work of political authority.

A recent article by Shaun Casey revisits and expands Curran's line of attack. His most damaging criticism highlights the way that "A Political Ethics Context" treats the Babel/Noah narratives in reverse order. Ramsey says that "the confusion of tongues, taken alone, meant that what happened was bound to happen: that by the time of Noah every imagination of

22. This line occurs in a heated exchange over the Barmen Declaration between Ramsey and Arthur Cochrane of Yale during the 1960s. Ramsey writes of Barth's document: "Where his statement misleads is that it is apt to tempt us into supposing that the *polis,* Christologically viewed, is now already the heavenly *polis,* and that the use of force is something less than a generally valid responsibility, whose limitations are to be Christologically reflected upon in the service of life in a fallen world (not derived from the Fall)" (Paul Ramsey to Arthur C. Cochrane, March 4, 1964, Box 3, Ramsey Papers). Ramsey returns to Cochrane on the subject of the Barmen Declaration several years later in "Liturgy and Ethics," *Journal of Religious Ethics* 7, no. 2 (1979): 139-71.

23. Curran, *Politics,* p. 15.

24. David Attwood, *Paul Ramsey's Political Ethics* (Lanham, MD: Rowman and Littlefield, 1992), p. 56.

25. Thielicke, *Theological Ethics,* p. 178.

the thoughts of men's hearts was only evil continually" (*Speak Up,* p. 185). This implies that the Noahic covenant of Genesis 9 follows the Tower of Babel narrative of Genesis 11. Casey says: "If the Noah episode displays the depravity of humanity and the need for government, then the Babel story must show that government didn't work very well."[26] While Casey's point is certainly on target, I am hesitant to conclude that it has a devastating effect on the essential argument that these Genesis narratives teach us about the futility of human strivings in light of divine judgment and the constructive (albeit limited) purpose of government as a good gift of God. Jeffrey Siker attempts a more comprehensive treatment of the role of Scripture in Ramsey's ethics, and I am content to defer to that study on the question of Ramsey's quality as an exegetical scholar.[27]

After voicing this initial criticism, Casey derives two further conclusions from Ramsey's use of the Genesis narratives: (1) "He gives no account of how the duty to love one's neighbor relates to international order and politics"; (2) "Instead the biblical warrants which are invoked are used to endorse a realist political view." The second claim is surely correct: Ramsey does use the narratives to endorse a realist political view. The problem is that he would not have thought that he needed to apologize for doing so. Thus, while Casey's term "realism transforming theology" is meant pejoratively, I suspect that Ramsey would have taken it as something of a compliment.[28] As *Who Speaks for the Church?* demonstrates, he certainly felt that there was a good deal of modern theology in need of healthy doses of political realism. This leaves Casey's first claim as the one requiring substantial engagement.

As I have observed above, Ramsey divides "A Political Ethics Context" into two halves. The first uses the covenant of Noah, the Tower of Babel, and a reading of H. Richard Niebuhr alongside Thomas Schelling to explain his theological interpretation of the political realm.[29] The second half opens with the heading "The Morality of War and of Deterrence," and it offers this introductory comment:

26. Shaun A. Casey, "Eschatology and Statecraft in Paul Ramsey," *Studies in Christian Ethics* 21, no. 2 (2008): 184.

27. Jeffrey Siker, *Scripture and Ethics;* see also Michael McKenzie, "The Bible and Paul Ramsey," in *Paul Ramsey's Ethics,* pp. 2-44.

28. Casey, "Eschatology and Statecraft," pp. 185, 183.

29. See Niebuhr, *The Responsible Self;* see also Thomas Schelling, *The Strategy of Conflict* (Cambridge, MA: Harvard University Press, 1960).

> The political ethics limits and determination of justice in war's conduct and in deterrence policy I have elaborated elsewhere. Readers who do not know this literature are my loss. That loss cannot be repaired here. I can only summarize certain theses which I have, I believe, proved elsewhere *in extenso.* The following are conclusions which I believe are demonstrable in any sound ethical reasoning about politics and warfare.[30]

What follows is a summary of Ramsey's lifelong wrestling with expressions of agape in the political sphere. Discrimination, immunity of noncombatants, proportion, and so on — these are the characteristic elements of purposive agapeic politics. Having already answered the request to "say something theological" in the opening section, and because the piece is composed for a secular audience, he does not explicitly connect each of these principles and ideas to the revelation of Christ or the work of Christian love.[31] Nonetheless, the introductory comment serves to make his point — that elsewhere he has proved *in extenso* the theological roots of this political ethic.

Only in light of these claims can we respond to Casey's suggestion that Ramsey "gives no account of how the duty to love one's neighbor relates to international order and politics."[32] That is, in point of fact, what the second section of the essay is about. Ramsey's opening qualification might as well have been intended to meet Casey's criticism directly. His work consistently emphasizes both the conditions of purposive political action *(esse)* and the purposive actions themselves *(bene esse)* in accordance with just-war criteria. The two halves of "A Political Ethics Context" take precisely this shape. He uses the Genesis narratives to drive his understanding of the context of right political action and then articulates "the political ethics limits and determination of justice in war's conduct."[33] It is the *esse* and the *bene esse* of political ethics, or, more directly, how agape relates to international order and politics.

30. Ramsey, *Speak Up,* p. 197.
31. Ramsey, *Speak Up,* p. 183.
32. Casey, "Eschatology and Statecraft," p. 185.
33. Ramsey, *Speak Up,* p. 183.

Covenant and Repentance in "A Political Ethics Context"

What I find most striking about Ramsey's use of the covenant of Noah and the Tower of Babel narratives is the way they reinvent and reintroduce several of the essential elements of his earlier development of covenant and repentance. I close this section by suggesting two ways that this takes place. First, we witness Ramsey revisiting the covenant theme of *Basic Christian Ethics*. His early writings struggle to explain how the covenant with Israel has political implications for all human communities. Here, with the help of Thielicke, he observes that the Noahic covenant includes "every living creature" (Gen. 9:12) even as it confirms to Israel the place their covenant with Yahweh holds in the created order. Inviting even secular readers into the wisdom of the text, Ramsey uses the narrative to reinforce his early claim that political authority is made possible by (and guided by) God's covenantal relationship with creation.[34]

Second, this reading provides an account of the tension between divine judgment and human political authority that stands on stronger footing than his appropriation of repentance as a political concept. Recall that Ramsey's aim in those early discussions was to keep in view the proper function of judgment in the Christian life. Repentance functions rightly when it calls attention to the hubris behind our moral endeavors without leveling the norms and principles with which we identify actions as right or wrong. He uses the Genesis stories to argue similarly that while human striving is always "subject to the divine overruling," the covenant also establishes a proper social function for government operating under norms of justice, law, and order.[35]

Consider these developments in light of Ramsey's correspondence in *Dialog* with Robert Hoyer over the issue of repentance (examined in the previous chapter). Ramsey notes that Hoyer uses justification by faith in Christ to "level" all earthly distinctions between relative (or ostensible) justice and injustice.[36] McKenzie interprets this comment: "Hoyer has confused the horizontal with the vertical. Or better, he has left no room for

34. As he says in *Basic Christian Ethics*, "Political decision . . . should be guided by the righteousness of the God we know through the covenant" (Ramsey, *Basic Christian Ethics*, p. 388).

35. Ramsey, *Speak Up*, pp. 184-85.

36. Paul Ramsey to Kent Knutson, May 10, 1967, Box 14, Ramsey Papers. The letter was later published as Paul Ramsey, "Two Extremes: Ramsey Replies to His Critics," *Dialog* 6, no. 3 (1967): 218-19.

the horizontal."[37] In "A Political Ethics Context" Ramsey says, "the verdict at Babel only suppressed man's 'vertical' aspiration to high heaven; it did nothing to allay the resulting chaos on the horizontal plane." The covenant of Noah, too, subverts our vertical pretensions: "To prevent that vertical turn upward toward unbridled expansion, the law of move and counter-move . . . was established for the good of mankind always."[38] In both his earlier and later discussions, Ramsey's principal aim is to maintain the transcendence of "vertical" relations between humanity and God without erasing the significance of "horizontal" relations governed by the relative justice of human judgments.

Ramsey's reading of the Genesis narratives provides a powerful example of the scriptural reasoning that marks his later political work. Through it he reintroduces several of the driving theological concepts behind his earlier work, including those of covenant and repentance. His sources have shifted from Barth to Thielicke and from Rousseau to a firmer footing in the biblical narratives. Of course, the language of repentance has disappeared altogether. Nonetheless, he upholds several of his most consistent observations about the political realm: that it is characterized by radical contingency and susceptible to corruptions of power; that the work of agape cannot be wholly abandoned; that preservation of justice and order are central political goods. There is, however, an even more important text for understanding Ramsey's later scriptural reasoning. He repeats this story, as well as his unique interpretation, in a number of different settings to hone in on the essential features of his theological perspective. I believe it captures some of his most important contributions to political theology.

Contingency and Temporality in Luke 14

On April 9, 1967, Ramsey delivered a sermon at the National (Episcopal) Cathedral in Washington, D.C. He entitled it "Counting the Costs" and took as his text the story of the builder and the king from Luke 14:28-33. Later that year the sermon was published in *The Vietnam War: Christian*

37. McKenzie, *Paul Ramsey's Ethics,* p. 127.

38. Ramsey, *Speak Up,* pp. 185, 186-87. Again, this is not to overlook the difficulties with his reading of the Babel and Noah narratives in reverse order. It is simply to recognize that they are being put to essentially the same theological purpose as his discussion of repentance.

Perspectives.[39] The following year he placed it as the concluding essay in his *The Just War,* and then, four years later, a similar exposition appeared in "Force and Political Responsibility."[40] Again, in 1973, he repeated the story in his contribution to *Strategic Thinking and Its Moral Implications* (which he then abbreviated and placed as an appendix to *Speak Up for Just War or Pacifism* in 1988).[41]

Ramsey offered a commentary on Luke 14 in at least six publications on political ethics over the last twenty years of his career. In appreciation of his evident fondness of the story and in recognition of its prominent place in his later political writings, I will explore his reading of the parable in Luke 14:28-33 in the second half of this chapter. I will argue that Jesus' description of the builder and the king supplies, for Ramsey, a scriptural rationale for theological conclusions about the realities and possibilities of political responsibility in a violent world. This will not only illuminate the ways that he reasons about war and statecraft through the text, but it will also supply one material response to the suggestion that modern advocates for a Christian understanding of justified war lack such forms of scriptural reasoning.

A Plain Sense Reading of Luke 14

David F. Ford argues that, within the practice of scriptural reasoning, "the first task of the interpreter of scripture is to try to do justice to its plain sense."[42] While Ramsey's work predates the interdisciplinary movement Ford describes, he begins his reading of Luke 14 with a similar impulse to capture the kind of faithful discipleship that is the "main point" of the parable.[43] I will first reprint the wider text from Luke 14:25-33 (RSV) that he takes as his prompt in order to frame his interpretation of this plain sense.

39. Paul Ramsey, "Counting the Costs," in Michael Hamilton, ed., *The Vietnam War: Christian Perspectives* (Grand Rapids: Eerdmans, 1967), pp. 24-44.

40. See Paul Ramsey, "Force and Political Responsibility," in *The Just War: Force and Political Responsibility* (New York: Charles Scribner's Sons, 1968; reprint, Lanham, MD: Rowman and Littlefield, 1983), pp. 523-36.

41. Ramsey, "A Political Ethics Context," pp. 101-47.

42. David F. Ford, "An Interfaith Wisdom: Scriptural Reasoning between Jews, Christians and Muslims," in David F. Ford and C. C. Pecknold, eds., *The Promise of Scriptural Reasoning* (Malden, MA: Blackwell Publishing, 2006), p. 14.

43. Ramsey, "Force and Political Responsibility," p. 49.

> Now great multitudes accompanied [Jesus]; and he turned and said to them, "If anyone comes to me and does not hate his own father and mother and wife and children and brothers and sisters, yes, and even his own life, he cannot be my disciple. Whoever does not bear his own cross and come after me cannot be my disciple. For which of you, desiring to build a tower, does not first sit down and count the cost, whether he has enough to complete it? Otherwise, when he has laid a foundation, and is not able to finish, all who see it begin to mock him, saying, 'This man began to build, and was not able to finish.' Or what king, going to encounter another king in war, will not sit down first and take counsel whether he is able with ten thousand to meet him who comes against him with twenty thousand? And if not, while the other is yet a great way off, he sends an embassy and asks terms of peace. So therefore, whoever of you does not renounce all that he has cannot be my disciple."

Ramsey begins by distinguishing between disciples, on one hand, and kings and builders, on the other. Disciples principally bear allegiance to the kingdom of God, which "is not a pearl of great price; it is a pearl of *inestimable* price for which one sells *all* that he has." The kind of "calculation" required of discipleship is, in fact, not calculated at all. It is impassioned, reckless, and in radical service to those in need. It forsakes family bonds and self-preservation. Against this approach is that of the kings and builders who "determine whether the costs are worth it in a world in which nothing is worth everything."[44] Their path is one defined by the need for precise calculation and management of resources in an imprecise world.[45]

The plain sense of these teachings from Luke is found here, in their demand for the radical sacrifices required of those who would be disciples of Christ. As this section is often subtitled, it is the cost of discipleship. It can be understood in these particular verses as a general call to surrender everything for the life of discipleship or, more concretely, as the relinquishing of all earthly (economic and material) possessions.[46] Thus Ramsey notes that Jesus "remarks upon this world in which the costs and

44. Ramsey, *The Just War,* p. 523.

45. Thus, he says, "the task of the statesman and builder is, in a sense, a more calculating one; it requires . . . more exactitude amid less certitude and greater ambiguity in measuring costs to goods that are irremediably relative" (*The Just War,* pp. 523-24).

46. See, for instance, Richard Hays, *The Moral Vision of the New Testament: A Contemporary Introduction to New Testament Ethics* (San Francisco: HarperSanFrancisco, 1996), pp. 122, 465, 466.

expected goods *can* be *compared,*" yet he speaks "instead of man's ultimate good and its inestimable worth."[47]

Counting Costs and Taking Counsel

Despite his primary recognition of this plain-sense meaning of the text, Ramsey also identifies and appreciates a secondary distinction between the tower-builder and the king. The differentiation between these "two sorts of worldly wisdom" stems from the fact that even within the realm of material pursuits there are varying degrees of contingency and various requirements according to one's social role.[48] I will examine them both, beginning with the tower-builder.

Ramsey argues that what is required of the tower-builder is a "comparatively simple calculation, and one that can be tallied up ahead of time." He is "the builder of a project that he can control or complete." This approach draws on a kind of consequentialist logic, and Ramsey speaks of the "ascendancy of technical reason in cost-counting."[49] A builder weighs and estimates each aspect of the project before initiating construction. Furthermore, there is a point at which the building is complete. Accordingly, in the parable Jesus indicates that those builders who fail to calculate rightly will be mocked.

In contrast to the builder who estimates the costs, Jesus describes the king as taking counsel. In one sense, this stems from the fact that the king already operates within a world of preexisting political relationships. Even though Jesus describes the king "first" sitting down to take counsel, Ramsey notes that "a very peculiar 'first' that would be, while he is already going to 'encounter' another king!" Thus he says that the king operates "in the midst of the interaction and forces already at play in the world."[50]

Additionally, the king takes counsel rather than counting costs because statecraft lacks the control and precision of tower-building: "In politics there are no completed towers." For this reason, "Jesus spoke not of measurable calculation, or proof or disproof of one's ability to finish an edifice, when he mentioned the predicament of a king. Instead, a king or statesman

47. Ramsey, *The Just War,* p. 524.
48. Ramsey, *Speak Up,* p. 193.
49. Ramsey, *The Just War,* pp. 525-26.
50. Ramsey, *Speak Up,* p. 194.

needs wise 'counsel.' "[51] While both kings and builders operate in worlds that require calculation, the radical indeterminacy and unpredictability of political endeavors mean that kings can receive, at best, only prudent counsel on the course they should follow.

Ramsey illuminates the unique predicament of the king with reference to a line from former U.S. Secretary of State Dean Acheson. Acheson, who was also a furniture-making hobbyist, said, "A chair is made to sit in: when you've made it you can tell whether you made it right; there is no such definitive test of the rightfulness of a political policy-decision."[52] Ramsey found this to be particularly helpful imagery for appreciating the lack of "completed towers" in the political realm. He adds: "This is not the case with international *policy.* Politics is a kind of *doing.* It is not a kind of *making* — like building a tower."[53]

Politics as a Kind of Doing

We must be careful not to overstate the conclusions that Ramsey will allow us to draw from his reading of Luke 14. He does not present a conclusive argument for the New Testament witness about justified war or pacifism, nor does he subvert the fact that the radical cost of discipleship is the primary aim of Jesus' teaching. After all, there were no kings in Jesus' audience. He does allow, however, that "in drawing one parabolic point from the tower-builder and the king on his way to a larger question, Jesus in some sense, and even if in passing, commended their practical wisdom and took note of its nature. This perhaps gives us warrant for focusing attention . . . upon the king — upon the direction of statecraft as among the tasks of men, of magistrates and citizens alike" (p. 524). If we follow his warrant and focus our attention on the king and on the nature of political judgment, we can observe three fundamental truths about statecraft and the political realm that Ramsey draws from the narrative.

First, the political realm is inescapably temporal — that is, it is characterized and governed by its movement through time. This explains why "Jesus described the king as already in movement" (pp. 524-25).[54] Ramsey

51. Ramsey, *Speak Up,* p. 194.

52. Ramsey, "Force and Political Responsibility," p. 49.

53. Ramsey, *The Just War,* p. 525. Hereafter, page references to this work appear in parentheses within the text.

54. Ramsey elsewhere suggests that this sense of things in movement requires "taking

takes note of "the nature of the encounters coming upon the statesman into which he is always going," and argues that statecraft requires "a ceaseless and perhaps changing appraisal of the stakes at issue and a ceaseless and perhaps changing appraisal of the costs proportionate to what is at stake, going on at the same time that action is being put forth in the context of the actions coming upon us, itself shaping and shaped by those actions" (p. 527). This is a complex statement, but his aim is to capture the way temporal moral relationships and a continual flow of actions and reactions surround every new political initiative. There are also matters of timing, patience, and expediency involved in prudential determinations of justifiable action. To express it more succinctly, magistrates operate "in a world whose *steady state* is that of encountering powers" (p. 525).

Second, the political realm is characterized by radical contingency. Ramsey observes that a magistrate "must always, unlike builders of towers, posit his decision and action in a world in which there is always the action, interaction, and counteraction of others and other forces and influences coming upon him" (p. 526).[55] Even in situations where the magistrate may judge rightly and in accordance with principles of justified war, that judgment does not *necessarily* lead to the desired or intended outcome. In Ramsey's words, the magistrate "is no builder of a project that he can control or complete; he cannot very clearly count the costs because he cannot — he simply cannot — predestinate the benefits he seeks" (p. 526). This sensitivity to the radical contingency and indeterminacy of statecraft is fundamental to his belief that politics is a kind of "doing."

It is crucial to hold alongside these two points of emphasis Ramsey's heightened sensitivity to the importance of political judgment. He is equally suspicious of those who abandon political relationships to moral chaos or conflicts of unrestrained power as he is of those who believe they can be controlled by "technical reason."[56] Therefore, his third observed truth from Luke 14 is that the political realm is governed by moral norms. He insists that Jesus' commendation of the king points the way toward limitations on justifiable war. The king's wise judgment to send an embassy and ask terms of peace is suggestive of the nature of political wisdom: "It is largely a matter of correctly counting the costs in relation to the goods

time seriously as a relation among creatures and the measure of the activity of creatures" (Paul Ramsey, *Nine Modern Moralists* [Englewood Cliffs, NJ: Prentice-Hall, 1962], p. 69).

55. See also Ramsey, "Force and Political Responsibility," p. 50.

56. Ramsey, *Speak Up*, p. 194.

to be obtained. This is, in fact, a principal word that through all the centuries Christians have addressed to the world, and to themselves in their offices as magistrate or citizen . . . the *principle of proportion*" (*Just War,* p. 524). This principle cannot, for Ramsey, erase the contingency of political judgments. "It is simply not at all clear that one may not be able with ten thousand to meet him who comes against him with twenty thousand. This is only what one should take counsel about" (p. 526). It does mean, however, that even an indeterminate political realm is subject to determinate moral limitations.

Notice that this reading of the text both highlights the central role of practical reasoning in the political realm and informs the content of that reasoning with the principle of proportion. That is to say, Ramsey reasons that the parable theologically underwrites not only his observations about the contingency and temporality of war and statecraft, but also the establishment of moral limitations on political judgment. This is his way of situating the "awesome responsibility of political leadership" in relationship to the judgment of God (p. 526). He frankly acknowledges that "those words uttered by the Lord of Heaven and Earth [in Luke 14] . . . do more than *point the way* politics should go. Those words also bring under judgment the whole of humankind and they reveal in one lightning flash that ours is a fallen existence" (p. 529). The two layers of Jesus' teaching suggest that "a Christian will think politically in the light of Christ, and he will think politically in the light of the revealing shadow thrown by the cross of Christ over our fallen human existence" (p. 529). Thus, for Ramsey, Luke 14 offers an unavoidable message from Jesus about the radical and inestimable cost of discipleship: the plain-sense meaning of the text. Yet, in the shadow of that light, Ramsey also discovers wisdom about the nature of statecraft in fallen human existence.

Conclusion

If we aim to investigate the role of Scripture in theological reasoning about war and political conflict, "Counting the Costs" and its numerous subsequent variations offer a significant example of such reasoning. Ramsey reads the story from Luke 14 as a revelation on the nature of political authority — its structure, purposes, and limitations in a temporal and indeterminate world. I conclude this chapter by suggesting how renewed interest in this line of argumentation might stimulate further conversation both in scholarship on Ramsey and wider debates regarding the role of Scripture in Christian justifications of war and pacifism.

Despite frequent appearances in later publications, Ramsey's reading of Luke 14 receives scant attention in scholarship on his work. Direct treatments of the role of Scripture in Ramsey's ethics are rare, and the most comprehensive of these, Jeffrey Siker's *Scripture and Ethics,* does not mention the passage or its influence. Furthermore, the common criticism that Ramsey's later work abandons his early theological commitments in *Basic Christian Ethics* often neglects to recognize these later theological forms of scriptural reasoning. In this chapter I have not tried to provide a comprehensive account of the role of Scripture in Ramsey's political theology, but I have offered several responses to criticisms of his later work.[57]

In addition to the corrective vision for scholarship on Ramsey, there are also wider implications for debates regarding the role of Scripture in Christian political ethics. In most modern discussions of this kind, especially those concerning the New Testament witness about war and political authority, references to Luke 14:28-33 are largely absent. For instance, there is no mention of it in Richard Hays's discussion of violence in *The Moral Vision of the New Testament,* nor in several lengthy recent exchanges on this subject in *Studies in Christian Ethics* between Hays and Nigel Biggar.[58] John Howard Yoder does not mention it in his pacifist reading of Luke in *The Politics of Jesus* (nor, according to my modest survey, anywhere else in his writings). Roland Bainton's seminal text only uses it (under the heading of "Texts for the Just War") to note that "in matters military Luke was also the most favorable."[59] Perhaps most notably, recent attempts to emphasize the significance of practical reasoning for Christian political

57. I have emphasized the way his attentiveness to the plain-sense reading of the text warns us against imposing a wider reading of his interpretation than he wants to allow. I maintain, however, that increased attention to his use of Luke 14 in future scholarship on Ramsey could go a ways toward correcting some of his critics.

58. Richard Hays, *The Moral Vision of the New Testament;* Nigel Biggar, "Specify and Distinguish! Interpreting the New Testament on 'Non-Violence,'" *Studies in Christian Ethics* 22, no. 2 (May 2009): 164-84; Richard Hays, "Narrate and Embody: A Response to Nigel Biggar," *Studies in Christian Ethics* 22, no. 2 (May 2009): 185-98; Nigel Biggar, "The New Testament and Violence: Round Two," *Studies in Christian Ethics* 23, no. 1 (February 2010): 73-80; Richard Hays, "The Thorny Task of Reconciliation: Another Response to Nigel Biggar," *Studies in Christian Ethics* 23, no. 1 (February 2010): 81-86.

59. John Howard Yoder, *The Politics of Jesus* (Grand Rapids: Eerdmans, 1972); Roland H. Bainton, *Christian Attitudes toward War and Peace* (Nashville: Abingdon, 1960), p. 61.

ethics by Oliver O'Donovan and Daniel M. Bell Jr. omit reference to Luke 14.[60] The lasting contribution of Ramsey's analysis lies in the lingering questions it raises about the place of Luke 14:28-33 in these contemporary efforts to reason about war and statecraft.

I will delay the attempt to place Ramsey more firmly within the discussions that occupy contemporary Christian ethics until the final section of this book. At the moment it is enough to observe the significance of these two later efforts at scriptural reasoning in Ramsey's political writings. As I have suggested above, Ramsey reads both the Genesis narratives and the story from Luke 14 as revelations on the nature of political authority — its structure, purposes, and limitations in a temporal and indeterminate world. In so doing he calls attention to the transcendent judgment of God and the role of relative human judgments in political communities. Most pointedly, Ramsey reasons through Luke 14 in arguing that the challenge of statecraft is not simply cost-counting or tower-building; instead, it is a kind of "doing" that requires taking counsel. Taking counsel, of course, requires the work of prudence, and so these reflections call for a richer description of human agency and moral psychology. I turn to the challenge of moral theory and Ramsey's account of virtue and agency in the next section.

60. Oliver O'Donovan, *The Just War Revisited* (Cambridge, UK: Cambridge University Press, 2003); Daniel M. Bell Jr., *Just War as Christian Discipleship: Recentering the Tradition in the Church Rather Than the State* (Grand Rapids: Brazos, 2009).

PART II

Politics and Practical Reasoning

CHAPTER FOUR

Against Situationism: Temporal and Interpersonal Bonds

In 1967, the United International Press released an article by Louis Cassels reviewing Ramsey's latest book at that time, *Who Speaks for the Church? A Critique of the 1966 Geneva Conference on Church and Society.*[1] The article ran in a number of papers across the United States, and local editors were responsible for supplying their own titles for the piece. Albion, Michigan's *Recorder* titled it "Ministers Should Not Just 'Pop Off,'" while Youngstown, Ohio's *Vindicator* gave it the headline "Churchmen Should Bite on Tongues." Perhaps most pointedly, the *Courier Times* of Bristol, Pennsylvania, gave it the heading "Advice to a Minister: You Talk Too Much."[2]

Such provocative titles in small-town papers were only the start of Ramsey's troubles with the release of *Who Speaks?* Franklin Sherman suggested in *The Christian Century* that Ramsey could be called "the angry young man" of Christian ethics and that the book was "annoyingly repetitious."[3] Roger Shinn said that Ramsey replaced "the church militant with the church studious," and D. L. Munby called it "too donnish and academic."[4] Richard Johnson observed that even Ramsey's admirers "must

1. Paul Ramsey, *Who Speaks for the Church? A Critique of the 1966 Geneva Conference on Church and Society* (Nashville: Abingdon, 1967).

2. See the published book file for *Who Speaks for the Church?* Box 25, Ramsey Papers; see also Paul Ramsey, *Deeds and Rules in Christian Ethics* (New York: Charles Scribner's Sons, 1965; reprint, Lanham, MD: University Press of America, 1967).

3. Franklin Sherman, "Geneva Jeremiad," *The Christian Century,* September 6, 1967, Box 25, Ramsey Papers, 1131.

4. Roger Shinn is quoted in Henry Clark, "Out of the Vineyard, Back to the Big House: A Review Essay." This review and D. L. Munby's "Review of *Who Speaks*" appear in Box 25, Ramsey Papers.

admit there is something a little 'ivory tower' about his call for the Church to remove itself so completely from the arena of specific policy decisions."[5]

These newspaper titles and critical reviews reflect the fact that *Who Speaks for the Church?* is at once a very straightforward and yet obscure and difficult book. Ramsey is quite clear that he is displeased with the ecumenical pronouncements from the 1966 Geneva Conference of the World Council of Churches. He thinks ministers are talking too much. At the same time, his arguments are arduous, and Ramsey fails to make clear the theological and systematic foundations on which he calls for such strict limitations on ecumenical pronouncements. His target is so clearly in view — the specific political "directives" issued by the WCC conference — that it can be difficult to see how the project fits into his wider theological considerations of Christian political ethics. In short, Ramsey does his readers few favors.

The substance of *Who Speaks for the Church?* is not explicitly doctrinal; Ramsey shields his theological commitments behind argumentative engagements with the Geneva conference. Nonetheless, I believe that it marks an important contribution to his political theology by virtue of the connections he makes between his developing moral theory and his understanding of political authority. The best way to read *Who Speaks for the Church?* is alongside *Deeds and Rules in Christian Ethics.*[6] Only a careful examination of his wrestling with situation ethics in the 1960s makes clear the systematic and theological foundations of his arguments in *Who Speaks for the Church?* Furthermore, this interpretive approach reveals that *Who Speaks?* is the ecclesiological outworking of the deeper theological commitments examined in the previous three chapters. The limitations he places on the church have everything to do with his elevation of judgment (i.e., political decision-making) as the central task of political authority and his appreciation for the responsibilities, obligations, and limitations that accompany moral and temporal bonds.

My aim in this chapter is to explore Ramsey's protection of the "magistrate's conscience" and ask what that protective instinct reveals about his broader framework for political theology and moral theory. In so doing I set the stage for the arguments of the two subsequent chapters of this

5. Richard N. Johnson, "Ramsey's Mirror," *Unity Trends,* November 15, 1967, Box 25, Ramsey Papers.

6. I will also keep in view Paul Ramsey, "The Case of the Curious Exception," in Gene H. Outka and Paul Ramsey, eds., *Norm and Context in Christian Ethics* (New York: Charles Scribner's Sons, 1968), pp. 67-135, though it will occupy a more significant place in the argument of chapter 6.

section, where I will explore the role of deontology (rules) and teleology (through the virtues) in Ramsey's later writings. Most importantly, however, I aim to help readers understand the complicated arguments of both *Who Speaks?* and *Deeds and Rules,* as well as how they intertwine. To this end I will examine his objections to "act-agapism" and situation ethics, including his emphasis on temporal and interpersonal bonds in Christian ethics.[7] Subsequently, I take up his strict limitations on ecumenical pronouncements and appreciation for political authority, and I suggest that his position on these matters stems from anxieties about "atomistic" individualism and sensitivity to the role of properly framed and informed choice (read: judgment) in political agency. Finally, I argue that his description of the church as theoretician is best understood as an outworking of his theological perspective on the structure and direction of political morality that I have detailed in the chapters of the preceding section.

Temporal and Interpersonal Moral Bonds in the Critique of Situationism

In the 1960s the adequacy of moral rules and principles for ethics came under fire from situation ethicists such as Joseph Fletcher and Paul Lehmann. Fletcher taught at Harvard Divinity School throughout that decade, and his *Situation Ethics* was a seminal contribution to the debate.[8] Lehmann, a Presbyterian minister who studied with both Reinhold Niebuhr and Karl Barth, worked at Harvard University and Union Theological Seminary until the 1970s. His *Ethics in a Christian Context* frustrated Ramsey, who judged that it failed to understand correctly the significance of covenant relations of life with life.[9] Ramsey initially contributed to the debate via selected essays, though he later arranged two book-length treatments of the subject.[10]

7. I opt for the less frequently used "interpersonal" over the gendered phrase "between man and man" (Ramsey, *Deeds and Rules,* pp. 66, 44).

8. Joseph Fletcher, *Situation Ethics* (London: SCM, 1966).

9. See esp. Paul Lehmann, *Ethics in a Christian Context* (London: SCM, 1963). Ramsey wrote to Fletcher in 1965: "My quarrel with Paul Lehmann is not over any natural law norm of truth telling, but over what faithfulness, agape, covenant, require in this regard" (Paul Ramsey to Joseph Fletcher, June 29, 1965, Box 8, Ramsey Papers).

10. Of the early essays, see Paul Ramsey, "Lehmann's Contextual Ethics and the Problem of Truth-Telling," *Theology Today* 21, no. 4 (1965): 466-75; "Two Concepts of General Rules in Christian Ethics," *Ethics* 76, no. 3 (1966): 192-207.

The earliest of these was originally published in 1965 as an occasional paper for the *Scottish Journal of Theology.* A substantially enlarged version was released in 1967 as *Deeds and Rules in Christian Ethics.* His second treatment was an edited volume entitled *Norm and Context in Christian Ethics,* which included his lengthy essay "The Case of the Curious Exception."[11]

The key to understanding Ramsey's response to situation (and/or "contextual") ethics lies in his assertion that Christian ethics involves the determination of "love-embodying" moral rules. He also calls these "rules of practices" and insists that "an inquiry into the *meaning of practices* is of the utmost importance for the whole of Christian ethics."[12] Before I take up Ramsey's explicit criticisms of situation ethics, however, I believe it is important to have a clear view of his appropriation of William Frankena's distinctions among "pure act–agapism," "summary rule–agapism," and "pure rule–agapism."[13] These are difficult distinctions to resuscitate today, since the word "agapism" has nearly disappeared from contemporary discussions of Christian ethics. Ramsey's writing on the issue does not do readers any favors either, as it is, to put it bluntly, often tedious and boring. Readers longing to explore the more technical aspects of the debate that so consumed moral theory in the 1960s will not find a shortage of secondary literature to consult.[14] My aim here is simply to lay down the basic structure of that debate so that we might hear clearly Ramsey's distinctly theological voice within it. Accordingly, I begin with his use of Frankena's technical descriptions.

11. Ramsey began with grand visions for the volume. He repeatedly pressed for a contribution from Reinhold Niebuhr, who declined, saying, "I was not interested partly because I thought so little of Joe [Fletcher]'s book; and partly because I am bored with emphasizing the whole Catholic tradition of Natural Law norms which Protestants should have taken more seriously long ago" (Reinhold Niebuhr to Paul Ramsey, May 26, 1966, Box 20, Ramsey Papers). Ramsey invited John Rawls, who also declined (John Rawls to Paul Ramsey, June 12, 1966, Box 20, Ramsey Papers).

12. Ramsey, *Deeds and Rules,* pp. 5, 8.

13. William K. Frankena, "Love and Principle in Christian Ethics," in Alvin Plantinga, ed., *Faith and Philosophy* (Grand Rapids: Eerdmans, 1964), pp. 203-25.

14. For starters, consult Paul F. Camenisch, "Paul Ramsey's Task: Some Methodological Clarifications and Questions," in David H. Smith and James T. Johnson, eds., *Love and Society: Essays in the Ethics of Paul Ramsey* (Missoula, MT: Scholars Press, 1974), pp. 67-89; Donald Evans, "Paul Ramsey on Exceptionless Moral Rules," in Smith and Johnson, *Love and Society,* pp. 19-46; James M. Gustafson, "Context Versus Principle: A Misplaced Debate in Christian Ethics," *Harvard Theological Review* 58 (1965): 171-202; Gustafson, "How Does Love Reign?" *The Christian Century* 83, no. 20 (1966): 654-55; Charles E. Harris, "Love as the Basic Moral Principle in Paul Ramsey's Ethics," *Journal of Religious Ethics* 4 (1976): 239-58.

Pure act–agapism is, in Ramsey's terms, the "purest form" of situation ethics. It assesses the facts of each moral "situation" independently in such a way that "the facts of other similar situations, or generalizations drawn from such situations, or from previous moments of loving obedience, are simply irrelevant or misleading."[15] Because pure act–agapism cannot appeal to general principles, rules, and so on (because they lie outside the independent situation itself), the primary moral task is to identify the facts of each situation. Elsewhere Ramsey describes this sort of reasoning as "the business of getting moral facts."[16]

Summary rule–agapism (or modified act–agapism) is akin to pure act–agapism in that there can be no limits placed on the working of agape in each individual situation. It does allow that certain "rules of conduct" can be derived from "summaries of past experience." But such summary rules lack the authority to restrict the freedom of love. The rules are mere repositories of past experience, and they in no way bind the moral agent. In Ramsey's view, summary rule–agapism fails to offer an improvement over pure act–agapism to the extent that the rules serve only the limited function of "aids to love."[17]

Against pure and modified forms of act-agapism, so-called pure rule–agapism upholds the notion that each situation is to be governed by a set of rules. This makes the primary task of moral theory not the determination of the most love-embodying action but the most love-embodying rule (pp. 106-7). I leave aside at the moment Ramsey's arguments against pure rule–agapism; in subsequent chapters I show how his emphasis on prudence and the role of judgment in the moral life made him suspicious of simplistic deontological approaches to ethics. The criticisms most relevant for this discussion are those directed at pure act–agapism and its sibling, summary rule–agapism (or modified act–agapism).

Objections to Act-Agapism

Ramsey's attack on situation ethics focuses on its "unexamined assumptions" (p. 23). This is evident in two explanations he offers for his disap-

15. Ramsey, *Deeds and Rules,* p. 106.

16. Ramsey, *Who Speaks for the Church?* p. 109.

17. Ramsey, *Deeds and Rules,* p. 106. Hereafter, page references to this work appear in parentheses within the text.

proval of pure and modified act–agapism (and in the work of Fletcher and Lehmann). Toward the beginning of *Deeds and Rules,* while speaking of two quotations from Frankena that he takes to be emblematic of situation ethics, Ramsey notes:

> There is nothing wrong with any of these statements except their two silent, unexamined assumptions: (1) that Christian love has in itself no *breadth* to match its personal depth and therefore no rule-implying power, and (2) that love "homes in" only upon *the moment* in the neighbor's reality, for which it cares. (p. 23)

Later he adds:

> But for all that, the basic philosophy of act-agapism is drawn from no Christian source. It is drawn rather from the atomistic individualism of secular thought in the modern period. This continues to be the acid that eats away at moral relations, and at the very idea that there are moral bonds between man and man, or between one moment and another. (p. 44)

Notice that in each quotation the rejection of act-agapism includes two parts: a criticism of situation ethics' inability to account for the moral aspects of interpersonal relationships and an insistence that those relationships must be viewed across time rather than in distinct (separable) moments. Both parts require further explication.

Ramsey's first complaint about situation ethics concerns the lack of "breadth," or any recognition of the moral bonds between individuals. The emphasis on the facts of the individual situation in act-agapism may allow for "personal depth," but it lacks a wider account of moral descriptions expanding beyond each specific situation. That is to say, in any particular situation it cannot account for the trans-situational moral claims arising out of human relationships and interactions.

He identifies Rousseau as the father of this "ethic of atomistic acts in Christian clothing" (p. 45) when he says: "For Rousseau there can be no bond (but only bargains) between two contracting individuals because there can and should be no bond established between one atomistic moment of willing, or consenting, and the next, and the next after that" (p. 45). Ramsey has turned his back on Rousseau. Where he was once drawn to the role of consent in the social contract (as I detailed in chapter 1), he now protests the protection of individual freedoms and elimination of moral bonds. Against this view he advocates an account of binding and morally significant human relationships. As he says in "The Case of the Curious Exception," "in the Christian life we are driven deeper and deeper into the meaning of covenant obligations. . . . We are therefore driven ever deeper into the meaning of the bonds of life with life."[18] Recognition of the moral significance of those bonds accounts for the breadth of Christian covenant love stretching beyond unrestricted individualism.

His second criticism of act-agapism concerns temporal moral bonds. Act-agapism and situation ethics fail because they "can find no sustaining moral bond between the present moment of action and a later moment of action." In other words, Ramsey understands Christian ethics as a discipline that must make judgments across time and sustain notions of obligation and responsibility that extend beyond individual moments.

The fundamentally temporal character of human action means that all such actions "are in fact already morally joined together" (p. 45). This theme in *Deeds and Rules* revisits and extends several early observations that Ramsey makes in an essay on Marxism in *Nine Modern Moralists.* There he expresses the inescapably temporal character of ethics by noting the importance of "taking *time* seriously as a relation among creatures and the measure of the activity of creatures." He also writes that "linear, temporal history and all the events that happen upon this plane have basic significance."[19] Situation ethics neglects this basic significance of moral reflection by obscuring the relationship "between one moment and another" (*Deeds and Rules,* p. 44).

In short, Ramsey's fundamental points of contention with situational (and contextual) ethics concern the significance of interpersonal relationships and the passage of time for a proper theological perspective on ethics. He says: "It is of the very greatest importance that we understand the connection between the presence or absence of bonds or structures between man and man, and the presence or absence of bonds or structures relating one moment to another" (p. 45). Act-agapism, even in its modified form, fails on both points.

18. Ramsey, "The Case of the Curious Exception," p. 125.

19. Paul Ramsey, *Nine Modern Moralists* (Englewood Cliffs, NJ: Prentice-Hall, 1962), p. 69.

Covenant Theology and the Problem of Choice

In Ramsey's view, no situation is ever *just* a situation. Yet, if this discussion yields nothing more than a rejection of pure and modified act–agapism, the reader may rightly ask whether there is any use for it now that situation ethics has come and gone. There are many ways of rejecting the movement, and other thinkers have done so more quickly and concisely than did Ramsey. (Arriving at the conclusion that situation ethics is a failed enterprise requires significantly less effort than reading *Deeds and Rules*!) In fact, there are two things Ramsey's line of argument helps us see more clearly. The first, as I suggested at the outset of this chapter, is that it helps us understand the arguments of *Who Speaks for the Church?* We will get to that shortly. Second — and of more immediate concern — is that the debate over situation ethics illuminates what Ramsey calls "the problem of choice itself" (p. 91). The failure of "atomistic" ethics is so clearly a *theological* failure — an insufficient "interpretation of the covenants of life with life" — that we require a richer theological account of moral agency (p. 163). In Ramsey's terms, this is more than a debate about the deficiencies of a particular form of secular reasoning. It is a question of whether Christians can provide a coherent account of moral agency by illuminating the relationship between decision-making and the wider network of temporal and interpersonal bonds that define and constitute our creaturely existence. I observed at the close of the last chapter that this question would drive us further into an account of human agency and the importance of prudence. While we are not yet at a full account of prudence, the emphasis on choice takes us squarely into a discussion about covenant theology and the contours of human agency.

In order to understand what Ramsey means by "choice," we must first understand his claim that "to be born means to be born among practices" (pp. 143-44). Practices are rule-governed activities, for example, driving on the highway, playing a card game, or voting in an election. There is an important distinction, however, between "justifying a *practice* and justifying an action falling under it" (p. 133).[20] For instance, the belief that voting is a morally justifiable, rule-governed social practice in many countries does not require the additional belief that *all* actual acts of vote-casting are morally justified (e.g., casting a vote under a fraudulent name). The

20. Ramsey takes this distinction from John Rawls.

difference between the "practice" and the "act" is an exercise of the will, or what Ramsey elsewhere calls "the production of a deed."[21]

His aim here is to highlight the fact that we are surrounded by all manner of rule-governed activities, even in the most basic habits of life. The problem with situation ethics is that it strips away any role for these practices in the determination of right actions. It attempts to account for an exercise of the will without attending to the fact that "everywhere, and at all recorded times, practices precede individual choice" (*Deeds and Rules,* p. 144). Ramsey pulls the curtain back on situation ethics to reveal that its supreme interest in the particular moment voids all possibility of identifying resources (i.e., temporal bonds and moral relations) for the particular choice required in that moment. He says that situation ethics "has therefore little or no light to shed upon any particular choice or upon the *problem of choice itself.* It does not tell us how to get on track (or do the good)" (p. 91). It simply cannot account for the world in which we find ourselves as moral agents.

Covenant is the driving theological concept behind Ramsey's description of the practices and moral relationships that constitute human existence and uphold the role of choice in moral agency. Thus he notes that situation ethics fails to offer "a sufficient interpretation of the covenants of life with life enacted and mandated by God's covenant with men" (p. 163). Just as with his earlier work in *Christian Ethics and the Sit-In,* a covenant theological foundation is inseparable from the doctrine of creation. "Situation ethics neglects our creation in covenant. It neglects that we were 'enmeshed' when God created out of nothing his covenant folk, or when he saw that man was alone" (p. 163). An adequate account of moral obligation will necessarily entail recognition that we are "enmeshed" in relations with God and each other across time. In other words, it will entail the recognition that we are *creatures.*

At this point Ramsey turns again to Barth, noting that "in Barth, the moral agent is bound, obliged; in [Fletcher's situationism], he chooses, if he does, to be bound (which is to say he is not bound at all). . . . But God stooped to the condition of the isolated and free moral agent. We are placed on notice that we cannot and may not and must not be alone with the act *in situ*" (p. 63). Fletcher's nonbinding choice resembles Rousseau's nonbinding consent. In both cases Ramsey uses Barth to emphasize that the act of choosing only becomes intelligible in the presence of obligation. Thus, "only obligation can *oblige* one moment to be connected with

21. Ramsey, "The Case of the Curious Exception," p. 106.

another, or reliably forecast any route. . . . Love must be able to adduce, produce, or discover these universal requirements" (p. 163). To translate: a workable social (and political) ethic relies on an account of obligation rooted in the "enmeshed" character of our created existence.

Notice the interplay between doctrines of creation and Christology here. The incarnation places us on notice that we are not, and never have been, creatures beyond God's relentless desire to be in relationship with us. Further, the very character of the relationship between creatures and their Creator is centered in Christ. Therefore, he notes that our creation is "toward *steadfast* covenant, toward the image of Christ" (p. 164). Where Ramsey begins with an insistence on interpersonal and temporal bonds, here he draws back the curtain to reveal the theological foundations of that position. Moral theory, indeed all human agency, is only intelligible in light of the Creator's unending commitment to be in covenant relationship with its creatures. That steadfast commitment is made flesh in Jesus, and thus we witness to the image of the Christ by entering and upholding steadfast covenants. We see now why the locus of choice — the heart of moral agency — is not found in particular situations, particular moments. There is no "light to shed," no way to "get on track," with the problem of choice unless you begin with a robust account of moral obligation rooted in the covenant-love of God (p. 91). The heart of moral agency lies in "forms of steadfastness in responsibility and accountability one to another" — and to God (p. 164).

Only with these broader theological commitments in mind can we speak of "choice." This should ease any fears that Ramsey's use of the term draws too closely to a neoliberal, market-driven version of the word. Given his sharp critique of situation ethics, it should be clear that he wants little to do with individualism. Prudence emerges in this context as an important regulating virtue, but we cannot move to it too quickly. As early as in *Nine Modern Moralists,* Ramsey saw that "prudence, or practical wisdom in actual exercise, is always in the service of prior insight, conviction, or principle. Its function is the application in living action of something prior which governs our choices."[22] For Ramsey, just as a situation is never just a situation, a choice is never just a choice. Rather, choices are always

22. Ramsey, *Nine Modern Moralists,* p. 5. Michael McKenzie explains the components of Ramsey's concept of prudence understood in political agency. He says, "Prudence is defined by two characteristics. One, they must have a full *understanding* of just what politics is about — its limitations and expectations must both be looked at realistically. Two, they must have what I call an *informed* (or, better, *informable*) *conscience.* This is the ability to listen to the political *ethos* which — both good and bad — comes out of society's moral underpinnings"

made intelligible by prior rules, commitments, and — most important — obligations.

What Ramsey means by "choice" is, in contemporary Christian ethics, called judgment. Nowhere is this clearer than in his protection of the office of political authority. In the early 1980s he wrote sharply to a critic that he was the kind of ethicist "who happens not to believe that choice among alternative military policies can itself be deduced from just war criteria."[23] Whatever "choice" is, it must be properly informed and governed by the limitations, justifications, and obligations of just-war criteria. Just as a belief in voting as a social good cannot validate every vote cast, the inevitable judgments involved by those authorizing and waging war are not made valid by just-war criteria. Neither strict attention to the facts of any individual moment (situation ethics) nor emphasis on the inflexibility of transcendent norms (just-war criteria) can be allowed to mitigate its role in political morality. The place of choice, or judgment, remains.

Who Speaks for the Church? Ecumenism and Political Pronouncements

This brings us to the task of interpreting *Who Speaks for the Church?* in light of these developments in moral theory. Ramsey's principal concern in that book is to reject the practice of offering specific policy advice to politicians in the name of the church. He lambasts the church's movement from particular issue to particular issue as "trying to compile a Christian social ethic by leap-frogging from one problem to another."[24] He directs these criticisms explicitly at the 1966 Geneva Conference's irresponsibility in issuing condemnations of U.S. military intervention in Vietnam and possession of nuclear weaponry: "There is no way to speak for the church

(Michael C. McKenzie, *Paul Ramsey's Ethics: The Power of 'Agape' in a Postmodern World* [Westport, CT: Praeger, 2001], p. 20).

23. Paul Ramsey to Ronald J. Sider, December 15, 1981, Box 25, Ramsey Papers. As William R. Stevenson Jr. observes of Ramsey's approach, "The delineation of the moral limits on warfare 'is the *context* for policy decision' and not the policy decision itself" (Stevenson, *Christian Love and Just War: Moral Paradox and Political Life in St. Augustine and His Modern Interpreters* [Macon, GA: Mercer University Press, 1987], p. 130).

24. Ramsey, *Who Speaks for the Church?* p. 156. Hereafter, page references to this work appear in parentheses within the text.

. . . and address particular prudential recommendations to the leaders of nations" (p. 34). Why such stark protection of the magistrate's conscience?

Two of Ramsey's criticisms of the Geneva Conference are particularly important for this discussion. One is that the church blurs "the distinction between itself and all other groups in the society" (p. 31). Ramsey observes that, when the church pretends to offer specific political advice, she joins the chorus of secular voices hoping to have their particular judgments mimicked by political authorities. He unsympathetically condemns such ecumenical pronouncements as "the most barefaced secular sectarianism and but a new form of culture-Christianity" (pp. 54-55). His concern on this point is for the integrity and distinctiveness of the church in its witness to the political realm.

The other significant consequence of making specific recommendations is that, as mentioned above, the conscience of the magistrate is "faulted" (p. 108). While this term is somewhat obscure, he uses it to voice his concern that specific political pronouncements from ecumenical councils will deprive the office of the magistrate of its proper function in the determination of particular political judgments. He tries to capture this by speaking of "two sorts of competence" with respect to moral political insight (p. 128).

I want to reflect on these two objections found in *Who Speaks for the Church?* in light of the previous discussion of Ramsey's moral theory in *Deeds and Rules.* First, I suggest that his rejection of situationism and promotion of interpersonal and temporal moral bonds provides a framework for understanding the inability of particular political pronouncements to sustain an adequate account of political authority. Second, I argue that his protection of the magistrate's conscience and assertion of two competencies is based on his understanding of choice as central to moral political reasoning.

Ecumenical Pronouncements and the Magistrate's Conscience

For Ramsey, ecumenical pronouncements on specific policy initiatives mirror the inability of situationism to account for ethics from moment to moment and person to person. Just as situation ethics obscures the reality of practices shaping and governing moral existence, so also the "bag of specifics" issued by ecumenical councils cannot be "brought to bear upon the realities in the midst of which the statesman lives and must decide and act" (pp. 35-36). Ramsey rejects the false assumption that increasing specificity and particularity in moral deliberation (whether of situations or policies) necessarily produces a more "realistic" perspective.

One problem with the "bag of specifics" mentality is its inability to account for a theologically informed understanding of Christ, creation, and time. The phrase Ramsey uses to capture this inadequacy is "truncated Barthianism" (not to be confused with the constructive appeal to Barth in the debate with situation ethics). He says that "the revolutionary theology pervasive at the conference was, of course, a truncated Barthianism, stressing Christ and the revolutionary situation, lopping off Barth's own 'prolongation' of his Christocentric ethics into a doctrine of man and of creation and many a principle and structure" (p. 77). In this case, "prolongation" means a theological understanding of the work of Christ in creation and throughout history as opposed to limiting it only to the "revolutionary situation."

He calls this truncated Barthianism "a quite definite narrowing of the bases of ecumenical theology," because it organizes "the Christian understanding of life and of politics under the second article of the Creed only (reducing the first, 'creation,' to the processes of historicized 'nature' and the third to Christ's ever coming present triumph over the powers)" (p. 77). Instead, ecumenical statements should witness to the political realm by representing more fully the theological resources of the Christian tradition. The blunted theological character of specific pronouncements marks the difference between "true prophecy" and "the way to succeed as prophets without really trying" (pp. 55, 38). Of course, as one commentator notes, the call for greater attention to the role of doctrine in shaping ethics is "like Mother's Day. Nobody is against it."[25] The question is what is at stake in the loss of the theological breadth and depth of ecumenical pronouncements.

Ramsey's concern is principally with the integrity of the church, which it maintains by attending "first of all . . . to the business of Christian reflection upon all sorts and structures of human activity" (p. 109). Later he provides a more substantial description of such reflection:

> [Ecumenical pronouncements] should clarify the grounds on which government must rest. They ought to open wide the articulation of

25. Paul Abrecht, "Some Notes on the Book by Paul Ramsey, *Who Speaks for the Church?*" July 26, 1967, Box 25, Ramsey Papers.

> structural elements in that human reality which statesmanship must govern and the range of alternatives it is legitimate for statesmen to have in mind as they rule by specific decree. They should inform the ethos and conscience of the nation, and thus aid in forming the conscience of its statesmen. (p. 154)

The integrity of the church is upheld not by issuing specific decrees but by articulating the proper theological significance of the structures and ends of political action.[26]

He cleared the ground for claims like this in debates over situation ethics, where he insisted that "the problem of choice" required a prior theological account of obligation and responsibility. Without a "prolongation" of Christian insight — a movement beyond specific directives into the structure and ends of political actions — we will obscure "the ultimates of the Christian faith."[27] As became clear in the earlier discussion, this is not an abdication of concern for particular moral actions. It is not the eradication of moral judgment. Rather, it is an effort to highlight the pitfalls of parachuting into particular situations without broader and deeper understanding of Christian commitments and obligations, without an appreciation for the structure and aim of political authority. Thus Ramsey does not eschew political action altogether in these claims; rather, his principal call is for witness to theological truth that is "made ready for action" (*Who Speaks?* p. 46).[28]

Even as we might appreciate Ramsey's call for broader and deeper theological reflection on the structure of political authority, we cannot overlook the fact that he aims to curtail sharply the church's issuing of particular political pronouncements. Here I want to look carefully at what he means when he accuses the church of "faulting" the magistrate's conscience and to suggest that his position is an outworking of the commit-

26. Ramsey says in an unpublished paper that "theological ethics, of course, must go as far as it can (and therefore only as far as it can) in clarifying the meaning of political responsibility on the part of the international system. But I do not believe that Christian ethics can justify or incriminate particular wars without the addition of certain presumptions about the fact situation; and I do not see how fact-finding can be made a matter of conscience or a part of the clarifying work of Christian ethics or the witness of the church." Ramsey, "Apologia Pro Vita Sua — One decade, that is," Box 39, Ramsey Papers, p. 42a.

27. Ramsey, "Apologia Pro Vita Sua," p. 42a.

28. Ecumenical "attempts to influence decision" lead the church away from the meaning of the "*esse* and *bene esse* of politics" that "might have been drawn forth from Christian understanding" (p. 53).

ment to the ineradicable role of "choice" in moral agency (established in *Deeds and Rules*). This also involves a closer look at his assertion that there is a distinctive form of competence in political agency.

For Ramsey, the "majesty of political rulership" includes "the right of persons in their official capacities of magistrate or citizen not to have their consciences faulted" (pp. 153, 108). The church should thus avoid the "fascination with decision making exercises" that undercuts the proper role of judgment in political authority (p. 84). If we stop there, we will miss that he pairs this concern about faulting the magistrate's conscience with a similar concern to avoid easing it. He writes that no ecumenical insights should attempt to "supplant the office of political judgment and decision on the part of magistrate and citizens, bind or fault their consciences, or in the slightest degree ease their special responsibility for deciding" (p. 119). As I have mentioned above, the role of judgment, properly understood, is central to Ramsey's understanding of "the integrity of the office of political prudence" (p. 108). Ecumenical pronouncements should not usurp that office with specific policy directives.

Seizing upon this aspect of his work, Ernest Lefever rightly observes that Ramsey is "more concerned about the overburdened statesman than the under-represented layman."[29] That much is true. But we must not read him too narrowly and presume that he is promoting a kind of moral political aristocracy. As Paul Camenisch observes, "Ramsey's case for respecting the integrity and role of the specialists' prudential judgments is at the same time a case for respecting the integrity and role of every moral agent's prudential judgment."[30] Ramsey says in a later essay, "The mantle of magisterial authority [falls] upon the shoulders of every citizen. We are all, in our degree, decision-makers, magistrates."[31] This serves to emphasize the way the "special responsibility for deciding" falls upon even those outside offices of political authority (*Who Speaks?* p. 119).

When Ramsey protects the magistrate's conscience, he is attempting to uphold "the majesty of political rulership" (p. 153). Ecumenical pronouncements must not usurp or collapse this proper function of authority, and what stems from this strict sense of limitation is an appreciation

29. Ernest Lefever, "Protestant Political Pronouncements Under Fire," October 6, 1967, Box 25, Ramsey Papers.

30. Camenisch, "Paul Ramsey's Task," p. 86.

31. Ramsey, "Some Rejoinders," p. 187. He frequently reads democratic citizenship through John Calvin's language of "lesser magistrates." See McKenzie, *Paul Ramsey's Ethics,* p. 19.

for the unique "competence" of political agency. He speaks of "two sorts of competence, between the moral and political insights that may come from the heart of the Christian faith and the competence we all may have, in varying degrees, to make the decisions that belong to the exercise of political prudence" (p. 128). There are two principal forms of justification for this division.

On one hand, he tends to argue that the difference in competences is based on knowledge or access to information. For instance, he rejects specific proposals "that attach labels 'right' or 'wrong,' 'moral' or 'immoral,' to innumerable particular choices of the statesman about which churchmen *as such* know less than he" (p. 152). They, as he observes elsewhere, lack "the services of an entire state department" and so can only offer "supposedly expert specific advice."[32] In *War and the Christian Conscience,* he says, "There are questions of fact in diplomacy and in weaponry . . . which the moralist as such knows nothing about."[33] This suggests that access to facts differentiates the competence of the magistrate from that of the citizen.

On the other hand, he also suggests that the distinction is based on the unique responsibilities of political office. As Stephen Long notes, the competence distinction is "making a descriptive claim about who actually makes governmental decisions."[34] Ramsey says that the church "inordinately seeks to assume . . . decisions that belong in the realm of the state" (*Who Speaks?* p. 31). This is not to say that "magistrates . . . are always wise. It means only that they are magistrates, which the church is not" (p. 153). The distinction of competences in this case depends on the authority to choose rather than on knowledge or expertise.

These two forms of justification converge when considered in light of my earlier discussion of moral theory. It is not simply choice, or the act of judgment, that marks the political competence; if decision-making is not to be arbitrary or baseless, it must be properly framed by structures identifying and upholding positions of authority. It must also be properly informed by particular facts and governing moral norms. Both contribute to a proper understanding of political judgment. Here Ramsey's insistence that the church attend to the proper structure of political authority becomes evident. The church simply cannot set for itself the task of instruct-

32. Ramsey, "Apologia," p. 35; *Who Speaks for the Church?* p. 43.

33. Paul Ramsey, *War and the Christian Conscience: How Shall Modern War Be Conducted Justly?* (Durham: Duke University Press, 1961), p. 138.

34. D. Stephen Long, *Tragedy, Tradition, Transformism: The Ethics of Paul Ramsey* (Boulder, CO: Westview Press, 1993), p. 110.

ing political authorities on the matters of fact — even in the information age, those who do not occupy high levels of political authority do not have access to the same information. The politics of the church is not an information game. Thus Ramsey writes in another setting: "I do not see how fact-finding can be made . . . a part of the clarifying work of Christian ethics or the witness of the church."[35] But the church *can* play a special role in illuminating the structure of authority, the role of the use of force, and the moral obligations and limitations that accompany political authority. This is a "competence" that Ramsey firmly believes that we all share — and one that Christians should robustly exercise.

This should make clear that Ramsey's protection of the magistrate's conscience is not an abdication of involvement in public debate about political affairs, including suggestions of when and where moral norms governing political authority have been grossly violated. His call for the church to attend to the structure and norms of political authority is a call to be mindful of precisely where the "clarifying work" of Christian ethics lies. It does not lie in fact-finding or in ignoring the reality that some of us hold political office and some do not. Rather, it is the wise appreciation of the difference between "the moral and political insights that may come from the heart of the Christian faith" and "the decisions that belong to the exercise of political prudence" (*Who Speaks?* p. 128).

Understanding Ramsey's Limitation of Church as Theoretician

To follow this line just a little further, in light of the "competence" assigned to political authority, what becomes of the "competence" designated to provide moral and political insights "from the heart of the Christian faith" (p. 128)? In other words, what does it mean for Ramsey to claim that in the realm of politics the church is a theoretician? Answering this question will draw together the various observations and assertions that I have made in this chapter in a way that makes clear what *Deeds and Rules* and *Who Speaks?* have to offer to this discussion of his political theology.

His comments are worth quoting at length:

> In politics the church is only a *theoretician.* The religious communities as such should be concerned with *perspectives* upon politics, with political

35. Ramsey, "Apologia," p. 42a.

> doctrine, with the direction and structures of the common life, not with specific directives. They should seek to clarify and keep wide open the legitimate options for choice, and thus nurture the moral and political ethos of the nation. Their task is not the determination of policy. Their special orientation upon politics is, in a sense, an exceedingly limited one; yet an exceedingly important one. (p. 152)[36]

On the basis of the idea that increased specificity and particularity produce more useful moral judgments for the political realm (the view driven by situation ethics), Ramsey's limitation of the church appears to render it irrelevant to the determination of political morality. Yet, in light of his theology of covenant, we have a clearer picture of what he means by the "direction and structures" of the common life. He is acknowledging the importance of a theological account of political morality that does not mitigate the inescapable contingency and temporality of the political realm. The "exceedingly limited" role of the church is a product of a proper sensitivity to the complexity of moral decision-making.

To put it another way, Ramsey's limitation of the church does not mean that, in the face of war and political conflict, she is reduced merely to reciting the Nicene Creed or the *Gloria Patri*. He suggests no such thing. The articulation of "political doctrine" is the identification of good and legitimate political ends — the *bene esse* of politics. It is also holding those in political office accountable for their "special responsibility for deciding" (*Who Speaks?* p. 119). That is what it means to say "every saving word but no more than can be said upon this basis" (p. 43). The point is that the church should not fall into the same traps that ensnare moral thinkers in atomistic individualism. Rather, the church's task is to provide a rich theological account of political decision-making that is governed not by situationist thinking but by steadfast commitments and obligations, enduring moral norms, and, most important, steadfast covenant love in the image of Christ.

This is made clear by the fact that, despite his sharp criticisms of the Geneva Conference, there are other church pronouncements that Ramsey finds more than satisfactory. One prime example is his positive endorsement of the perspective on war in the Pastoral Constitution on "The

36. Ramsey also places this paragraph at the beginning of "The Ethics of Intervention," in Paul Ramsey, *The Just War: Force and Political Responsibility* (New York: Charles Scribner's Sons, 1968; reprint, Lanham, MD: Rowman and Littlefield, 1983), p. 19.

Church in the Modern World" adopted by Vatican II. He is pleased with the statement's perspective on "the morality of deterrence and the need for new security arrangements." He is also supportive of the "signal reassertion of the principle surrounding noncombatants with moral immunity from direct attack."[37]

He is not pleased simply with the structural form of these pronouncements; he is most delighted that these conclusions are "the fruit of Christian political reason connecting every political consideration with the *whole* idea of God."[38] It is the opposite of the "truncated Barthianism" of the Geneva Conference. In *Who Speaks?* he says: "The Vatican Council was able to place equal moral force behind the need for new directions in international politics and the need for world public authority, without being betrayed into making demonstrably false statements about Christian responsibility in the meanwhile before these are established."[39] By understanding the proper limitation of their task, the council speaks for the church and witnesses to the political realm.

The limitation of the church as theoretician contains within it all the elements of this discussion: an emphasis on properly framed and informed choice as evidence of a right perspective on political ethics; an understanding of the balance between the structure of created existence and the direction toward which that existence is being drawn in historical time; an appreciation of the church's role in illuminating the *bene esse* of politics. There are deeply resonant continuities between Ramsey's later work in moral theory and ecclesiology and his earlier work on covenant and repentance that we examined earlier. Across these discussions I have tried to demonstrate Ramsey's significance as a theological commentator on the essential features of political agency. While he does not use the language of covenant heavily in these two discussions in *Deeds and Rules* and *Who Speaks?* it is there, and I believe that the arguments of each piece reveal the extent to which he articulates his political ethics from that theological perspective.

There is a line of thinking in Ramsey's work that begins with Rousseau, produces the *esse/bene esse* construction, takes shape in his scriptural reasoning, and informs his particular insights into moral theory and ecclesiology. I have tried to trace that line and identify it with his distinctive contribution to a theological perspective on politics. However, the line

37. Ramsey, *The Just War,* p. 388.

38. Ramsey, *The Just War,* pp. 388-89.

39. Ramsey, *Who Speaks for the Church?* pp. 133-34.

does not end with *Deeds and Rules* and *Who Speaks?* He continues to develop his theological perspective; indeed, he shifts his use of covenant (not to mention repentance and contingency) in the final years of his career. Understanding these shifts in theological perspective is not only helpful for appreciating his development as a theologian, but it also helps clarify his enduring commitments to contemporary conversations in Christian ethics.

CHAPTER FIVE

Political Obligation, Tragedy, and Rules of Conduct

I mentioned in chapter 2 that several of Ramsey's most important writings on political realism and justified war wrestle with the public significance of theological claims and the problem of dirty hands. Central to this wrestling is his allegiance to the "Pauline prohibition" never to do evil in order that good may come out of it (Rom. 3:8).[1] I observed in that earlier discussion that he navigates the problem of dirty hands with reference to three central commitments. The first is his belief in the possibility of faithful Christian obedience, even within the political realm. The second is his commitment to an understanding of the "structural difference between personal moral agency and political agency."[2] This arose from his efforts, as Jeffrey Stout notes, "to make his writings acutely sensitive to the responsibilities and concerns of the powerful."[3] The third tempers the second: in it Ramsey imposes onto the Niebuhrian public/private distinction a strict allegiance to fixed moral concepts. Staunch refusal to compromise these concepts, such as the inviolable principle of noncombatant immunity, is Ramsey's way of upholding the Pauline prohibition and refusing to identify politics as a realm hopelessly abandoned to conflicting pursuits of lesser evils. As I noted above, the corollary to his belief that right action is possible in the realm of politics is an adherence to the prohibition of doing evil that good may come.

1. "And why not say (as some people slander us by saying that we say), 'Let us do evil so that good may come'? Their condemnation is deserved!" (Rom. 3:8, NRSV).

2. Paul Ramsey, *War and the Christian Conscience: How Shall Modern War Be Conducted Justly?* (Durham: Duke University Press, 1961), p. 9.

3. Jeffrey Stout, "Ramsey and Others on Nuclear Ethics," *Journal of Religious Ethics* 19, no. 2 (1991): 213.

Ramsey revisits these early theological and moral convictions in his last — and in many respects most significant — book, *Speak Up for Just War or Pacifism.*[4] Some earlier tropes disappear in this volume; two omissions that are notable here are the notion of deferred repentance and any appreciation for Jean Jacques Rousseau. Other themes appear within in a richer theological framework, such as the insights into moral agency gained in the philosophical debate over situation ethics. In that respect, it is Ramsey's most purposefully theological book since *Basic Christian Ethics,* and he makes deliberate use of a broad range of theological doctrines and perspectives.

The aim of this chapter is to provide a clear picture of how the interpersonal and temporal bonds mentioned in the preceding chapter animate (and regulate) Christian participation in the political realm. Doing this requires that we move beyond Ramsey's early use of repentance and his later debates over situationism and ecclesial pronouncements. Instead, we will examine his turn to tragedy as a regulating concept in *Speak Up.* This is a new effort: neither *War and the Christian Conscience* nor *The Just War* use tragedy in systematically descriptive ways.[5] But it also draws heavily on an old influence, that of Reinhold Niebuhr.

Scholars such as Jeffrey Stout and Stephen Long read Ramsey's realism through his debts to Niebuhr, and they suggest that his increasing attention to the Pauline prohibition draws him away from this influence. How does Niebuhr understand tragedy, and in what sense does Ramsey inherit this

4. Paul Ramsey, *Speak Up for Just War or Pacifism* (University Park: Pennsylvania State University Press, 1988).

5. In *War and the Christian Conscience,* Ramsey uses the term only once to reject any suggestion that murder can be excused (or justified) by the description "tragedy." See *War and the Christian Conscience,* p. 213; see also Paul Ramsey, *The Just War: Force and Political Responsibility* (New York: Charles Scribner's Sons, 1968; reprint, Lanham, MD: Rowman and Littlefield, 1983), p. 159. One significant misstep in Stephen Long's treatment of Ramsey is his repeated use of the phrase "Ramsey's view of tragedy." For instance, Long observes: "In 1946, Ramsey did publish an essay based on his dissertation entitled, 'Theory of Democracy: Idealistic or Christian?' In that essay, he demonstrated that Reinhold Niebuhr's 'realism' did not represent an epistemological rupture from late nineteenth-century thought, but that nineteenth-century thought was as capable as Niebuhr to take into account 'tragedy.'" This statement makes it appear as though Ramsey uses the term "tragedy" in the article, which he does not. In the footnote, Long adds: "I continue to use the term 'tragedy' rather than 'sin,' because I am convinced that Niebuhr's theological realism was not indebted to Christian notions of sin, but to pagan notions of tragedy that effectively removed God from human history" (D. Stephen Long, *Tragedy, Tradition, Transformism: The Ethics of Paul Ramsey* [Boulder, CO: Westview Press, 1993], p. 40).

tradition of thought? Further, if Stout and Long are right about Ramsey, how are we to read his later discussion of the concept of tragedy? These questions will drive the move toward a more coherent account of political bonds and rules of conduct in this chapter. In short, the task ahead of us is to understand this interplay of the Niebuhrian inheritance, Ramsey's unwavering commitment to the Pauline prohibition, and the way these produce a peculiar political theology of tragedy.

Niebuhr on Christian Realism and Moral Norms[6]

Niebuhr developed his most important work on Christian realism and politics in the prime of his career against a post–World War II backdrop and the change in global politics associated with the cold war. The writings from this period are generally continuations of earlier theological themes from *The Nature and Destiny of Man* and *Moral Man and Immoral Society,* such as human nature, pride, and the perennial problem of power in human relationships. However, once the conflicts of the mid-twentieth century erupted, Niebuhr's thought was pitted against a previously unfamiliar world order in which superpowers remained in constant tension with one another. Thus tragedy (which Niebuhr sometimes spoke of coincidentally with irony) occupied a significant role in the development of his mature public theology. While Niebuhr's concept of tragedy was most fully developed in his later thought, elements of it are evident in all of his work.

The first point I want to make about Niebuhr's understanding of tragedy regards the possibility of fixed moral norms and their relationship to moral judgment. Niebuhr is a "realist" in the sense that he affirms the reality of such norms, which serve as a guide for moral discernment and exist objectively and independently of human conceptions about them. In other words, Niebuhr embraces the traditional stance of moral realists who affirm that goodness exists as a set of facts about the order of the universe.[7] What

6. I am indebted to John K. Burk for his contributions to our jointly written essay, from which much of the material in this chapter is taken. John is the "Niebuhr scholar," and I am the "Ramsey scholar," and I am grateful for the ways that he has helped me see the connections between the two thinkers. See Adam Edward Hollowell and John K. Burk, "Paul Ramsey and Reinhold Niebuhr on a Public Theology of Tragedy and the Problem of Dirty Hands," *International Journal of Public Theology* 5, no. 4 (2011): 458-75.

7. For more on Niebuhr and moral realism, see Robin W. Lovin, *Reinhold Niebuhr and Christian Realism* (Cambridge, UK: Cambridge University Press, 1995), pp. 11-18.

makes this way of thinking specifically *Christian* realism is that, for Niebuhr, the existence of moral goodness is irrevocably tied to Christianity's "law of love."[8] Niebuhr's is thus both a moral and a theological realism in the sense that the objective good that serves as the plumb line of moral agency originates with the law of love in God. Put differently, "In a theological realism which culminates in the divine nature as love, a moral resolution unifies all human aims and interests in a harmony of life with life which conforms to the unity and love of the divine nature itself."[9]

Niebuhr and Ramsey differ on the use of objective moral norms, however, when it comes to the applicability of the norms to moral judgment. Where Ramsey finds no a priori conflict between individual Christian moral obligation to act in accordance with the demands of the law of love (agape) and public political demands, Niebuhr does. Niebuhr says: "Although we affirm that any specific conflict between persons is susceptible to a resolution in accordance with the law of love, we cannot argue directly from the law of love to the requirements of love for that situation."[10] The law of love in Niebuhrian realism is thus what he frequently refers to as the "impossible ideal": what we strive toward, but what remains beyond realization in human life. It is the problem of human sin — the "ideological taint" — that affects all areas of life, including politics, and prevents the simple application of the theology of the law of love to the complex circumstances of human moral judgment.[11] Robin Lovin notes: "In [Niebuhr's] thought, the theological concepts function more like virtues than like foundational propositions. They indicate habits of judgment and observation."[12] Therefore, the Niebuhrian realist understands public theology as the task of rendering judgments in the face of difficult moral situations that approximate the law of love, but that never fully embody it. Ramsey clearly appropriates this sense that theological concepts function like virtues that inform particular judgments. But Niebuhr's realism falls short of Ramsey's call for

8. Reinhold Niebuhr, *An Interpretation of Christian Ethics* (New York: Harper and Brothers, 1935), p. 136.

9. Lovin, *Reinhold Niebuhr and Christian Realism,* p. 24.

10. Lovin, *Reinhold Niebuhr and Christian Realism,* p. 24.

11. Reinhold Niebuhr, *The Nature and Destiny of Man,* vol. 2: *Human Destiny* (Louisville: Westminster John Knox Press, 1996), pp. 241-44.

12. Robin W. Lovin, "Reinhold Niebuhr: Does His Legacy Have a Future?" *Speaking of Faith,* National Public Radio: http://speakingoffaith.publicradio.org/programs/niebuhr-rediscovered/lovin-hauerwas.shtml (accessed May 30, 2010). This public discussion offered by NPR is a particularly helpful commentary on Niebuhr's relevance today.

magistrates to enact judgments in accordance with bonds of covenant love, as we examined previously. (This difference stems, in part, from Niebuhr's tendency to speak of "nations" — "the selfishness of nations is proverbial" — and Ramsey's tendency to speak of "magistrates.")[13]

This brings me to a second point concerning Niebuhr's understanding of the problem presented above, of a politics of dirty hands. As with Ramsey, Niebuhr does not use the term "dirty hands," but few public thinkers have wrestled with the problem so thoroughly. For Niebuhr, there are definite moments of political judgment in which an act of a greater evil may be done for the sake of some greater justice, because the acts of political judgment are themselves morally ambiguous. This does not mean, however, that Niebuhr replaces justice with love as the normative standard of judgment in public theology. Drawing on Augustine, Niebuhr argues that love is indeed the highest of all moral norms, especially when understood as self-sacrificial agape love. But it is facile sentimentalism to believe that the responsibilities found in the political sphere can be met by the demands of agape love. The genius of Augustine, Niebuhr believes, is that "he takes account of the power and persistence of egotism, both individual and collective, and seeks to establish the most tolerable form of peace and justice under conditions set by human sin."[14] In other words, Augustine embodies best what Niebuhr believes is true realism: the recognition that sin persistently inhibits even the best moral judgments. As Niebuhr puts it, "Men do have to make important decisions in history upon the basis of certain norms, even though they must recognize that all historic norms are touched with both finiteness and sin; and that their sinfulness consists precisely in the bogus claim of finality which is made for them."[15]

What this means in terms of the problem of dirty hands, then, is that Niebuhr believes that all public theologies are marked by a sense of tragedy in which public officials sometimes inevitably choose undesirable moral options. Niebuhr takes note of this phenomenon at the beginning of *The Irony of*

13. Cf., e.g., Reinhold Niebuhr, *Moral Man and Immoral Society* (New York: Charles Scribner's Sons, 1932), p. 83; Ramsey, *The Just War,* p. 84. Interestingly, Robert Markus notes that Augustine "speaks of emperors rather than of empire, of kings and magistrates rather than of state or government" (Markus, *Saeculum: History and Society in the Theology of Saint Augustine* [Cambridge, UK: Cambridge University Press, 1970], p. 149).

14. Reinhold Niebuhr, "Augustine's Political Realism," in *Christian Realism and Political Problems* (Eugene, OR: Wipf and Stock, 1999), p. 131.

15. Reinhold Niebuhr, *The Nature and Destiny of Man,* vol. 1: *Human Nature* (Louisville: Westminster John Knox Press, 1996), p. 284.

American History, where he wonders whether there could "be a clearer tragic dilemma" than the one embroiling America at the height of the cold war. This tragic dilemma is indicated by the notion that "though confident of its virtue, [America] must yet hold atomic bombs ready for use so as to prevent a possible world conflagration."[16] There is thus a moral ambiguity pervasive in political judgments, particularly with regard to decisions about violence and war. Niebuhr notes this ambiguity in *The Nature and Destiny of Man:* "Not all wars are equally just and not all contestants are equally right. . . . The very same war which fails to yield an absolutely clear case of 'justice' may yet concern itself with the very life and death of civilizations and cultures."[17] It is the proclivity for sin that makes all moral judgments tragic in some sense.

The point is that sin is never necessary, but it is always inevitable. Applied to the moral judgments of his public theology, this does not mean for Niebuhr that the realm of politics is one of necessary immorality separated from a pure Christian community. For Niebuhr, we are always already sinful before ever entering into public moral judgments.[18] He says: "We are responsible for making choices between greater and lesser evils, even when our Christian faith, illuminating the human scene, makes it quite apparent that there is no pure good in history, and probably no pure evil either."[19] This fact is only an indication of the inevitability of sin in political judgments, and the moral ambiguity associated with them.

For Niebuhr, the consequences of moral judgment should always reflect modicums of restraint and responsibility. Thus he was fond of suggesting that "[t]he common currency of moral life is constituted by the 'nicely calculated less and more' of the relatively good and the relatively evil."[20] That is, we live ambiguously between the poles of righteousness and depravity. I will return to this Niebuhrian account of tragedy, sin, and ambiguity shortly. First, however, it is important to establish Ramsey's later theological definition of tragedy.

16. Reinhold Niebuhr, *The Irony of American History* (New York: Charles Scribner's Sons, 1952), p. 1. This is not only tragic for Niebuhr, but also ironic; for it highlights the absurd element that the threat of evil violence might secure a tentative peace between warring nations.

17. Niebuhr, *The Nature and Destiny of Man,* vol. 1, pp. 283-84.

18. For instance, he notes, "Sin presupposes itself" (Niebuhr, *The Nature and Destiny of Man,* vol. 1, pp. 250-51).

19. Reinhold Niebuhr, "Theology and Political Thought in the Western World," in Ronald Stone, ed., *Faith and Politics* (New York: George Braziller, 1968), p. 56.

20. Niebuhr, *An Interpretation of Christian Ethics,* p. 37.

Defining Tragedy in *Speak Up for Just War or Pacifism*

I mentioned above that Ramsey's adherence to the Pauline prohibition, and his increasing attentiveness to its impact on political ethics, shaped his later thought on a public theology of tragedy. In order to substantiate that claim, I turn to his description of tragedy in *Speak Up for Just War or Pacifism.* Ramsey initiates the discussion with reference to a common topic of discussion among ethicists in the 1970s, the idea that pacifists and just-war theorists share a "presumption against violence." Simply stated, Ramsey remains unconvinced that the logic of that "presumption" is a helpful starting point for an ecumenical discussion aimed at transcending the "two options for Christian conscience" — just war and pacifism.[21]

Ramsey suggests that "the one thing Christian pacifists and just warriors have in common is that if anything is shown to be *per se* a moral atrocity, or to have no 'just cause' *now,* it should be given Christian endorsement *no moment more*" (p. 52). He recognizes that no anticipation or calculation of justice or peace can justify the perpetrating of moral atrocity. Such calculation would patently violate the Pauline prohibition. Pacifists and just-war thinkers are thus united under the prohibition by a presumption against moral atrocity (rather than a presumption against violence per se).

The categorical limits set by the promise to consider immoral acts "no moment more" generates his definition of tragedy. In *Speak Up* it follows upon an expression of frustration with the idea that just-war criteria can be applied as "a thoughtless, legalistic way of condemning all wars at one time, and any war test-by-test" (p. 71). This viewpoint is particularly susceptible to the "most deplorable failure" of omitting "any sense of tragedy or sorrow Christians have to endure, and should cultivate under the tutelage of these norms" (pp. 71-72). This point is crucial: *tragedy does not describe the performance of immoral acts with a heavy heart.* Rather, it describes the situation where "resort to violence in a palpably just cause cries to high heaven for us to rescue the perishing and *we cannot do so* because in the attempt greater evil would be caused than prevented or corrected" (p. 72).[22] Tragedy describes the situation where, by pain of conscience, one who would intervene to stop moral atrocity is restrained by just-war limitations

21. Ramsey, *Speak Up,* p. 51. Hereafter, page references to this work appear in parentheses in the text.

22. See also Ramsey, *The Just War,* pp. 14-15.

(i.e., by the realization that intervention would *necessarily* entail violation of the moral norms of war).

Ramsey highlights "the sense of tragedy inculcated by a proper use of just-war political wisdom." Such tragedy is productive of "*moral anguish* over inevitable clashes between *justice* — reasons for going to war, and *disproportion* — reasons prohibiting it." What is noteworthy about this claim is that he assumes that pain of conscience in the face of moral atrocity is something that the Christian magistrate "should cultivate" while under the restraints of just-war criteria (p. 72). This is a remarkable claim, especially given the outcry over Ramsey's protection of the magistrate's conscience in *Who Speaks for the Church?* Tragedy describes an occasion when one cries out for wrongs to be put right, all the while suffering the anguish of a conscience restrained by the Pauline prohibition.

This becomes evident in his claim that "the sounder our understanding, the more the moral anguish over suffering we *ought* to let continue *unrelieved* because to topple the oppressor would bring on as great or greater suffering" (p. 72). Tragedy requires "thoughtful reflection on the 'just' and right thing to do" because of the "tension among just-war teachings, by the fact that we are obliged to observe *all* the norms" (p. 73).[23] The anguish of tragedy is, in part, evidence that the moral norms prescribed by covenant fidelity are weighing appropriately on the (justifiable) options for purposive political action. It is also evidence of faithful protection of the neighbor in a world of conflicting political relations.

As Ramsey so frequently reiterates, justified war must fall within a matrix of obligation (to the neighbor and to God), justification (the course of action adheres to the norms that regulate and authorize militant action), and limitation (in short, the course of action does not violate the principles of proportion and discrimination). One is not allowed to go to war justly without all three, and commitment to their rigidity may require inaction in the face of conflict or surrender amidst it.[24] An inability to square obli-

23. In Ramsey's account of tragedy, the limits on human agency are more moral than they are existential. By comparison, Charles Mathewes writes: "The fact of tragic conflict does not simply delimit the realm of human capacities, and thereby reveal to us that there are things beyond our control; it further reveals that that very realm is itself vulnerable to destruction. . . . The possibility of tragedy not only reveals the limited extent of our power; it also reveals the fragility of what power we *can* have (Mathewes, *Evil and the Augustinian Tradition* [Cambridge, UK: Cambridge University Press, 2001], p. 29).

24. As early as *War and the Christian Conscience,* Ramsey says: "The test is whether we are willing to limit ends and means in warfare and yet sustain the burden of this evil neces-

gation and justification with limitation marks the anguish of a conscience in the face of tragedy. It is a tragic situation that is made more tragic by the inability to intervene justly. The tension of tragedy is thus characterized only by a proper understanding of and adherence to obligation, justification, and limitation in the political realm.[25]

Ramsey on Tragedy, Sin, and Indeterminacy

Ramsey's refusal to identify all acts of violence as moral atrocities in the above discussion may frustrate pacifists.[26] He maintains a category of violence that is morally ambiguous — that is, that "risks" conceivable (unintended) evil in pursuit of more proportionate, probable, and achievable (intended) good.[27] Where there is a choice between right and wrong per se, a Christian of any ethical persuasion is obligated to choose what is right. But Ramsey believes that political choices are more frequently of an indeterminate kind.

Two obstacles make it difficult to locate continuity between Ramsey's early political writings and these later theological reformulations. The first

---

sity, whether we as a people are willing, if war comes, to accept defeat when our fighters cannot win the hoped-for victory rather than venture more and exact more than the nature of just endurable warfare requires, whether we can mount the resources for action with at most small effect and plan surrender when none is possible" (Ramsey, *War and the Christian Conscience,* pp. 151-52).

25. As Ramsey often says, "What justified also limited!" (Ramsey, *The Just War,* p. 143).

26. I am thinking of Long's claim: "Yet for Ramsey, unlike Aquinas and Augustine, the presence of evil — force, coercion, violence — becomes the essence of politics" (Long, *Tragedy, Tradition, Transformism,* p. 44). Ramsey would reject the claim that all force and violence are inherently evil, and perhaps request a more nuanced reading of this claim: "The use of power, and possibly the use of force, is of the *esse* of politics" (Ramsey, *The Just War,* p. 5).

27. Although some of Ramsey's early writings fail to make these points clear, "The Politics of Fear" (an essay reprinted in *War and the Christian Conscience* under the title "The Politics of Fear, or, the End Is Not Yet") illuminates this later discussion. He distinguishes between "the great *evil* of all out war and the *risk* of such a war, and between the *evil* of destroying mankind by human action and the *danger* that this may happen" (Ramsey, "The Politics of Fear," *Worldview* 3, no. 3 [1960]: 5). His point is that the "possible effects of modern war must not reduce us to inaction" (p. 4). *Definite and intended* immoral effects can and may and must reduce us to inaction — the Pauline prohibition insists so. Yet, "to choose liberty by means that could conceivably threaten the existence of mankind . . . is not yet the same as choosing death" (p. 5).

is that, as we have seen throughout this book, Ramsey does not make it easy on his readers. The foundations of these commitments are evident in early writings, for instance, when he says in *War and the Christian Conscience,* "It was to be expected that political vocation and participation in war, if these were justified and motivated by what love required the Christian to do, would at the same time be surrounded by very severe limits on what love permitted him to do."[28] Yet selected statements in his early work fail to make his sensitivity to the limits of political action explicitly clear.

David H. Smith brings to light one example of this in his parallel reading of Ramsey and Aquinas in "Paul Ramsey, Love and Killing." He calls attention to Ramsey's early declarations in *Basic Christian Ethics* that, in service to the neighbor, "all things are now lawful, all things are now permitted."[29] Smith says that "it would make sense for Aquinas to describe a case of a neighbor who 'needed' saving, yet whom one could not save as an act of charity, since the saving act was sinful. For Ramsey the total commitment to neighbor entailed by agape makes such a limitation of the requirements of love a contradiction in terms."[30] The account of "moral anguish" in *Speak Up* certainly marks a departure from this early view inasmuch as Ramsey explicitly describes the tension of obligation, justification, and limitation in political endeavors. By the late 1980s he is, at least on this point, a Thomist. He bases his definition of tragedy on the inability to intervene in a "palpably just cause" due to restraint by the moral limitations of justified war.

The maturity of these later efforts also makes evident the distance Ramsey has traveled from the early struggle with "deferred repentance" outlined in chapter 2. In *Speak Up* he drops the suggestion that moral norms can be temporarily suspended without also losing the insistence that political authority requires proper sensitivity to the unpredictability and systemic contingency of the political realm. That early emphasis on the tension of political office wrought by allegiance to just-war norms is repackaged here in terms of tragedy and moral anguish without the baggage of his creative (and, at times, troubling) reinterpretation of the theological category of repentance. This is directly connected to the debates about situation ethics in the 1960s, where he located moral agency within a broader account of obligation stemming from covenant theology. These themes run throughout

28. Ramsey, *War and the Christian Conscience,* pp. xviii-xix.

29. Ramsey, *Basic Christian Ethics* (New York: Charles Scribner's Sons, 1950), p. 184.

30. David H. Smith, "Paul Ramsey, Love and Killing," in David H. Smith and James Turner Johnson, eds., *Love and Society: Essays in the Ethics of Paul Ramsey* (Missoula, MT: Scholars Press, 1974), p. 9.

the political arguments in *Speak Up*. Actions outside the formal limitations of political agency are to be considered "no moment more."[31] This means that right political judgments are only possible within a sustained ethos of normative principles. Whereas his principal concern in *Who Speaks?* is to protect the magistrate from the particular pronouncements of the church, the theology of tragedy presses the issue more directly to those who hold political office. Here, those in positions of political authority must operate within the matrix of obligation, justification, and limitation.

The second obstacle to seeing continuities between *Speak Up* and Ramsey's early work on the problems of political conflict and moral limitation is critical misunderstanding of his theology of tragedy. The most prominent example here is Stephen Long, who describes Ramsey's work with the phrase "ontology of tragedy." Long declares: "Just war is not merely an ethic about war for Ramsey, it is also a political practice necessary because of tragedy."[32] But the argument in *Speak Up* is precisely that the "practice" of fighting a just war is absent in tragic situations. Indeed, tragedy describes the state of affairs where a moral atrocity leads to cries for forceful intervention, but it remains morally impermissible. The fact that Ramsey is so frequently mischaracterized on these issues makes belaboring the point important. Tragedy, for Ramsey, is a description that can only be used by a conscience appropriately bound by the moral limitations, obligations, and justifications of the just-war theory (Long's "ethic"), including the Pauline prohibition.

Ramsey's establishment of the upper limit — where the Christian says, "No moment more" — means that inviolable rules of conduct always restrict his Christian political realism. Under the limits of the prohibition of moral atrocity, tragedy in Ramsey's political theology cannot describe a situation where inherently wrong actions serve some greater or preferred good (i.e., a kind of sinister utilitarianism). Rather, the problem is that those who hold political offices trade in a number of currencies that are unavoidably ambiguous in their potential for moral good or evil (i.e., they cannot be classified as immoral per se or unjust *now*). The most fundamental point of agreement between pacifists and just-war thinkers is a promise to consider per se immoral acts no moment more. Beyond that promise is a realm of actions with intended (but not guaranteed) consequences, purposive (but not unassailable) decisions, and desired (but nonetheless contingent) outcomes. In Ramsey's mind, what to do amid these contex-

31. Ramsey, *Speak Up*, pp. 72, 63.

32. Long, *Tragedy, Tradition, Transformism*, pp. 44, 143.

tual ambiguities and uncertainties represents the true point of contention in the pacifist/just-war debate.

We must not forget that both of these ideas, in their own way, stem from Ramsey's allegiance to Niebuhr. For Niebuhrian realists, the admission that sin marks all political judgments does not generate a moral carte blanche to do as we please. For instance, in *Moral Man and Immoral Society,* Niebuhr observes:

> An adequate political morality must do justice to the insights of both moralists and political realists. It will recognize that human society will probably never escape social conflict, even though it extends the areas of social cooperation. It will try to save society from being involved in endless cycles of futile conflict, not by an effort to abolish coercion in the life of collective man, but by reducing it to a minimum, by counseling the use of such types of coercion as are most compatible with the moral and rational factors in human society and by discriminating between the purposes and ends for which coercion is used.[33]

I have noted above that Niebuhr does not hold consistently to the inviolability of this process of discrimination. There are simply too many places where he takes a utilitarian line. Yet roots of Ramsey's increased attentiveness to the morality of means lie in Niebuhrian claims such as these.[34]

More importantly, however, is the way in which Ramsey's insistence on the ambiguity of political judgments draws on Niebuhr. Here again we have to avoid the temptation of Long's reading: Long notes that Ramsey "did not ontologize evil, but [he] did ontologize tragedy! If evil should not be ontologized, neither should tragedy be written into the fabric of political being."[35] If Ramsey "ontologizes" anything in his description of tragedy, it must be the inescapable indeterminacy that plagues the public responsibilities of political office-holders. He concedes (even insists) that judgments

33. Niebuhr, *Moral Man and Immoral Society,* p. 234.

34. Some accuse Niebuhr's influence of tempting Ramsey to shield his theological commitments. For instance, "Ramsey's Niebuhrianism led him to play down the theological convictions behind his deontological stance" (Samuel Wells, *Transforming Fate into Destiny: The Theological Ethics of Stanley Hauerwas* [Eugene, OR: Cascade Books, 1998], p. 8).

35. Long, *Tragedy, Tradition, Transformism,* p. 47. This particular comment comes in a discussion of H. Richard Niebuhr, but Long's description of Ramsey's "ontology of tragedy" runs throughout the book and is similarly attributed to influences from Reinhold Niebuhr elsewhere.

within the political realm will often be ambiguous and uncertain. But this does not lead him to collapse the significance of agency or promote the purchasing of good with evil. Rather, he reinstalls agency as principally important through acts of right political judgment. The magistrate should thus pursue a conscience plagued by anguish stemming from the inviolability of the Pauline prohibition. The magistrate acts with purpose within the bounds of a theory of justified war and laments the tragic situations where intervention remains incompatible with faithful obedience.

Here we see that Ramsey's refusal to describe violence as inherently morally atrocious inherits Niebuhr's argument that the use of force in and of itself cannot be singularly responsible for the ambiguity of political judgments.[36] Rather, that ambiguity stems from the "bogus claim of finality" mentioned earlier, and the difference between the two thinkers lies in how their sensitivity to ambiguity defines their notion of tragedy. For Niebuhr, the "bogus claim of finality" involved in political judgments undermines the rigidity of moral norms in human experience and allows for their tragic violation in certain pursuits of justice. For Ramsey, on the other hand, Niebuhr's "bogus claim of finality" takes the shape not of tragedy, as Long suggests, but of *indeterminacy.* Ramsey reinstalls the significance of agency in political judgment by refusing to suspend moral norms, even in the face of indeterminate and ambiguous circumstances — what he elsewhere calls "the incalculable determinants" of moral judgments.[37]

Conclusions on Tragedy and Political Conflict Situations

Earlier in this chapter I suggested that Jeffrey Stout highlights the problem of dirty hands as a way of linking political judgments to the moral life of

36. "It is wrong to assume, however, that the ambiguous ethical position of the state is due primarily to its use of physical force. The real cause of its questionable moral worth lies in the fact that the real power which it wields (composed of both force and majesty) is ostensibly derived from the total community and justified by its service to the community. But practically this power is always in the hands of a particular oligarchy, of some group which possesses the most significant form of social power" (Niebuhr, "Do the State and Nation Belong to God or the Devil?" in *Faith and Politics,* ed. Ronald H. Stone [New York: George Braziller, 1968], p. 86).

37. Paul Ramsey, "Indeterminacy and Incommensurability in Moral Choice," in Richard A. McCormick and Paul Ramsey, eds., *Doing Evil to Achieve Good: Moral Choice in Conflict Situations* (Chicago: Loyola University Press, 1978), p. 70.

the community. This is most clear in his expression of anxieties about a "supreme-emergency exception" to moral limitations that would weaken "democratic culture by undermining its ability to sustain a genuinely democratic politics, here and now."[38] By genuinely democratic politics, of course, Stout means the exchange of reasons in public. He is arguing that the moral norms governing emergency situations should be congruent with the moral life of the democratic community and the reason-giving practices of that community. Therefore, the determination of what kind of people we want to be influences how we locate the upper limits on the moral judgments of a democratic culture. (This is unavoidably a question of the relationship between judgment and virtue, to which I will return in later chapters.)

In response to this anxiety about the moral substance of the democratic community, public theology can supply a methodology in which the community of the church helps articulate an upper limit on such judgments. Ramsey, in part through his debts to Niebuhr, offers the language of tragedy as a helpful resource as the church seeks to articulate this methodology. To be fair, the account of tragedy has its flaws, and I have suggested several ways in which Ramsey could have offered a more thoroughgoing *theological* rendering of the term. But the most significant element of this discussion is the significant challenge it offers to the idea that "tragedy" can be used to describe the liberal failings of either Niebuhr or Ramsey as political theologians. In contrast, the following conclusions assert the potential helpfulness of their arguments as the church seeks to exchange reasons in a democratic culture. In fact, the foregoing analysis provides several starting points for the way that Ramsey's account of tragedy helps to describe realities of political context and to establish limits on morally permissible political behavior.

First, Ramsey's language of tragedy reflects firm moral limitations in a violent world under divine judgment. Long argues that tragedy "usurps God's place over creation, and this constrains how Christians should act in the world."[39] Rather, in Ramsey's hands, the language of tragedy acknowledges God's place over creation, and this constrains how Christians should act in the world. It describes a world governed *by* God's judgment and living *under* God's judgment. Thus, when Niebuhr points to the tragic nature of human existence, he has in mind that life is tragic precisely be-

38. Stout, *Democracy and Tradition,* p. 200.

39. Long, *Tragedy, Tradition, Transformism,* p. 192.

cause it has falsely attempted to usurp God's sovereignty but does not realize that such coups are figments of distorted imaginations. Therefore, he suggests: "Sin is occasioned precisely by the fact that man refuses to admit his 'creatureliness' and to acknowledge himself as merely a member of a total unity of life. He pretends to be more than he is."[40] For Ramsey's part, his descriptions of just war as obligation, limitation, and justification are born out of a recognition of God's sovereignty, not in defiance of it. Divine love dictates which actions are to be considered "no moment more," as well as those in service to the neighbor that are to be pursued in faithful obedience. Political authority is always subject to God's greater judgment and therein governed by principles of justice. Ramsey's use of tragedy does not ignore that reality, but helps describe it.

Second, if the language of tragedy appreciates the constant cloud of indeterminacy hanging over political judgments, this does not legitimate sin or waive the moral demands on political judgments. I admit some difference between Ramsey and Niebuhr here, though the two share more in common than not. Neither thinker saw entry into the political realm as requiring any loss of human agency or moral responsibility.[41] Both articulate a sense of sin as something inevitable in human endeavors. But that is never a unique feature of the political realm! Nor should it be excluded from any viable public theology. Inevitability functions as a descriptive term meant to convey the broken character of human agency. As Niebuhr suggests, "The Christian estimate of human evil is so serious precisely because it places evil at the very center of human personality: in the will. This evil cannot be regarded complacently as the inevitable consequence of his finiteness or the fruit of his involvement in the contingencies and necessities of nature."[42] In other words, tragedy never functions as a prescriptive term that liberates the agent from moral restraint or responsibility. Such a position, strengthened by both Ramsey and Niebuhr, refuses to see the political realm as one where representative agents bear no responsibility for the demands of faithful obedience. Their emphasis on moral norms in an indeterminate world — and especially Ramsey's insistence on the inviolable status of the Pauline prohibition — attempts to address the pervasive nature of

40. Niebuhr, *The Nature and Destiny of Man,* 1:16.

41. Rather, political ambiguity stemmed from the fact that "power is always partial. It always has a particular locus. Yet power would degenerate into naked force if it could not pretend that it is universal and not partial and particular" (Niebuhr, "Do the State," p. 87).

42. Niebuhr, *The Nature and Destiny of Man,* 1:16.

evil in the world without making it a kind of necessary ally within a constructive political ethic.[43]

Finally, one of the reasons why Stout's account of politics in a democratic culture is so compelling for those interested in influential public theologies is that he captures the widespread anxiety that politicians can justify anything under the heading of a political emergency. He judges that "the necessity excuse almost always turns out to be false."[44] In their attempt to ward off such excuse-making as moral justification, Ramsey and Niebuhr use the language of tragedy to similar ends. (I will explore Ramsey's response to the emergency situation as an "exception" to moral rules in the following chapter.) Both ethicists are concerned about providing a public language capable of simultaneously voicing lament over moral atrocity and rejecting political judgments discordant with moral norms. This similarity helps us remember that both thinkers write theology for the public. That is to say, they write to supply the community with a language of tragedy as a creative theological resource for describing faithful obedience in a violent world.

Stout's analysis of the problem of dirty hands renders into a secular language a concern for the pervasive nature of evil in the world and the need to address it. He supplies a narrative of responsibility for the moral life of the democratic community capable of appreciation by anyone — assenter to religious belief or not. Because Ramsey and Niebuhr are so frequently criticized for their respective ecclesiologies, it is easy to miss that they, too, display a strong sense of connection between political judgments and the moral life of the community. Both insist that the moral community bears responsibility that is directly related to, though not equivalent to, the individual's responsibility for making judgments. They both believe that the community of the church stakes out important territory in helping discern the limits of permissibility in moral judgments.

For Stout's purposes, this theologically grounded limitation of moral

43. Though frequently criticized for being more fundamentally determined by pagan concepts than theological accounts of sin, both Ramsey and Niebuhr suggest that tragedy can be a theologically informed description of the fundamental realities of political and social existence. For more on this particular criticism of Niebuhr, see John Milbank, "The Poverty of Niebuhrianism," in *The Word Made Strange: Theology, Language, Culture* (Oxford: Blackwell, 1997). For a response to Milbank on this issue, see John K. Burk, "Moral Law, Privative Evil, and Christian Realism: Reconsidering Milbank's 'The Poverty of Niebuhrianism,'" *Studies in Christian Ethics* 22, no. 2 (2009): 208-25.

44. Stout, *Democracy and Tradition,* p. 187.

atrocities may not represent a consensus of the entire democratic populace. However, the voice of public theology can contribute to the reason-giving exercises inherent in a genuinely democratic politics. And theological descriptions of tragedy such as we encounter in Niebuhr and Ramsey can be helpful to this effect. Within a democratic society, the church can present political leaders with an inviolable moral standard against which moral judgments are measured. It provides resources to contextualize the problem of dirty hands by offering the moral ceiling of the Pauline prohibition in which no evil may be done in the name of some putative democratic good.

The challenge facing all liberal democracies is the need to balance a range of perspectives on public issues by which the moral character of a particular people is defined. Ramsey and Niebuhr provide similar ways of thinking publicly and theologically about the particular problems of violence and coercion that a liberal democracy will confront. In this chapter I have identified and emphasized the elements of Ramsey's and Niebuhr's work that are instructive to a coherent public theological stance with regard to the problem of violence and the attendant issue of tragedy. In the following chapter, I will continue to explore the challenges of public theology by examining the possibility of a justified "exception" to the same rules of conduct Ramsey finds inviolable. This will bring the importance of practical reasoning and the necessity of the virtue of prudence clearly into focus.

CHAPTER SIX

Ramsey's Practical Reasoning and the Necessity of Virtue

The 1960s saw the rise of situation ethics in philosophical and theological debates, and along with it came an attack on the adequacy of norms, rules, and principles for moral deliberation. With roots in philosophical pragmatism and strong consequentialist impulses, the situation ethics movement sought a "third way" between legalism and antinomianism.[1] Union Theological Seminary's Paul Lehmann supplied a theological framework for the movement with *Ethics in a Christian Context* in 1963. However, Joseph Fletcher's *Situation Ethics* (1966) captured the full force of the argument for an ethic of contextual decision-making.[2]

Ramsey, who exhibited his share of tendencies toward antinomianism in *Basic Christian Ethics,* came to view situation ethics with great skepticism. He remarked in a personal letter to Reinhold Niebuhr in 1966 that it represented "a sort of nervous breakdown in present-day theology and ethics, and our flight from careful, disciplined reflection."[3] Ramsey's contributions to the debate included a number of essays that he collected in the publication *Deeds and Rules in Christian Ethics* in 1967.[4] In that book he

1. See James F. Childress, introduction to Joseph Fletcher, *Situation Ethics* (Philadelphia: Westminster, 1966; reprint, Louisville: Westminster John Knox Press, 1997), pp. 1-10.

2. Paul Lehmann, *Ethics in a Christian Context* (London: SCM, 1963); Joseph Fletcher, *Situation Ethics* (Philadelphia: Westminster, 1966; reprint, Lousiville: Westminster John Knox Press, 1997).

3. Paul Ramsey to Reinhold Niebuhr, May 18, 1966, Box 20, Paul Ramsey Papers, Special Collections and Manuscripts, Perkins-Bostock Library, Duke University. See also Paul Ramsey, *Basic Christian Ethics* (New York: Charles Scribner's Sons, 1950).

4. Paul Ramsey, *Deeds and Rules in Christian Ethics* (New York: Charles Scribner's Sons, 1965; Lanham, MD: University Press of America, 1967).

argues that Christian ethics should attend "in very great measure" to questions of "which rules of action are most love-embodying."[5] This argument did not include support for so-called summary rules, that is, rules that offer no particular moral limitation but merely an account of past practices. Ramsey suggests that, because such rules have no legitimate moral claim over new situations, they fail precisely where their success is needed: in the determination of the moral landscape in which the agent acts.

In spite of his rejection of summary rules, the arguments of that collection of essays left several questions unanswered concerning the place of rules within moral and practical reasoning. These included anxieties about the captivity of Protestant ethics to the consequentialist tendencies of situation ethics, debates concerning the distinctive contributions of Christian convictions to discussions of philosophical ethics, and confusion about the precise character of love-embodying rules. Perhaps most importantly, *Deeds and Rules* failed to answer fully the question of *exceptions:* "Is it possible to speak of justifiable violations of moral principles [or moral rules]?"[6]

With this question in mind, Ramsey wrote "The Case of the Curious Exception" for inclusion in a volume he edited with Gene Outka, entitled *Norm and Context in Christian Ethics.* In that essay he offers elaborate technical analysis of the difference between "directions" of action and "directives" of action, as well as "moral-species-term" and "moral-genus-term." More broadly, he provides a negative answer to the question about the viability of justifiable exceptions and instead proposes a model of practical reasoning rooted in a covenant theological framework. It is a lengthy, complicated, and arduous essay that some have said slams the door shut on the situation-ethics debate.[7] The question facing us, more than forty years

5. Ramsey, *Deeds and Rules,* p. 5. Indeed, this was also against the grain of some of Ramsey's earlier arguments, e.g., in *Basic Christian Ethics.*

6. Paul Ramsey, "The Case of the Curious Exception," in Gene H. Outka and Paul Ramsey, eds., *Norm and Context in Christian Ethics* (New York: Charles Scribner's Sons, 1968), p. 67.

7. Oliver O'Donovan observes that "The Case of the Curious Exception" "spoke the last word on the formal questions which had been agitated in the debate about situationism" (O'Donovan, *Resurrection and Moral Order,* 2nd ed. [Grand Rapids: Eerdmans, 1994], p. 196). Stanley Hauerwas suggests that the debate slowly came to an end not because "the issue has been settled, but as so often happens in intellectual disputes, the adversaries simply become bored and begin to turn their interests elsewhere" (Hauerwas, "Situation Ethics, Moral Notions, and Moral Theology," in *Vision and Virtue* [Notre Dame, IN: University of Notre Dame Press, 1974], p. 11).

after "The Case of the Curious Exception" was published, is whether it has any abiding value beyond the debates that occupied philosophical ethics at the time. It is not at all clear that readers need to master the more technical elements of the essay in order to appreciate its overall interpretive gains. Furthermore, contemporary writers such as Jean Porter have examined the place of rules and exceptions in Christian ethics with degrees of clarity and accessibility that surpass Ramsey's efforts.[8]

In this chapter I will suggest that the arguments in "The Case of the Curious Exception" remain lively for two reasons. The first is my belief that Ramsey's theological emphasis on covenant remains a helpful resource for resisting the temptation toward "escape-clauses" and exceptions in moral deliberation that is still with us today. This element of the discussion will draw together a number of threads on covenant and moral agency that have been present throughout the preceding chapters. The second is my belief that Ramsey's account of practical reasoning helps illuminate the turn toward the virtues in contemporary moral theology. This element of the discussion lays the groundwork for subsequent chapters that put Ramsey in conversation with several contemporary virtue thinkers, including John Bowlin, Jennifer A. Herdt, Charles Mathewes, and Daniel Bell Jr.

In order to defend both of these claims, I find it necessary to sidestep a good deal of the technical argumentation that occupies the majority of the essay. (As with *Deeds and Rules,* readers curious about the precise contours of the debates over antinomianism and contextualism from the 1960s will find ample critical analysis elsewhere.)[9] Instead, my argument will unfold as follows: First, I will establish the theological foundations of Ramsey's commitment to practical reasoning by examining the role of covenant in the closing section of that article. This will highlight the way he roots Christian behavior in the world within a properly eschatological response to God's steadfast covenant faithfulness. Second, I will locate the philosophical questions surrounding morally justifiable exceptions, including his account of practical reasoning, within this broader theological framework. Recent debates about exceptions to the prohibition of

8. Jean Porter, *Moral Action and Christian Ethics* (Cambridge, UK: Cambridge University Press, 1995).

9. See esp. Paul F. Camenisch, "Paul Ramsey's Task: Some Methodological Clarifications and Questions," in David H. Smith and James T. Johnson, eds., *Love and Society: Essays in the Ethics of Paul Ramsey* (Missoula, MT: Scholars Press, 1974), pp. 67-89; Donald Evans, "Paul Ramsey on Exceptionless Moral Rules," in Smith and Johnson, eds., *Love and Society,* pp. 19-46.

torture will here help to highlight the continued liveliness of Ramsey's arguments for the distinctiveness of Christian convictions. Finally, I will suggest that "The Case of the Curious Exception" helped clear conceptual ground for the turn toward the virtues in contemporary moral theology. In doing so, I make no claim that Ramsey alone is responsible for this turn. Alasdair MacIntyre's *After Virtue* is nearly unrivaled in its impact; and, of course, any so-called return to virtue theory must account for the monumental legacy of Aristotle, Augustine, and Aquinas.[10] Still, it is noteworthy that "The Case of the Curious Exception" plays an important role in the early work of two of the most significant voices in contemporary Christian virtue ethics, Jean Porter and Oliver O'Donovan.[11] As I will show, both Porter and O'Donovan provide foundational accounts of the virtues that appropriate central features of Ramsey's argument, especially his conviction that creativity and flexibility in practical reasoning must stem from an exploration of foundational theological commitments rather than a pursuit of exempting conditions.

Covenants and Consequences: Against the Grain of the Present Age

As I mentioned above, the prompt for "The Case of the Curious Exception" is this: "Is it possible to speak of justifiable violations of moral principles?"[12] Never one to assume that theologians have a monopoly on truth, Ramsey begins by warning readers that his approach will be "bifocal." By this he means that on occasion he will side with the philosophers against the theologians, and at other times he will use theological insights to challenge and clarify philosophical arguments (p. 70).[13] However, he also warns that

10. Alasdair MacIntyre, *After Virtue: A Study in Moral Theory* (London: Gerald Duckworth, 1981; 2nd ed., Notre Dame, IN: University of Notre Dame Press, 1984).

11. I trace Ramsey's importance through Porter and O'Donovan for two reasons. The first is that they are on the leading edge of the contemporary turn to the virtues in Christian ethics. Second, Porter and O'Donovan actually *use* Ramsey's work. As I engage more recent work from virtue thinkers in subsequent chapters, I will show that they often nod to Ramsey's importance without substantially engaging his arguments.

12. Ramsey, "The Case of the Curious Exception," p. 67. Hereafter, page references to this work appear in parentheses within the text.

13. "It ought not to be surprising if there are philosophical analyses that are useful in repairing some of the worst aspects of theological ethics, and Christian ethical understanding that may improve some of the best philosophy" (p. 70).

his concluding response to the question will run against both the philosophers' "*consequence*-features" or "*justice*-features" and "the current vogue of 'exceptionism' in theological ethics" (pp. 70, 68).[14] Instead, any properly Christian approach to the question of justifiable exceptions must arrive at its conclusions through an examination of foundational theological commitments.

What are those prior commitments? The theological proposal in "The Case of the Curious Exception" consists of the following three movements. First, he argues that Christian behavior in the world should be rooted in a theological account of God's behavior in the world. The "ultimate warrant" of Christian ethics is "an appeal to what the Lord of heaven and earth is believed to have been doing and to be doing in enacting and establishing His covenant with us and all mankind" (p. 125). God's steadfast faithfulness to the covenant with creation is a witness and pattern for Christian faithfulness. The name for this kind of ethics is "eucharistic" (p. 123),[15] and it is located in the church, where God's "performative actions" are "celebrated in the action and worship of the Christian community through all ages" (p. 125). Although God's "mandates" remain a part of this divine witness, it is ultimately "the nature of His self-involvement with us in our history" that dictates the character of Christian obedience (p. 123). (It is interesting that in this respect he presents a position not unlike the one taken by John Howard Yoder in *The Original Revolution:* "We do not, ultimately, love our neighbor because Jesus told us to. We love our neighbor because God is like that."[16])

14. Ramsey included Karl Barth's ethics among this "current vogue." Oliver O'Donovan has argued that Ramsey misunderstood Barth's theological ethics on this point. See O'Donovan, "Karl Barth and Paul Ramsey's Uses of Power," in Oliver O'Donovan and Joan Lockwood O'Donovan, eds., *Bonds of Imperfection* (Grand Rapids: Eerdmans, 2004), pp. 246-75.

15. Ramsey is both acknowledging and correcting Joseph Fletcher's use of this phrase. He agrees with the suggestion that "in Christian ethics it is more than a doctrinaire formality to insist that before we ask the ethical question "What shall I do?" comes the *pre*-ethical question "What has God done?" (Fletcher, *Situation Ethics,* p. 157). However, Ramsey is also correcting Fletcher's suggestion that a "eucharistic ethics" is "distinct from other moralities only because of its reason *for* righteousness, not by its standards *of* righteousness" (p. 156). In fact, Ramsey is here demonstrating the way Christian "faithfulness obligations" run against the grain of contemporary moral deliberation.

16. John Howard Yoder, *The Original Revolution* (Scottdale, PA: Herald Press, 1971), p. 52. Of course, Yoder continues: "It is not because Jesus told us to that we love even beyond the limits of reason and justice, even to the point of refusing to kill and being willing to suffer — but because God is like that too." In chapter 9, I explore the conflict between Ramsey and Yoder concerning Christology.

The second feature of this theological proposal follows from the first. If Christian witness in the world is rooted fundamentally in the imitation of God's steadfast faithfulness, then it is also fixed on the eschatological hope of God's promised redemption of all creation. Ramsey says, obscurely, "The grain of things cannot ultimately prove unsupportive of the doing of our fidelities under the moral constitution God makes known in His word-deeds toward us" (p. 133). He is careful here to avoid linking God's promises to the contemporary philosophical interest in the calculable consequences of behavior. Eschatological hope is no rational calculus, and it is "far and away different from supposing that the final worldly consequences of faithful deeds will show the success of the good" (p. 133). On the contrary, Christians should not expect faithfulness to yield programmatically a better world. Yet the sure promises of God's "word-deeds" should lead Christians to expect that *"ultimate* consequences cannot be such as to render [the] performance of fidelity obligations *wrong"* (p. 133). Therefore, eschatological hope seals the conviction that God's steadfast faithfulness sets the pattern for Christian behavior in the world.

The third component makes explicit the turn toward ethics in this moral theology. If Christian behavior is patterned after God's dealings with the world and sealed with God's eschatological promises, Ramsey says, "it follows that in Christian ethics we can and may and must be enormously disinterested in any exception, or openness to exceptions, that would have to be justified primarily by future-consequence features" (p. 125).[17] He considers this search for "escape-clauses" and the distaste for fixed moral rules to be "one of the chief presuppositions of the present age" (p. 135). Where the impulse of contemporary philosophy and theology is to pursue "relevant moral features" justifying exceptions to covenant obligations, he argues that Christian ethics should pursue "occasions of faithfulness." In the Christian life "we are driven deeper and deeper into the meaning of covenant obligations" (p. 125). In other words, Christians seek not exempting conditions, but bonding conditions.

Against the grain of the present age, Ramsey argues that a properly Christian discussion of exemptions to moral rules must first recognize

17. Mark Storslee suggested to me that this might be written as the following syllogism. Major: Right action is premised on God's dealings with creation, and the shape of those dealings is steadfast faithfulness. Minor: Ultimate (eschatological) consequences will surely work toward God's purpose, but an emphasis on immediate (and calculable) consequences is unlikely to mirror God's steadfast fidelity. Therefore: Christians ought to be "enormously disinterested" in exceptions that find their justification in "future-consequence features."

the moral implications of our foundational theological convictions. I have highlighted the essential features of these convictions, including the primacy of God's "word-deeds" toward the world, the eschatological hope in God's good future, and the movement deeper and deeper into covenant obligations. We must now turn to see how these convictions shape his response to the particular question of justifiable exceptions and the role of practical reasoning in the moral life.

Practical Reasoning and Inviolable Moral Rules

Careful attention to the lengthy middle sections of the essay (almost fifty pages!) suggests two broad conclusions: first, that the notion of a "justifiable exception" is logically incoherent; and second, that the far more pressing concern is a proper account of practical reasoning and what Ramsey calls "the subsumption of cases" or "the actual production of particular deeds" (p. 125). I will address these two consecutively.

The "curious exception" under investigation concerns the justification of an action that is incongruent with moral rules relevant to the situation. Ramsey suggests that we are immediately faced with a dilemma. If there are no "relevant moral warrants" for the action, how can it be *justifiable?* At the same time, if there are such moral warrants, by what criteria is the action *exceptional?* It seems that a justifiable exception is a contradiction in terms. To justify an action — that is, to make the judgment that the action, however unique, is morally permissible — is at once to classify it as a *sort* of action. Thus he says: "The effort to locate a *justifiable* exception can only have the effect of utterly destroying its exceptional character" (p. 78).[18] A justifiable exception is thus a "misnomer" (p. 77).

Another way of saying this is to call moral justifications generic. In Ramsey's terms, if a situation has "the same justifying features" and "the same verdict," then "the same general judgment upon this sort of conduct should again be forthcoming" (p. 78). This leaves us with a more challenging question than the one concerning the possibility of justifiable exceptions. If morality itself is *generic,* what is the relationship between general moral rules and *particular* actions? In other words, how are we to give an account of practical reasoning in connection with moral justifications?

18. Earlier he says, "To justify any action one must be able to characterize it as a *sort* of action that should be done by anyone who is in a similar situation" (p. 68).

Here we need not use Ramsey's technical terms to grasp his response to the question; a few examples will do the trick.

First, we can explore the character of generic moral rules, beginning with a rather simple one: One should not steal a car. We can add features to this rule that are morally irrelevant: One should not steal a car while chewing gum. Or we can add features to this rule that are morally relevant: One should not steal a car by threatening mortal violence. We can also add features that appear to create exceptions: One should not steal a car unless doing so is necessary to transport a severely injured person to medical care, when no other transportation is available. Ramsey, of course, has instructed us that this is not truly an exception-creating feature, but rather a clarification and deepening of the original rule. We know this because there are moral warrants for the apparently exceptional action: Someone is severely injured and no other transportation is available! These moral warrants make such an action *generally* commendable, which, of course, means that it is no longer strictly *exceptional.*[19] Allow me one final example. We may continue to add features to the rule until it becomes elaborately specific: One should not steal a car from a teenage driver accompanying infant children unless doing so is necessary to transport a gunshot victim to medical care, when no other transportation is available. Notice that this increased *specificity* does not erase the *generic* character of rules. Either there are moral warrants for the action that appears to be an exception, in which case those warrants make the action generally commendable, or there are no moral warrants for the so-called exception, in which case it is not an exception but simply a morally atrocious violation of the rule. In short, moral rules, even those describing rather unlikely circumstances, are still generic in character: they reject a *kind* of behavior.

The question we must answer is whether the proper task of the ethicist is to clarify moral rules with such increasing specificity as to leave no doubt about which course of action the agent is to pursue. Can narrowly specific moral rules eliminate the final element of moral judgment about how to act in a particular situation (e.g., to steal the car or not)? Ramsey clearly suggests that the answer is no.[20] He says: "No matter how narrowly

19. The point about exceptions here is not that Ramsey wants a reductive account of absolutely simple moral rules (e.g., one should not steal). In fact, he is trying to help us understand how our moral language works, thereby allowing us to see clearly how the language of exceptions can easily mislead us into morally atrocious behavior.

20. In Ramsey's terms: "There can be no *subsumption-ruling* rules" (p. 103). In 1961, Ramsey wrote in a letter to Byron Johnson that prudence "is not a derogatory word. . . . It

defined may be the multiple terms or qualifications of the meaning of a moral permission or prohibition that has been elaborated or stated as fully as possible . . . such specification of action is never a *particular.*" He continues: "Moral reasoning is always a matter of . . . increasing illumination — for the direction of concrete actions." The acting itself is the result of practical reason ("Curious Exception," p. 76).

We should pause to note the oddity of Ramsey's use of the term "subsumption of cases" to describe this element of moral judgment. He clearly links the term with the production of a particular deed, but there is no reason why "subsumption" might not also reasonably describe a judgment that a particular past action ought to be classified under this moral rule and not that one. Oliver O'Donovan helps capture the odd specificity of Ramsey's intentions for the phrase: "Curiously, [Ramsey] goes so far as to say that subsumption is not part of moral reason at all, but of 'actual practice,' though he also consistently describes it as the work of 'prudence or practical wisdom.' It is clear what the point of forcing this distinction is: it is to protect against the suggestion that there is to be found in the particular case any *other* kind of moral wisdom than knowledge of the moral law itself."[21] Interestingly, Ramsey's frustration with situation ethics does not include the suggestion that particular cases — or particular moments of decision — are unimportant. In fact, only the foolish will elide the quite demanding work of moral judgment. Situation ethics errs instead where it says that *everything* the moral agent needs lies in the moment of decision, or in the features of that particular situation. Against the trends of contextual decision-making, Ramsey is eager to keep our attention squarely on the enduring commitments and rules that stem from covenant faithfulness. As we saw in earlier in this study, right judgment requires the ability to know the depths and complexities of steadfast covenant love, as well as the ability to generate a concrete action responsive to that moral wisdom.

What we discover amid Ramsey's obsessively technical descriptions of such matters is a call to explore the depths and contours of moral rules — and of Christian theological reflection about moral rules. Ramsey flatly refuses "our contemporary penchant for escape-clauses and exception

is 'practical wisdom' in applying ethical principles to actual cases. Without prudence there would be no morality at all put forth into actual practice and decision-making" (Paul Ramsey to Byron Johnson, Feb. 17, 1961, Box 12, Ramsey Papers).

21. O'Donovan, *Resurrection and Moral Order,* p. 197.

generating criteria" because he sees our reliance on them as a perverted way "to introduce creativity and sensitivity into the moral life" ("Curious Exception," p. 92). We have already seen that turning toward the language of exceptions erodes, rather than strengthens, enduring moral commitments. So-called exceptions are a mirage; they are evidence that "somebody stopped thinking morally" (p. 67). More important, for Ramsey, is the fact that Christians can discover moral creativity and sensitivity in the face of rapidly changing contemporary challenges by probing more and more deeply into faithfulness obligations and covenant bonds. Theological reflection on God's steadfast faithfulness and Christian eschatological hope in God's final victory animate us away from the temptations of consequentialism and exceptionalism. That is the work of covenant faithfulness in the world.

Temptations toward Exceptionalism

Lest anyone think that the temptations toward exceptionalism in Ramsey's time have receded along with the passing of situation ethics as a viable philosophical position, it may be helpful to point briefly to a relatively recent public issue of some concern, in which justifying exceptions figure prominently. (It is also one in which Ramsey would have been deeply invested as a political theologian.) In the wake of the release of "torture memos" from the George W. Bush administration (beginning in 2002) and the subsequent passing of the Detainee Treatment Act of 2005 (introduced by Senator John McCain), the question of whether torture should be categorically prohibited emerged as a topic of significant and continuing public debate. Advocates of the moral permissibility of torture in emergency situations frequently invoke the language of justifiable exceptions. For instance, columnist Charles Krauthammer wrote in *The Weekly Standard* that "the problem" with a categorical legal prohibition of torture is that "it is going to be very difficult to publicly carve out exceptions."[22] Jeremy Waldron has written about attempts by lawyers working in the White House and the Departments of Justice and Defense in 2002 and

22. Charles Krauthammer, "The Truth about Torture: It's Time to Be Honest about Doing Terrible Things," *Weekly Standard,* December 5, 2005. See also Alan M. Dershowitz, "Should the Ticking Time Bomb Terrorist Be Tortured?" in *Why Terrorism Works* (New Haven: Yale University Press, 2003), pp. 131-63.

2003 to "narrow the definition of torture . . . so the prohibition would cover much less than most people supposed." He rightly locates this debate as one concerning "the integrity of the rules and standards of positive law."[23] Even former president Bill Clinton entered the debate, saying on NBC's "Meet the Press" in 2007, "If you have any kind of formal exception [to a prohibition against torture], people just drive a truck through it, and they'll say 'Well, I thought it was covered by the exception.'" But Clinton refused to make the legal prohibition a categorical moral prohibition: if someone is in an emergency situation — "and it was six hours to the bomb or whatever . . . you'll do whatever you do, and you should be prepared to take the consequences."[24]

At the center of the torture debate are questions about the use of exceptions to uphold the creativity and sensitivity of the law in emergency situations. Ramsey warned that the most enticing of those escape clauses would appear in the language of consequentialism. This is nowhere more apparent than in suggestions that, when it comes to the permissibility of torture, "all that's left to haggle about is the price."[25] While the philosoph-

23. Jeremy Waldron, "What Can Christian Teaching Add to the Debate about Torture?" *Theology Today* 63 (2006): 333. See also Jeremy Waldron, "Torture and Positive Law: Jurisprudence for the White House," *Columbia Law Review* 105 (2005): 1681-1750.

24. Bill Clinton, interview with Tim Russert, "Meet the Press," website, 30 September 2007. Of course, there are two ways to try to "get around" a prohibition against torture. The first plays a consequences game, suggesting that the prohibition is not *categorical.* Based on a certain calculation of loss/reward in a particular political situation, torture may be understandable, even justifiable. Clinton endorses this approach while displaying precisely the kind of erosion of moral commitments through the language of exception that Ramsey has in view. (The moral rules have surely been thrown out the window when someone says, "You'll do whatever you do.") The second plays a language game by challenging the *definition* of torture. Of course, torture is categorically prohibited, but who said waterboarding is torture? Here Clinton seems to take a harder stance, saying that people will "drive a truck" through those kinds of generic ("formal," as he puts it) exceptions. In the first approach you're haggling over the *price* of torture, and in the second you're haggling over the *definition* of torture. Ramsey has consequentialism so strongly in his grasp here that it's difficult to make a judgment about his posture on the second kind of exception. One suspects (anxiously perhaps) that Ramsey might have taken a line similar to Jean Bethke Elshtain's in recent years, which uses the language game to create space for waterboarding. I'm grateful to Mark Storslee for making this distinction clear to me.

25. Krauthammer clearly roots his justifiable exception in the calculation of consequences. The full quotation reads as follows: "However rare the cases, there are circumstances in which, by any rational moral calculus, torture not only would be permissible but would be required (to acquire life-saving information). And once you've established the principle, to paraphrase George Bernard Shaw, all that's left to haggle about is the price. In

ical debates concerning situation ethics have passed, rendering much of Ramsey's technical analysis outdated, the torture debate is evidence that we still face the same erosion of moral deliberation by a reliance on escape clauses and exceptions. If this is true, and I believe it is, then we are confronted with the continued liveliness of Ramsey's insistence that Christians will discover the true creativity and sensitivity of moral law by probing the bonds of our covenant with God and the created order, including obligations of faithfulness to our neighbors. This involves growing in the virtues, both cardinal and theological.

Clearing Ground for a Turn toward the Virtues

I dedicate the final section of this chapter to showing how the arguments in "The Case of the Curious Exception" helped facilitate calls for the compatibility of virtues and rules in moral theology. As I observed above, no one would dare to suggest that Ramsey alone is responsible for this contemporary turn to virtue ethics, and I do not intend to make that claim here. However, it does appear that his dense work in "The Case of the Curious Exception" helps clear conceptual ground for some contemporary virtue-based accounts of moral judgment. To put it another way, Ramsey's attentiveness to the importance of practical reasoning within a theological account of moral obligation enables others to articulate renewed accounts of the centrality of the virtues to the Christian life. To demonstrate this, I will now briefly examine two early works of moral theology, by Jean Porter and Oliver O'Donovan, respectively.

In *Moral Action and Christian Ethics,* Porter sets her sights on the "criteria by which actions are described in moral terms." This enterprise begins with the rejection of the "Kantian ideal of moral reasoning," by which she means the view that "moral rules are to be understood as functioning . . . in the same way as mathematical functions."[26] Here she finds a friend in Ramsey, as they share the conviction that moral problems are not "resolved for good" nor "in a way that everyone can see to be rationally compelling."[27]

the case of torture, this means that the argument is not whether torture is ever permissible, but when — i.e., under what obviously stringent circumstances: how big, how imminent, how preventable the ticking time bomb" (Krauthammer, "The Truth about Torture").

26. Porter, *Moral Action,* pp. 3, 8.

27. Porter, *Moral Action,* p. 9. Hereafter, page references to this work appear in parentheses within the text.

Furthermore, she echoes Ramsey's belief that such indeterminacy does not undermine moral rules, but rather forces us to give a richer account of what it means to act in relationship to them.[28]

Porter's grasp of this basic indeterminacy leads her to several important conclusions about the place of rules within moral reasoning. For starters, it commits her to the belief that moral concepts are generic. Here Ramsey's "The Case of the Curious Exception" enters the discussion as an example of an argument supporting "the fact that generic moral concepts can only be applied through the exercise of a kind of judgment that cannot be expressed exhaustively in formulae" (p. 39).[29] With Ramsey, Porter agrees that there is "an ineliminable element of judgment in the application of moral rules" (p. 42). This commits her to the rejection of any talk of "hedging exceptions," because, as Ramsey has shown, this "is better understood as a process of deepening our understanding of the rationale of a rule, and applying it accordingly." Lastly, and most importantly, the indeterminacy of empirical concepts means that rules can only go so far in bearing the weight of moral concepts. That is to say, "it will be necessary to locate the distinctive stringency of moral rules in something other than their character *as rules.*" Rules may play a significant role in our understanding of moral concepts, but it is also necessary to look at the *"substantive content"* of such concepts. This drives us deeper into the question of "what we mean by 'moral' " (p. 43).

This turn toward the moral drives Porter to make several observations, two of which are worth highlighting for their relevance to the current discussion. First, she suggests that pursuit of a concept of morality requires us "to go beyond the considerations that inform our basic moral notions." Here "the long tradition of Christian ethics can offer a distinctive contribution to moral philosophy. The history of Christian ethics is precisely a history of reflections on a moral order which . . . must be placed in a wider theological context if it is to be rightly understood and valued" (p. 88). As with Ramsey, Porter faces the challenges of moral philosophy and the description of moral acts with a turn toward deeper theological

28. "It does not follow that there are no such things as moral rules, or that they have no force; but we must revise our understanding of what it means to understand and to follow a moral rule" (p. 34).

29. Rejecting Anscombe's suggestion that (exceptionless) moral rules are uniquely religious, Porter instead asserts that moral rules are simply uniquely *generic:* "Morality itself, in turn, is understood this way not because it is originally a religious conception, but because it is a *generic* conception" (p. 37).

commitments. Where Ramsey chooses covenant as his framing concept for this theological turn, Porter orients her account around theological developments in Thomas Aquinas's *Summa Theologica*. I will return to this decision shortly.

Second, and more important, Porter argues for the compatibility of rules and virtues in the discernment of right moral judgment. Rejecting any forced dichotomy between quandary ethics and virtues as "wrongheaded," she suggests that "the distinction between following a rule and acting out of a virtue presupposes a mistaken idea of both the traditional moral rules and the virtues" (p. 126). At the center of this misunderstanding is the assumption that "the indeterminacy of concepts of the virtues constitutes a critical difference between a form of moral judgment that is grounded in the language of virtues, and moral reasoning that is governed by moral rules" (p. 133). This is, of course, precisely the opposite of her insistence that both virtues and rules are indeterminate with respect to "concrete applications." She says: "There is no fundamental difference between following a moral rule and acting out of a virtue. In each case, the intellect is guided by a set of paradigmatic examples of kinds of actions, which must be applied to a specific choice through an act of judgment" (p. 156). "It will not do, therefore, to turn from the language of moral rules to the language of the virtues, as if these were two alternative approaches to moral judgment, one of them problematic and the other unproblematic" (p. 137). Against a separation of rules and virtues, Porter suggests that in an indeterminate moral universe both can help sustain and inform moral judgment.

We need not follow Porter's account all the way through to its end in order to see how she narrates a turn toward the virtues in Christian ethics through attentiveness to the complexity of the moral act. It is enough for now to take note of her insistence that virtues function, as do traditional moral rules, by providing "criteria by which to evaluate our actions, either prospectively or in retrospect. In order to make use of these criteria, we must use judgment to apply general notions of kinds of actions" (p. 133).

What should be clear at this point is how Porter arrives at these conclusions, in part at least, by reasoning through the arguments in "The Case of the Curious Exception." Ramsey clears conceptual ground for Porter's work by illuminating the generic character of rules and the role of practical reasoning in the structure of the moral act. Porter acknowledges these debts, though surely few will fault her for relying much more heavily on Thomas than on Ramsey as her work develops. In fact, a theological framework as robust and complex as a Thomistic one would have helped Ramsey considerably in his effort to replace contextualism with a richer account of moral reasoning.[30] It certainly would have taken him deeper into virtue theory at a time when few considered that to be a viable option. Nonetheless, my point here is to show that Porter appropriates arguments from "The Case of the Curious Exception" in her call for a return to the virtues in contemporary Christian ethics. She uses Ramsey to argue for the importance of wider theological considerations to analysis of the moral act, as well as for the ineliminable role of moral judgment. She also introduces the virtues as distinctly helpful resources for such judgment, though neither at the expense of moral rules nor at the displacement of practical reasoning.[31]

Oliver O'Donovan presents a similar pattern of response to "The Case of the Curious Exception" in *Resurrection and Moral Order.* While he, like Porter, replaces Ramsey's covenant theology, he adopts the fundamental assertion that Christian behavior in the world should be imitative of God's behavior in the world. In the preface he writes: "My teacher, Paul Ramsey, once wrote: 'Christian theological ethics is metaethics, and the Christian community in all ages is a standing metaethical community of discourse.' It required only a little reflection to turn this proposition around, and to conclude that the exploration of Christian moral concepts must always, in the first place, be the work of theology."[32] Where his theological framework differs from Ramsey is in his insistence that "when we think quite specifically about Christian *action,* we have to single out the resurrection

30. In other words, while Ramsey succeeds in leveling a devastating critique of contextual moral thinking, his reliance on a covenant theological framework does not seem to be able to do the heavy lifting necessary for a fuller account of virtue theory. That critique may be anachronistic given the debates that commanded Ramsey's attention, though Thomas was there, of course, all along.

31. Porter also squarely retains the force of Ramsey's argument that creativity and flexibility in practical reasoning must stem from a deepening commitment to foundational theological considerations rather than a pursuit of "hedging exceptions." In fact, Porter takes a thoroughly Ramseyan approach to the public debates on the prohibition of torture mentioned earlier. See Jean Porter, "Torture and the Christian Conscience: A Response to Jeremy Waldron," *Scottish Journal of Theology* 61, no. 3 (2008): 340-58.

32. O'Donovan, *Resurrection and Moral Order,* pp. vii-viii. (Hereafter, page references to this work appear in parentheses within the text.) Although the first edition of *Resurrection and Moral Order* was published nearly a decade before Porter's *Moral Action and Christian Ethics,* I examine it second because it includes the more substantial appropriation of Ramsey's argument.

moment which vindicates the creation into which our actions can be ventured with intelligibility" (p. xviii).[33]

We can read within O'Donovan's emphasis on "liberated action" an endorsement of Ramsey's account of practical reasoning and the production of "particular deeds" in "The Case of the Curious Exception." In fact, chapters 2 and 9 of *Resurrection and Moral Order* — titled "Created Order" and "The Moral Field," respectively — directly capture the force of Ramsey's arguments on these subjects. In the former we find O'Donovan arguing for concepts of created order as "end" and "kind" of "teleological" and "generic" order. Protecting, as Ramsey does, the current obscurity of the final relationship between human creative actions and the activity of their Creator, he nonetheless insists that "the Christian faith, calling us to respond appropriately to the deeds of God on our behalf, supposes that there is an appropriate conformity of human response to divine act" (p. 36). This is the teleological element of action within a vindicated created order. Furthermore, O'Donovan defends the "generic" concept of morality as fundamental to that created order. Accordingly, he says that "judgments will be made about kinds of things and situations, and about particulars only as instances of a kind" (p. 39). He rejects "making allowances" (read: exceptions) as "nothing other than specifying more exactly what circumstances might differentiate our situations from [others], an undertaking which is meaningless unless . . . set together within the same moral field" (p. 43). For O'Donovan, the vindication of creation through the resurrection renders Christian action intelligible, and his subsequent description of agency materially incorporates Ramsey's conclusions about the teleological and generic character of created order.

O'Donovan revisits these same features of Christian moral action in the chapter entitled "The Moral Field." Here he highlights the generic character of morality and the importance of casuistry, "the application of the moral law to action in particular cases" (p. 191). He emphasizes the role of wisdom in the moral life, saying that it "liberates us from the persistent fear of that unutterable and unknowable uniqueness by enabling us to interpret each particular thing, in all its newness to us, generically, and so measure

33. O'Donovan makes the same connection in the prologue to the second edition: "Purposeful action is determined by what is true about the world into which we act; this can be called the 'realist' principle. That truth is constituted by what God has done for his world and for humankind in Jesus Christ; that is the 'evangelical' principle. The act of God which liberates our action is focused on the resurrection of the dead . . . this we can call the 'Easter' principle" (p. ix).

its difference from other things and respond to it appropriately according to its kind" (p. 189). Thus, casuistry is "not just a matter of solving problems, but of growing in wisdom" (p. 190). Here the argument echoes Ramsey's distaste for the pursuit of "exceptions" to the moral law. O'Donovan describes the case where, upon recognition that "the categories of our moral understanding are no longer sufficient to interpret our situation," we "rebel wildly and disorderedly against them" (p. 195). He continues: "The form which this rebellion takes in moral theory is the positing of random and meaningless 'exceptions' to moral rules. The exception is the case which our understanding cannot encompass, the absurd contradiction of the rule for which we cannot account" (p. 195).[34]

Chapter 10 moves from a description of the "ordered moral field" to one of the "ordered moral subject."[35] Here he introduces an account of the virtues to complement the role of moral law examined in chapter 9. Referring to Mark 7 and Matthew 5, O'Donovan observes: "Jesus did not propose to *substitute* agent-evaluation for act-evaluation and leave it at that" (p. 205). Rather, the role of the virtues is to help place moral deliberation "in its soteriological context." That is to say, virtues focus our attention on the moral life "as a matter not merely of 'doing the right thing' but of 'saving one's soul'" (p. 224). There is much to be said, in another setting, about the differences between O'Donovan's repudiation of Neo-Aristotelian epistemological prioritization of character over act, as well as his insistence that character does not play a role in "a deliberative train of thought" (p. 222). The only thing we need notice for the moment is the way judgments of character cannot substitute for what Ramsey calls "the actual production of a particular deed" — that would be to go back on the coherence of vindicated created order. Rather, "[w]e can form judgments (partial, no doubt, but not valueless) on what kind of character our history has disclosed, and these, rather than judgments on particular acts, are what will make us feel most acutely the need of salvation" (p. 224).

Here O'Donovan introduces virtues, as Porter does, into an account of the Christian moral life without displacing the central role of practical reasoning. O'Donovan leans heavily on "The Case of the Curious Exception"

34. At the conclusion of these arguments we are at last granted citations of "The Case of the Curious Exception" and told that they "may be read as a modest footnote to Ramsey's article" (p. 197).

35. At the beginning of chapter 9, O'Donovan instructs us, with reference to Luke 3 and Acts 2, that "[t]he form of the moral life will be that of an *ordered moral field* of action on the one hand, and of an *ordered moral subject* of action on the other" (p. 183).

while making these arguments. As with Porter, Ramsey is not the only influence, and O'Donovan's work testifies greatly to his early intellectual engagements with Augustine. But the argument of this chapter remains: Ramsey's moral theory, while weighed down by his dense technical refutations of situation ethics, nonetheless clears important conceptual ground concerning the relationship of rules to judgments, and the central role of practical reasoning in Christian ethics.

Conclusion

O'Donovan observes that "The Case of the Curious Exception" "spoke the last word on the formal questions which had been agitated in the debate about situationism" (p. 196). What I have tried to suggest here is that while the essay may be the last word on situation ethics, it also appears to be a point of beginning for turns toward the virtues in contemporary Christian moral theology. I have insisted throughout that Ramsey is not the only point of beginning, and that is amply evident in his absence from prominent work in the virtues by Alasdair MacIntyre and Stanley Hauerwas. But I submit that it is noteworthy that Porter and O'Donovan, two central thinkers in contemporary Christian moral theology, use Ramsey's work on moral rules and practical reasoning to articulate a shift toward virtue theory. It is a testament to Ramsey's insight that both Porter and O'Donovan present positions largely in agreement with Ramsey's arguments and with the presumption that increased attention to virtues must complement, never eradicate, the role of practical reasoning in Christian ethics. That the performance of judgment plays such a central role in their accounts of the virtues is no accident. By working through "The Case of the Curious Exception" on their way to a renewed theory of the virtues, both Porter and O'Donovan refuse to elide the place of practical reasoning and the function of judgment in the moral life. Both also refuse to establish a firm dichotomy between virtue and obligation.[36]

We need not be surprised that Ramsey's practical reasoning in some ways contributed to a turn toward the virtues in contemporary Christian

36. These commonalities stand in stark contrast to the strand of contemporary virtue theory represented by Alasdair MacIntyre and Stanley Hauerwas. For instance, Hauerwas and Charles Pinches suggest that a contemporary turn to the virtues must reject the "attempt to combine virtue and obligation" (Hauerwas and Pinches, *Christians Among the Virtues* [Notre Dame, IN: University of Notre Dame Press, 1997], p. 58).

ethics. He admits at the beginning of *Deeds and Rules* that, despite his misgivings about the tendency to separate "being from doing" within theological and philosophical ethics, he will adopt the "manner of speaking" to inquire how we are to "do" Christian ethics.[37] While he rarely explicitly uses the language of virtue after *Basic Christian Ethics,* Ramsey understood the importance of character and welcomed the turn toward virtues in the field late in his career.[38] Perhaps we might say that Ramsey too easily allowed the pressing questions of his day to set the agenda for his work, though one suspects he would point us to the subversive function of covenant theology in the debates examined above. This suggests, at the least, that there is abiding value in both his emphasis on practical reasoning and his insistence that theological considerations supply creativity and flexibility in moral theology precisely where exception-seeking fails.

The resilience of these arguments may also shine light on what appears to be a mainstay in public debates: reliance on exceptions and consequence-calculations for flexibility in moral deliberation. It requires little work to sympathize with Ramsey's suggestion that keeping *all* human actions open to moral justification is "one of the chief presuppositions of the present age."[39] His wrestling with the place of rules and exceptions in Christian ethics continues to present moral theology with a lively challenge: amid our knottiest moral problems we are called to mimic the creativity and sensitivity exhibited in God's covenant faithfulness with creation — and therein humanity. Just as the marks of God's steadfast love are not demonstrated through exceptions or escape clauses, but deeper and deeper commitments to the covenant bond that began with Abraham and Sarah, we, too, are called to probe the depths of our responsibilities and obligations to creation and those created in the image of God.

37. Ramsey, *Deeds and Rules,* p. 1.

38. See Paul Ramsey, "A Question (or Two) for Stanley Hauerwas," Box 41, Ramsey Papers. Ramsey presented this paper in November 1982 at a symposium convened by the Center for Theological Inquiry, Princeton, New Jersey.

39. Ramsey, "The Case of the Curious Exception," p. 135.

PART III

Ramsey and Contemporary Christian Ethics

CHAPTER SEVEN

Contingency and Virtue: Engaging John Bowlin and Jennifer A. Herdt

In the preceding chapters I examined fundamental aspects of Ramsey's political theology. Against many of the cultural and intellectual trends of his era, Ramsey insisted that theological language can illuminate the structure of political agency and public goods. He steadfastly believed that Christians can (and should) explore the unique contours of political authority, even as they uphold the stringency of moral norms and limitations. Key among these developments is his recognition that time and chance shape all political endeavors. No legislation, movement, or leader can escape the contingencies of political life, and an appreciation of this reality can help ward off a simplistic Christian account of political ethics. More importantly, an appreciation of contingency inspires a serious exploration of the virtues necessary for those who would pursue faithful obedience in the political realm. Yet even as some of Ramsey's most profound insights point us in this direction, he lacks a formal account of contingency and its impact on political agency. Perhaps even more importantly, he fails to explain the relationship between contingency and virtue.

There can be no doubt that formulating an appropriate response to a contingent world is central to Ramsey's political project. It is also central among the concerns of contemporary Christian ethics. Princeton theologian John Bowlin labors, more than any other author among this generation of Christian thinkers, to illuminate the role that contingency plays in the Christian moral life. His *Contingency and Fortune in Aquinas' Ethics* charts territory previously unexplored, and we would do well to heed his insistence that virtue and contingency are deeply related concepts.[1] Jennifer A. Herdt broadens and expands several of Bowlin's core insights; her *Putting on Virtue* is one of the most important books of the last twenty years in Christian ethics.[2] Herdt shows how any coherent account of moral agency must include a place for habituation in the virtues, and she insists on the need for authenticity in virtue equal to its mimetic character.

I suggested in the preceding chapter that Ramsey's critique of situation ethics clears the way, in part, for a turn toward virtue in Christian ethics. I suspect that he would be deeply sympathetic with the suggestion that the cultivation of virtue is the appropriate moral response to the contingent status of our lives. If we are to reconsider the significance of his thought for contemporary discussions in the field, however, we must test his work against the recent contributions of thinkers such as Bowlin and Herdt to see what it offers and what it lacks. Where Ramsey lacks a formal account of contingency, Bowlin's work is of considerable help. Herdt's insights into virtue and agency offer distinct resources for his account of political judgment. Yet Ramsey's work remains lively. Even in his informal efforts at theorizing contingency, he offers resources that can help push the contemporary conversation on contingency and virtue forward.

The aim of this chapter is to explore Ramsey's lasting contributions to contemporary Christian ethics by placing his work alongside that of Herdt and Bowlin. He has much to learn from these two thinkers. I will also aim to retrieve distinctive resources delineated in earlier chapters to show how Ramsey can sharpen the contemporary conversation on these topics. I begin with John Bowlin and the matter of contingency.

Theorizing Contingency

Where Ramsey's efforts at describing contingency are a hodgepodge, Bowlin's are densely systematic. For Bowlin, contingent events are those whose causes are "periodically subject to accidental disruption."[3] There are two kinds of accidental disruptions. The first includes disruptions of an

1. John Bowlin, *Contingency and Fortune in Aquinas' Ethics* (Cambridge, UK: Cambridge University Press, 1999).

2. Jennifer A. Herdt, *Putting on Virtue: The Legacy of the Splendid Vices* (Chicago: University of Chicago Press, 2008).

3. Bowlin, *Contingency and Fortune,* p. 7. Hereafter, page references to this work appear in parentheses within the text.

external kind: difficulties that prevent us from achieving intended goods. (Think of the plea "I would have been on time for work if it had not been for the terrible traffic!") The second kind includes internal disruptions driven by the fickle and corruptible nature of our judgments. (Think of the reply, "Did you really expect an open road to the office on a Monday morning?") If the stain of sin fundamentally disorders our passions and desires, then contingency will never be purely external. It is, in other words, the internal and external character of events that distinguishes this world from one in which all events are necessary, where events occur "always and unavoidably when their sufficient conditions [are] in place" (p. 7).

Bowlin suggests, through Aquinas, that it is the unique role of the moral virtues to "cope" with both the internal and external contingencies of this world (p. 13). This is for two reasons. First, if external circumstances are perennially contingent, then achieving particular goods will require constancy in the face of difficulty. As he notes, the "functional dynamic" of virtue and difficulty is "largely a matter of constancy and chance, of contingent fear threatening our constant willing of the good and of courage keeping this contingency at bay" (p. 33). Thus virtue provides the stability necessary to remain persistent in the face of the unpredictability of external contingencies. Simultaneously, virtue works through the formation of character to address internal contingencies that inhibit good judgment. If the human will is indeterminate, then faithfulness will depend in no small part on the acquisition of "particular habits of affection that simply and absolutely dispose it to some particular goods and not others" (p. 58). Putting on virtue involves the development of habits that will dispose us toward judgments in accordance with right reason. In short, the cultivation of virtue is the most appropriate response to the contingencies of the self and the world around us.

Examining the virtue of courage will help illuminate the contours of Bowlin's proposal. Aquinas regards endurance as the "chief aspect" of courage, since endurance is more naturally associated with standing firm in the face of danger than it is with initiating danger by attacking an enemy. Perhaps even more importantly, endurance is central to courage because it "entails standing unmoved over a considerable span of time, while aggression is normally a sudden and decisive affair" (p. 27). True courage thus requires strength and resolve in response to dangerous external contingencies, such as an unexpected enemy attack. It also simultaneously involves the cultivation of enduring habits that can overcome internal difficulties such as an irrational response to fear or a disordered appetite for destruction. Bowlin notes: "Difficulties are legion, in some manner obstructing the virtuous pursuit and achievement of every good, and therefore it is easy to see how virtuous actions of all kinds normally include something like endurance" (p. 27). Like courage, every virtue requires cultivation and performance of habits over time.

Virtue is not simply about constancy, however, and it is here that prudence enters the frame. If contingent events are defined by their susceptibility to accidental disruptions, then they fall outside of what Aquinas calls "those things which are altogether determinate." It follows that there is a relationship between human agency and contingency, since, as Bowlin says, "choice is possible only when the end in question is not gained by certain and determinate means."[4] In other words, we act, by definition, in a world where we cannot guarantee with absolute certainty that we will achieve the intended outcome of our actions. We do not live in a world of such necessity. As I mentioned earlier, this external difficulty achieving the desired good is compounded by the internal one: our passions and desires are corruptible, and the objects of our will are multifarious — good in some circumstances and evil in others.

If these difficulties sound complicated, then welcome to the challenge of moral deliberation. Overlapping contingencies create a whole range of circumstances whose moral status can be difficult to parse. Take, for instance, an act normally considered good: the giving of alms. Aquinas notes that even if external contingencies do not intervene, disordered passions can corrupt almsgiving and render it an evil rooted in vainglory.[5] This places distinct limits on the usefulness of general moral classifications. To classify a type of action as good does not guarantee that it is good in every instance. In the example of almsgiving in pursuit of glory, the internal contingency of disordered passion is to blame. Bowlin points to a different example: "Returning a weapon kept safe for a friend, an action whose generic goodness is equivalent to promise-keeping, can be vitiated if, in the meantime, the friend becomes insane with rage or overcome with evil intentions" (p. 63). Here the agent's intentions are in good order, but the goodness of the act is nullified; external contingencies are to blame.

Readers will recognize in this concern over particular moral actions

4. Aquinas, *Summa Theologica* I-II.13.2, quoted in Bowlin, *Contingency and Fortune,* p. 57.

5. *ST* I-II.19.7.2; 20.1, quoted in Bowlin, *Contingency and Fortune,* p. 63.

deep similarities to Ramsey's work in "The Case of the Curious Exception." There he directs his attention to the generic character of moral rules and the incoherence of so-called exceptions to such rules. As we saw in the previous chapter, Ramsey insists that the work of the ethicist is both circumscribed and enlivened by the distance between generic rules and particular actions. Bowlin uses the language of internal and external contingency to capture these same ambiguities in the moral field. He also knows, as Ramsey does, that most specific actions do not fit neatly into generic categories. Most acts, unlike promise-keeping or almsgiving, are not possessive of an inherent moral species. In these cases — public speaking, ingesting prescription medication, wielding a knife, just to name a few — the contingency of the good becomes all the more obvious. To whom are you speaking? About what, and with what intention? Did a doctor prescribe the medication for you, and do you ingest it in the prescribed doses? Does the knife involve threat of violence, or is it for some other purpose? The moral praiseworthiness or blameworthiness of these behaviors is contingent. Bowlin recognizes that this is the case in nearly every instance of human behavior. Thus "the principal mark of the virtuous is their ability to consider an object good in one setting while silencing its goodness in another" (p. 64).[6] Choice becomes "largely a matter of determining whether some contingently good means is in fact good in a particular instance for the purpose of achieving some intended end" (p. 61).[7] Ramsey obscurely calls this "the subsumption of cases."[8]

Recognizing these layers of contingency and the challenge they present to the moral life reminds us of an important, if obvious, truth: achieving our proper good is difficult. Moral judgments are adrift without an anchor in the virtues, among them prudence. As Bowlin observes, "There is no substitute for prudential judgment, no procedure for discovering the good apart from its labors, no standard of concrete goodness in human action that we know apart from the judgments of right reason" (*Contingency*

6. Bowlin credits this insight to John McDowell.

7. It is precisely for this reason that Ramsey suggests: "Perhaps the term absolute should be banished forever from the discussion of moral questions" (Paul Ramsey, "Incommensurability and Indeterminacy in Moral Choice," in Richard A. McCormick and Paul Ramsey, eds., *Doing Evil to Achieve Good: Moral Choice in Conflict Situations* [Chicago: Loyola University Press, 1978], p. 83).

8. Paul Ramsey, "The Case of the Curious Exception," in Gene H. Outka and Paul Ramsey, eds., *Norm and Context in Christian Ethics* (New York: Charles Scribner's Sons, 1968), p. 125.

and Fortune, p. 79). No amount of philosophical or theological reflection on moral rules, duties, consequences, or calculations can eradicate this fundamental work of prudence.

Ramsey spilled far too much ink trying to articulate this point. His use of recondite language didn't help. (E.g., "There can be no *subsumption-ruling* rules.")[9] We might blame his entanglements with situation ethics, or his stubborn refusal to admit that these later developments conflicted with material in *Basic Christian Ethics.* We might blame his insistence on technical precision. But there is no fundamental disagreement between Ramsey and Bowlin on these points: Moral judgment is difficult, and contingency is the source of that difficulty. Judging rightly requires putting on virtue through habits of constancy and the cultivation of character. There is no avoiding the work of practical reasoning, and there is no greater aid to that work than the virtue of prudence.

Bowlin undoubtedly provides a more accessible account of the contingency inherent to the moral field than Ramsey does. But what of moral rules? To this point they have been of little significance for Bowlin's proposal, and we know that Ramsey fights hard for their inclusion in the Christian moral field. Does this insistence on the inescapable work of prudence undermine — or at least contradict — Ramsey's commitment to rules as the outworking of moral bonds? Must we choose between rules and virtues?

Contingency, Virtue, and Rules

It is important to remember that one feature of contingency is the instability of certain objects of the will. Think of the examples mentioned earlier, almsgiving corrupted by desire for vainglory and promise-keeping (in the form of returning an item to a friend) corrupted by the outcomes of that friend's rage. In both cases the pursuit of the good was corrupted. Indeed, the overriding challenge of contingency is that our pursuit of good ends is so unstable. Objects, both means and ends, are never simply good in and of themselves, regardless of circumstances. Except, Bowlin suggests, God. God is the single object of the will that is absolutely good. Here Bowlin is worth quoting at length:

9. Ramsey, "The Case of the Curious Exception," p. 103. A little clearer is his suggestion that there is "a sort of ambiguity that cannot be eliminated from moral choice" (Ramsey, "Incommensurability and Indeterminacy in Moral Choice," p. 69).

> Of the potential objects of the will, vast in number and kind, only God is "good universally and from every point of view," only God's goodness is perfect and necessary, and consequently the will, whose natural object is the universal good, "tends to it of necessity, if it wills anything at all." By contrast, all other potential objects of the will are good contingently, for the most part, from some points of view but not all, even those goods willed simply and absolutely. (*Contingency and Fortune,* p. 60).

God is the only object of the will that is beyond contingency; all other objects are only ever contingently good. It follows that "the goodness of every potential object besides God is potentially open for rational consideration in every circumstance of choice" (p. 82).[10]

This reality produces an exhausting amount of complexity in the moral field. As I mentioned earlier, the pursuit of constancy and habit through virtuous character is the most appropriate response to such complexity. But this is enough to bring even the exercise of virtue through prudent deliberation to a screeching halt at each moral decision. There are simply too many goods to be weighed, as means and ends, at every turn. Thus, Bowlin concedes: "Some ends must be held in place, their goodness assumed and intended, at least for now, before prudent deliberation over the means can proceed. And this must occur not only in individual instances of choice, but also over the course of many such instances" (p. 83).[11] This does not mean, as he is quick to remind us, that such assumed goods become (functionally) absolute goods. Just because we are right to judge that almsgiving is an act whose moral species is generally good does not mean we are foolish enough to think it free from the corruptions of vainglory. But the designation of some ends as generally of a certain moral species — good or evil — assists in the work of prudence.

10. Ramsey remarks similarly that the "indeterminacy among the ends of action" cannot be "removed." Later he adds: "Only God has absoluteness and aseity; and even in his case we scarcely know the meaning of those attributes" (Ramsey, "Incommensurability and Indeterminacy in Moral Choice," pp. 69, 83).

11. Bowlin reasons as follows: "If prudence is the virtue that describes a means, its circumstances, and the intended end all in order to find and preserve its goodness, and if the goodness of every end besides God is contingent, changing with its circumstances and with its status as a potential means to some other end, then prudence could, in principle, work on every end that comes before it. . . . Obviously, this would make action impossible, for no ends could be assumed and intended and thus there would be no stable principles to guide our deliberation over particular means" (p. 82).

The primary way that Bowlin refers to this designation of assumed ends is justice. True prudence requires justice, which "is needed as a kind of repository of moral wisdom that disposes us to will the good of our neighbor even when our passions direct us elsewhere" (p. 90). But unlike what Ramsey discards as "summary rules" in the debate about situation ethics, justice in this case is not merely a catalog of past decisions and outcomes. As a repository of wisdom it also has a regulating function that stringently marks off ends that can be pursued. Prudence requires that "some ends must be judged good, steadfastly willed, and consistently tended to over time if there is to be any action at all" (p. 83). Justice is precisely the virtue constituted by habits of steadfastly judging and willing the good. Its cultivation supplies some "stable principles to guide our deliberations over particular means" (p. 82). It also transforms the agent's character, inclining the will to true goods rather than simply apparent goods.

Again, this is not to suggest that the repository of wisdom is sealed shut or beyond reflection. "This does not mean that the goodness of these ends [that have been judged good] can never be reconsidered in light of other ends and circumstances." It does mean that if prudence is to do its proper work — if prudence is to get on with the business of taking counsel, making decisions, and *acting* in the world — it is "practically feasible only when the nearly infinite list of potential ends is reduced to a standard repertoire" (p. 83). Therefore, "prudence is not merely the ability to adjust contingencies to other contingencies in the circumstances of choice, it is also the ability to do this difficult work in pursuit of ends that are just, and thus often difficult" (p. 86).

Contingency and Covenant

It is not difficult to see the compatibility between Ramsey's account of moral rules and this view of justice as a repository of wisdom that remains open to reconsideration and reflection. In *Deed and Rules in Christian Ethics,* Ramsey repudiates the notion of summary rules, suggesting that they do not carry sufficient weight to govern moral behavior. Further, he advocates for Christian ethics to attend "in very great measure" to questions of "which rules of action are most love-embodying."[12] (He would not have

12. Paul Ramsey, *Deeds and Rules in Christian Ethics* (New York: Charles Scribner's Sons, 1965; Lanham, MD: University Press of America, 1967), p. 5. Indeed, this was also

thought there was tension between love and justice here.) Both Bowlin and Ramsey see the need for certain practical aids to the work of practical reasoning, and both believe that those aids must always be subject to further revision. But Ramsey's account of justice leans, from the start, more heavily on the language of covenant than the language of virtue to articulate the constancy and habits of a community patterned after God's faithfulness to creation. To that extent, he offers nowhere near the complex virtue theory that Bowlin offers through Aquinas. But we need not see his covenant theology in a negative light. In fact, it opens Bowlin's account to a richer and more thoroughly theological description of justice.

Recall that, as early as *Basic Christian Ethics,* Ramsey suggests that political judgments should be "guided by the righteousness of the God we know through the covenant."[13] He locates God's steadfast covenant love as the ground of all political identity and insists that it precedes and sustains all possibility of faithful obedience. In *Christian Ethics and the Sit-In,* he takes from Barth the insight that there is no teleology for the creature outside of covenant with the Creator. For Ramsey, justice begins and ends with God's enactment of the covenant in Christ, and our pursuit of justice for the neighbor must always imitate God's prior creative action on our behalf. Thus, where Bowlin suggests that justice is "a kind of repository of moral wisdom that disposes us to will the good of our neighbor," Ramsey sees clearly that there is no greater repository of wisdom than shared memory of God's embodied faithfulness to covenant (Bowlin, p. 90).

As I suggested in the preceding chapter, in "The Case of the Curious Exception," Ramsey pushes his commitment to moral rules further than he had previously, suggesting that Christian ethics "must be enormously disinterested in any exception, or openness to exceptions" that would be justified on consequentialist grounds.[14] The rationale for this move resides in his belief that love-embodying rules must be patterned after God's dealings with the world and sealed with God's eschatological promises. If prudence, as Bowlin says, is "practically feasible only when the nearly infinite list of potential ends is reduced to a standard repertoire," then Ramsey insists that Christians take their standard repertoire from God (Bowlin, p. 83). This complements Bowlin's claim that

against the grain of some of his earlier arguments in Ramsey, *Basic Christian Ethics* (New York: Charles Scribner's Sons, 1950).

13. Ramsey, *Basic Christian Ethics,* p. 388.

14. Ramsey, "Case of the Curious Exception," p. 125.

all contingent goods must be ordered to the only good end, which is God. I see no conflict between this account of justice and prudence and Ramsey's insistence that covenant is "the connecting link between divine righteousness and human justice."[15]

Undoubtedly, Bowlin captures poetically some of what Ramsey belabored obtusely. He offers a much richer account of contingency, and the vital link between contingency and virtue is clearer in his work. But Ramsey's account has its merits, and among them is a deep sense of the significance of covenant for moral reasoning. It is worth lingering on this connection a little longer before we turn to Jennifer Herdt's work. For while it is certainly true that Bowlin provides an account of contingency and virtue that is sorely missing in Ramsey, one concern remains. It involves Bowlin's suggestion that contingency is difficulty, which I fear obscures several broader theological realities about God's continual care for creation. Here some of the lessons Ramsey learned from Karl Barth's covenant theology will be of help in providing a corrective vision.

As I mentioned in chapter 1, Ramsey picks up Barth's suggestion that creation is the external basis of covenant, and covenant is the internal basis of creation. In its role as the internal basis, covenant works to define the character and shape of creation, including the limitations and possibilities of God's creatures. Thus, in *Church Dogmatics* III/1, Barth writes: "The covenant whose history had still to commence was the covenant which, as the goal appointed for creation and the creature, made creation necessary and possible, and determined and limited the creature."[16] Another way of saying this would be that creation may be contingent, but it is not ultimately indeterminate. Creation is not a necessary part of God's Trinitarian life, and yet, miraculously, God creates. Creation is *determined* by the covenant love of the Creator; yet, inasmuch as it remains something other than God, it is also *limited* by that same creaturely status.

Ramsey embraces this account of creation and covenant, albeit somewhat obscurely. He affirms the creative work of God, as well as the creaturely limitations that result. His account of humanity is such that "God who created me . . . at the same time gave me a nature in the form of fellow

15. Ramsey, *Basic Christian Ethics*, p. 5. Ramsey says: "The righteousness *(tsedeq)* of God provides the measure of true justice for all human justice *(mishpat)*." I will return to his use of these Hebrew terms in his definition of justice in chapter 9 below.

16. Karl Barth, *The Doctrine of Creation*, III/1 of *Church Dogmatics*, ed. G. W. Bromiley and T. F. Torrance; trans. J. W. Edwards, O. Bussey, and Harold Knight (Edinburgh: T&T Clark, 1958), p. 231.

humanity in the historical time and space of my existence in covenant."[17] These constraints of historical time and space present, for Ramsey, no small degree of difficulty in the pursuit of the good and the faithful upholding of the covenant. He repeatedly reminded readers of *Basic Christian Ethics* that Christians continue to play out the unfaithfulness to the covenant first told in the stories of the Israelites. But our difficulty, our unfaithfulness, is always a shadow thrown in the light of God's steadfast love. He points aptly to Isaiah chapter 24: "Israel's unusual share in the relationship is described as 'breaking the everlasting covenant,' breaking the unbreakable!"[18] Our creaturely status is, no doubt, limited. But as long as we remain *creatures,* that status reflects the enduring commitment of a sustaining Creator.

According to these insights, I find it challenging that Bowlin only ever refers to contingency as *difficulty.* It is difficulty, no doubt, but it is not only that. Contingency also points to our status as creatures. And that status is a gift of a good Creator. Scottish theologian T. F. Torrance writes: "Far from isolating the world from God, the contingent relation between them means that the world even in its creaturely otherness from God is held continuously in such an ontological relation to Him."[19] Bowlin acknowledges this "contingent relation," but only in an early footnote. There he says that his topic "is *not* the centerpiece of Thomistic metaphysics: the contingent being of all things created" (Bowlin, p. 6, n. 12). But this distinction too easily separates the contingent status of creation from the contingent circumstances and limitations that mar our decision-making. Again, Torrance is of considerable help: "The independence of the world depends entirely upon the free creative act of God to give it being and form wholly differentiated from Himself, but that is then an independence that is delimited by the dependence that anchors the world beyond itself in the freedom of the Creator."[20] Charles Mathewes puts it this way: "A true prudence — a proper use — involves treating things gratuitously, as more fundamentally contingent gifts rather than necessities, and hence imitating (and hence participating in) God's *ex nihilo* creation."[21]

17. Paul Ramsey, *Christian Ethics and the Sit-In* (New York: Association Press, 1961), pp. 37-38.

18. Ramsey, *Basic Christian Ethics,* p. 371.

19. T. F. Torrance, "God and the Contingent World," *Zygon* 14, no. 4 (December 1979): 332-33.

20. Torrance, "God and the Contingent World," p. 333.

21. Charles Mathewes, *A Theology of Public Life* (Cambridge, UK: Cambridge University Press, 2007), pp. 102-3.

Contingency is difficulty, and we experience this difficulty at every turn and in every moment. We are subject to the whims of time and chance, all the while doing what we do not want to do and avoiding what we desire. Ramsey's work shares deep agreement with Bowlin's descriptions of these internal and external difficulties. This is an author who once wrote that "*contingency* itself" is "the nature of all events we know or shall ever know."[22] But he also viewed creaturely status as an opportunity. After all, God continues to sustain us, and that sustaining Creator pursues its creatures with a relentless covenant love. This is why Ramsey clings so tightly to a theology of covenant. Covenant allows that the contingency of our lives can be at once difficulty and opportunity. Yes, we "cope" with contingency in putting on virtue, but the cultivation of virtue is also an expression of gratitude — a form of faithful response made possible by our gratuitously contingent lives. Habituation in virtue is both a response to the difficulties of a contingent world and a responsive pursuit of the good while there is time left for such pursuits.

Of course, to speak of putting on virtue in the face of contingency is to move directly into the matters of virtue and human agency. Here both Bowlin and Ramsey require richer accounts of agency, human ambition, and God's grace. Fortunately, we can take as our guide the book that Bowlin dubbed, "far and away, the best recent work in Christian ethics that we have," Jennifer Herdt's *Putting on Virtue.*[23]

True Virtue and Augustinian Anxiety

Herdt locates her study in the crosshairs of moral psychology and eudaimonism, and she traces broad theological and philosophical developments in both fields. Of sharpest interest for this study is her attention to differences between Augustine and Aquinas and how, in concert, they help direct us toward an account of virtue that is at once responsive and mimetic. Crucial to this effort is her fear that an "inflationary" worry about hypocrisy will produce paralysis by self-examination. As we know from his troubled theology of repentance, that was also one of Ramsey's chief concerns.

22. Paul Ramsey, *Speak Up for Just War or Pacifism* (University Park: Pennsylvania State University Press, 1998), p. 26.

23. Bowlin's dust-jacket endorsement of Herdt, *Putting on Virtue.* Hereafter, page references to this work appear in parentheses within the text.

At the root of Augustinian reflection on virtue are a variety of anxieties. These include: anxiety about the deceptiveness of pagan virtue, given that it is falsely ordered to the self rather than God; anxiety about the hypocrisy of Christian virtue, given that efforts to cultivate virtue may simply reinforce vices of self-love; anxiety about the psychology of habituation, given that all virtue must in some sense be "interruptive," that is, first given by God. These anxieties serve to illuminate core tensions at the heart of the Christian life, and in many respects they reflect the very greatness and complexity of Augustine's account, even as later writers aim to provide accounts of Christian virtue less ridden by anxiety. Before moving to Aquinas, and later to Ramsey, I want to explore briefly these Augustinian anxieties in order to show what they expose about the temptations of self-love, as well as the transformative love of God.

Herdt insists that Augustine's account of pagan virtue is exceedingly complex, and that complexity is further obscured by his notorious claim that pagan vices are *splendida vitia,* "glittering virtues" (p. 45). It is significant that the point at issue for Augustine is not the eudaimonism of pagan ethics but the determination of the self as the final good. The "fundamental disorder" of pagan virtue is that "it is pervaded by *superbia,* pride," which "orders all things to self" (p. 49). Thus he "finds pagan ethics guilty of hubris in its aspiration to self-sufficiency" (p. 51).

Here there is an important distinction to be made between contingent and constitutive goods. Pagan virtue serves to demonstrate that the self is worthy of honor, and thus it is driven — deceptively — by pride. Virtue becomes an instrument of acclaim. But Christian virtue is not demonstrative of worthiness. For Christians, "[t]o become virtuous is to be transformed into one enough like God to be capable of this loving relationship with God" (p. 55).[24] Virtue ordered to love of God is constitutive rather than contingent, that is, it "proves after all to be not just instrumental but partially constitutive of my happiness, my final end." In other words, instead of simply demonstrating love, or serving as a means to a loving end, virtue is itself loving.

Augustine's anxiety about the falsity of pagan virtue thus rests in his belief that it is fundamentally centered on the self rather than God. The end of Christian virtue is love of God, and love of God is not possible alongside a drive for self-achievement. "Christian imitation never at-

24. In other words, for Augustine there must be a relationship between "virtue, happiness, and our final end" (p. 54).

tempts to become independent of its exemplar, to achieve self-sufficient virtue" (p. 47). Only Christian virtue takes a fundamentally mimetic character, since only it assumes that God alone is the exemplar worthy of imitation.

Of course, Augustine's description of Christian virtue admits that Christians remain as susceptible to corruption by pride as pagans. Christians are "characterized by imperfect virtue," and "it is also the case that we often encounter the mere semblance of virtue among those within the church" (p. 59). This is a result of original sin, which "can never be extirpated in this life," and consequently it is the burden of Christians and pagans alike (p. 60). Even as Augustine draws a firm boundary "between true and false virtue," Herdt credits him with the recognition that "the imperfect virtue of Christians is often corrupted by the same ordering to self that rendered pagan virtue merely counterfeit virtue" (pp. 60-61).

The anxiety about false pagan virtue here spills over into the Christian life, which, under constant temptation toward pride, becomes characterized by inner strife. Hypocrisy becomes the great danger to Christian virtue precisely because it appeals to our disordered longing for human praise. The hypocrite desires (in vainglory) the appearance of virtue rather than true virtue (which brings glory to God). While vigilance against hypocrisy is necessary for the pursuit of virtue, it remains plagued by the paradox of self-examination. How can looking inward possibly rid one of *superbia?* Questions such as this one generate, as Herdt says, a worry "that ordinary habituation in virtue simply entrenches the vices of pride and self-love" (p. 2).

The first two anxieties drive Augustine to the third: concern about the psychology of habituation. He avoids the twin evils of passivity and ambition by insisting that Christian virtue "is active insofar as it is fundamentally responsive, responsive to the grace that converts us from love of self to love of God" (p. 47). This means that Christian virtue will always be "interruptive," that is, first given by God. Herdt says: "We find happiness in the perfected activity of receiving and returning God's gifts" (p. 57).[25] The form of human activity that most fully participates in this responsive relationship is, for Augustine, humility. Only humility can

25. Herdt goes on to say, "Augustine's perfected human agents will thus appear too passive from the perspective of pagan eudaimonism, while too active from the perspective of Augustine's anti-eudaimonist Christian critics" (p. 57).

"guarantee" that virtue is anything other than a manifestation of pride (p. 58).[26]

The challenge of habituation remains. But where he might be tempted to abstraction, Augustine is concrete: the exemplary humility of Christ is the locus of habituation in virtue. Herdt notes: "It is God's humility in Christ, God's willingness to become a servant rather than retain supremacy, that enables us to accept our own weakness, our utter dependency on God, even for that which we would most like to consider our own — our moral character" (p. 58). Imitation of the humility of Christ is a responsive act that involves "a chastening of human agency" (pp. 67-68). Christian virtue always points back to its true source and good end in God's grace, even as we are actively involved in receiving and returning that gift.

Although Augustine warns against the temptation of self-love, he does not eradicate the role of human agency in Christian cultivation of virtue. Rather, his "defense of Christian virtue as true virtue rests on the fact that we are responsive to grace rather than passive in the face of grace" (p. 48). But if this interruptive grace means that virtue "must first be given by God in some way outside of, and discontinuous with, ordinary moral psychology," then what are we to say about human agency (p. 3)? In other words, is there any constructive element to the cultivation of virtue beyond "honest confession of our own failure to attain virtue" (p. 1)? It is noteworthy that in Augustine's emphasis on humility as the form of Christian virtue, a moral psychology outlining the process of habituation remains elusive. Herdt sees lurking behind Augustine's anxieties a temptation toward paralysis in the moral life, even as she works to uphold his insistence that God is the sole author of Christian virtue. She affirms the claim that true cultivation of virtue must be understood as "a form of secondary causality or co-causation with divine agency" (p. 3).[27]

26. This is a move against not simply the pagans but the anti-eudaimonists more broadly, including Christian anti-eudaimonists. "The anti-eudaimonists recognize their dependence on God, but wrongly think that gift precludes activity, when in fact it requires it, calling it forth and enabling it. . . . It is finally only humility that can for Augustine guarantee that virtue is not simply a cunning mask worn by superbia" (p. 58).

27. Indeed, in the *Confessions*, "Augustine must learn that he cannot convert himself, that Christian humility consists in being willing to receive what we cannot get for ourselves, that the strong and intact will he desired so much to dedicate to God's service could not be won in battle, but would instead be a gift received through inspiration, for which he would always be indebted" (p. 69).

At the same time, she worries that Augustinian anxieties can lead us to abandon "any sense that grace can work through ordinary processes of habituation" (p. 3).

There is no escaping the inner strife of the Christian life, and there is no apprehension of true virtue apart from the grace of God. If there is any repair to be made of Augustine's account, it lies neither in his clarification of our final end, nor in the insistence that true virtue must be constitutive of that good. Herdt looks to Aquinas, however, for a subtle improvement on Augustine's account of moral psychology within Christian eudaimonism. She suggests that Augustine's approach suffers mainly from the fact that his conceptual categories lack differentiation between "the variety of semblances of virtue found among pagans (and Christians)" (p. 61). In short, his conceptual apparatus rules out, by necessity, "the possibility of true pagan virtue directed toward the common good of an earthly society" (p. 72). Aquinas, on the other hand, "was willing to consider the possibility not only of pagan virtue directed toward the common good and not vitiated by the love of glory but even of virtuous *self*-love among pagans" (p. 72).[28] Thus we turn to Aquinas.

Thomas Aquinas and the Moral Psychology of Habituation in Virtue

Aquinas echoes Augustine's emphasis on God as the author of all virtue, but he does so with less anxiety for the imminent danger of hypocrisy. He is, as Herdt says, "more willing to credit aspiration than dwell on impurity" (p. 72). This frees Aquinas to develop a richer account of the moral psychology of habituation in Christian virtue, even as he elaborates a more generous account of pagan virtue. The matter at issue here is Augustine's insistence that all pagan virtues are "simply sophisticated expressions of pride" (p. 74). Aquinas disagrees. For Aquinas, Herdt says, "while pagan virtues remain imperfect unless they are referred to the final and perfect good, the fact that they are capable of being so referred indi-

28. "By distinguishing between acquired and infused virtues, and by insisting on infused virtue as a necessary and sufficient condition for salvation," says Herdt, "Aquinas guards against the elitism of Aristotle's account of virtue. At the same time, by insisting that the infused virtues are intrinsic dispositions to act, by acknowledging that the ease of virtuous action is dependent on the acquired virtues, and by speaking of the increase of infused virtue, Aquinas affirms the importance of human moral agency" (p. 73).

cates that they are true virtues" (p. 74). Aquinas affirms a proximate end in pagan virtue that, while imperfect, does not in and of itself constitute a denial of God.

His extension of generosity toward pagan virtues does not include a free pass for Christians. As with Augustine, hypocrisy is a concern of any who would theorize virtue. If the hypocrite displays virtue without pursuing virtue as his or her true intention, then how are we to distinguish the hypocrites from the truly virtuous? Aquinas certainly condemns hypocrisy, but "he does not see hypocrisy looming as a global infection." He demonstrates less anxiety than does Augustine on this front, and Herdt describes the difference between the two thinkers as being between an "inflationary" and a "deflationary" account of hypocrisy (p. 81).

Aquinas's generosity toward pagan virtue and the deflationary account of hypocrisy stem from the same root: he aims to make clear that God's gifts "dispose rather than displace human agency. Grace heals and elevates human character, but always in ways that stand in an organic relation to human agency" (p. 73). Herdt rightly sees that this opens up breathing room in the pursuit of virtue that is not available in Augustine's account. She observes: "There is here a subtle but significant divergence from Augustine, for whom achieving purity of intention, a perfect match between character and action, is a more pressing concern. For Aquinas, habituation in virtue requires that we learn to focus more on our exemplars than on ourselves, imitating their actions as well as we can, keeping our eyes on the prize and trusting that our character will be transformed through our action" (p. 82). As with imperfect pagan virtue, Aquinas believes that imperfect Christian virtue need not always constitute a flagrant rebellion against God. Rather, just as pagan virtue can point beyond itself to true virtue, so too can the genuine but imperfect pursuit of true virtue point beyond itself to the true source of our perfection: God. This is a significant allowance, and it frees the agent for pursuit of virtue without an overburdening fear of hypocrisy.

As an example of the necessity of this conceptual opening, Aquinas points to one who has made a vow to perform works of perfection. Herdt says:

> The vow signifies not just an obligation to act in certain ways. If it is rightly made, the vow also signifies the intention to be transformed into one whose character does match up to those perfect actions. The person who makes such a vow has entered on a process, something not com-

> pleted in an instant. Performing certain actions will create new habits in this person, transforming her character. If the primary focus of such a person were on honest self-presentation and full self-disclosure, she would be reluctant to perform any action that seemed to reflect greater perfection than her own present state of character. But this reluctance would undermine the process of transformation on which she had set out in taking the vow. (p. 82)

Aquinas sees that an overbearing concern to avoid hypocrisy can undermine truthful efforts at genuine obedience. He does not underplay our capacity for weakness, sin, and vice. He simply allows that the failure of one who truly pursues virtue "is weakness but not itself additional vice" (p. 81). The work of divine grace on human agency must necessarily be interruptive, as Augustine saw, but it need not be antagonistic.

Herdt sees that what is at stake in this debate is a functional account of virtue, grace, and human agency. She is wary of the paralysis lurking behind an "inflationary" view of hypocrisy, and she upholds the primacy of God's authorship of true virtue. She says, in directly theological terms, "If the gifts of the Holy Spirit dispose human beings to act, they cannot displace human agency" (p. 91). For this reason, hypocrisy cannot be "endemic" to the cultivation of the virtues (p. 82). Rather, we must continue to explore the organic relationship between human agency and divine grace, trusting in the one who is our true end.

Contingency, Virtue, and Paul Ramsey

There are deep similarities between Ramsey's attempt to locate political judgment within a theology of repentance, examined at several points in this book, and Herdt's insistence that divine grace must have an organic, if interruptive, relationship to human agency. Readers should already sense that Herdt shares with Ramsey the conviction that the contingency of created existence is at once a grace-filled opportunity and sin-plagued difficulty. Her insistence that grace is as endemic to the pursuit of virtue as are sin and hypocrisy shows her tendency, like Aquinas's, to credit aspiration rather than dwell on impurity.

Even more important, both Ramsey and Herdt share deep concern for the potentially paralytic effects of extreme self-examination on the everyday lives of those who would be Christian. Recall the troubled concept of "deferred repentance" and the debates on moral agency that occupied chapter 2 of this study. While Herdt frames her discussion mostly in terms of hypocrisy, it is noteworthy that at a key moment she introduces language similar to Ramsey's theology of repentance: "Confessing at every instant how our characters fall short of the actions we are performing, insisting on the deceptiveness of our activity, obsessing over lack of purity of intention would short-circuit our movement toward perfection" (p. 82). Notice her sensitivity to time in that statement ("every instant"), and recall that Ramsey shares similar concerns over the crippling effect of perpetually "trying to be sickly sorrowful for what we are now doing."[29] Ramsey lingers on the issue of repentance precisely because he is wary of responses to sin that careen into endless cycles of self-hatred.

Ramsey develops his early thought on these matters with reference to Luther's claim that all of the Christian life is repentance.[30] In fact, Herdt helps us to see how closely several of his claims reflect Aquinas's moral psychology. Ramsey suggests that "we cannot remorsefully repent and put away from us *all* our sins, because this would mean ceasing to do what we are *now doing.*"[31] The above discussion reveals a similar concern at the heart of Aquinas's distinction between weakness and vice. While the movement from imperfection to perfection lies only in God's hands, our imperfect pursuit of virtue need not itself be classified as vice. For Ramsey, as for Aquinas, this simplistically collapses the Christian life into contrition.

Of course, Ramsey moves his theological commentary in a distinctly political direction. His principal example of one who understands that contrition is not the only response to sin is the Christian soldier who "repentantly fights the just war" but "is not one who is always blubbering over his gunpowder!" Here again Ramsey sounds distinctly Thomistic: "More fundamental than sorrow for our past sins is a repentant faith which *in act-*

29. Paul Ramsey, "The Manger, the Cross, and the Resurrection," *Christianity and Crisis* 3, no. 4 (1943): 3.

30. It is worth noting that Herdt's critique of Luther raises many similar points to Ramsey. She seeks an account of human agency that is sustained by grace, but not swallowed by an endless paralysis of self-reflection. This places her at odds with "certain paradoxes of passivity," which she attributes to Luther, where "human agency directed toward the acquisition of virtue is always potentially empty self-assertion rather than grace-filled sanctification, and agency is thus limited to the often paralyzing role of self-examination" (Herdt, p. 15).

31. Ramsey, "The Manger," p. 3.

ing nevertheless *waits* for the Lord to complete by His Divine Providence the goodness of our finite actions, and which still trusts Him when in His Divine Judgment our action is thwarted and rejected."[32] As I mentioned in chapter 2, Ramsey italicizes "in acting" precisely to highlight the importance of judgment about what is good, however short of perfect virtue that judgment may be.

Herdt provides us, indirectly, with a profound insight into Ramsey's work. Her subtle reading of the differences between Augustine and Aquinas reveals the fact that, while Ramsey's overall political theology is thoroughly Augustinian, on the matter of moral psychology he is deeply Thomistic. This goes even beyond her reading of Aquinas and into her core insights on virtue theory. For Herdt, the place of human agency cannot be eradicated in pursuit of virtue, just as the inexhaustibility of God's grace outstretches every human effort. In her conclusion she writes: "Given the prerequisite of passivity, of acknowledged evacuation of agency, human agency is channeled into the task of self-eradication, of understanding its own aspirations as sinful and rooting them out" (p. 341).[33] She rejects this narrow and pessimistic view of Christian habituation in virtue, and she corrects "hyper-Augustinian traditions of reflection on the false character of human virtue" with a profound sense of the significance of human agency (p. 342). Thus she helps us see why Ramsey's insights on repentance and moral agency fit most properly within a rich account of habituation in virtue.

Ramsey offers insight into Herdt as well, for he draws a straight line between moral agency and political authority. However troubled his account of deferred repentance may be, Ramsey insists that a theology of repentance must have profound implications for the work of political judgment. He insists that "an ethics grounded in justification in Christ has no . . . urgent need to avoid making judgments of right and wrong in politics."[34] Claims such as that draw him away from Augustine's emphasis

32. Ramsey, "The Manger," p. 4.

33. Herdt, of course, packages many of these insights into her analysis of Aquinas and others. I have not delved into her use of Erasmus and mimetic virtue, given that the point at issue here is Ramsey's Thomistic moral psychology.

34. Paul Ramsey, *War and the Christian Conscience: How Shall Modern War Be Conducted Justly?* (Durham: Duke University Press, 1961), p. 13. To put it another way, Ramsey would agree with Eric Gregory, who writes: "The realism of limits and the unmasking of vice, however, do not exhaust an Augustinian repertoire" (Gregory, *Politics and the Order of Love* [Chicago: University of Chicago Press, 2008], p. 31).

on humility, even as they retain the Augustinian insistence that all Christian action is responsive. As we will see in the following chapter, it also draws Ramsey away from Charles Mathewes's suggestion that Christians fundamentally "suffer" virtue.[35] Nonetheless, for Ramsey, there must be more to Christian political ethics than a call for repentance. Those who criticized him for being too permissive with political authority did so unfairly; his tendency to credit aspiration rather than dwell on impurity was driven by a particular moral psychology, one that refused paralysis by self-examination.

Bowlin's work shows that, for Christians, cultivation of virtue is the most appropriate response to a contingent world. Herdt insists that Christian reflection on moral agency must account for the work of grace through ordinary processes of habituation. Ramsey's work demands that we extend both of those insights into Christian reflection on political authority. Consider his comments in an early essay on political ethics, "Turn Toward Just War":

> It ought to be impossible for Christians to suppose that the political life of mankind is anything other than a realm of "patient endurance." . . . This puts politics in its place, and frees men for clear-sighted participation in it. . . . Then politics can be best conducted; decision and action can be what they are worth. This only *de-mythologizes* the role of politics, and men are free to think of it as highly as they ought to think, and not make unearthly demands of it.[36]

For Ramsey, political decision and action have ordinary "worth" only insofar as they are responses to God's prior decisions and actions on our behalf. This is, ironically, a demythologizing reality, for it puts politics "in its place." Still, the interruptive work of grace must have an organic relationship with political judgment, just as it does with all forms of human agency. This means, for Ramsey, that divine love is the ground of all political identity. It also means that covenant love binds and limits all political authority, driving Christians away from consequentialist exceptions. It both chastens judgment and makes judgment possible.

In some respects, this approach to political authority is one of cop-

35. Charles Mathewes, *The Republic of Grace* (Grand Rapids: Eerdmans, 2010), pp. 141-42.

36. Paul Ramsey, "Turn Toward Just War," *Worldview* 5, nos. 7-8 (1968): 8-9

ing with the difficulties of contingency. But, as I hope has become clear, Ramsey is neither a pessimist nor a quietist when it comes to the realm of politics. Instead, patient endurance in politics is a responsive pursuit of the good without paralysis or self-eradication. This is fundamentally an eschatological claim: it is the character of life sustained by hope.

CHAPTER EIGHT

Ramsey among the Augustinians: Engaging Charles Mathewes and Eric Gregory

What Robert Benne wrote in *First Things* fifteen years ago may be true of every new generation of Christian thinkers: "There is a rising strand in Christian social thought inspired by a fresh reading of Augustine's *City of God*."[1] Benne's claim is certainly as true today as it was then. As another author has written more recently, there is "a burgeoning movement to bring Augustinian themes to bear on contemporary political concerns."[2] Among those contemporary theologians who claim the label "Augustinian," few have commanded attention like Charles Mathewes and Eric Gregory. As we shall see, Ramsey's work provides significant impetus for their efforts, and they are as thoroughly "Ramseyan" as they are Augustinian, despite the preference of both authors for the latter description.

This chapter continues the theme of exploring Ramsey's lasting contributions to contemporary Christian political theology. I place his work alongside that of Mathewes and Gregory in order to ask not only how their work improves on Ramsey's particular brand of Augustinianism, but, more important, how lasting elements of his work remain relevant for the contemporary conversation. If our focus in the previous chapter was habituation in virtue, here political judgment takes center stage, including the responsive nature of all human judgments and the significance of prudence for the work of love in politics.

I begin with Charles Mathewes, in whose work Ramsey's influence is perhaps stronger but harder to detect. Mathewes rarely cites Ramsey,

1. Robert Benne, "The Neo-Augustinian Temptation," *First Things* 81 (March 1998): 14.

2. Gregory W. Lee, "Republics and Their Loves: Rereading *City of God* 19," *Modern Theology* 27, no. 4 (October 2011): 553.

though when he does so, it is usually in supportive ways. Instead, mention of Ramsey typically serves to reinforce a point Mathewes traces back to Augustine.[3] Before we move to his appropriation of Ramsey, however, it is important to understand the broad scope of his Augustinian project.

Mathewes positions himself amid deep commitments to the theological virtues — faith, hope, and love — and a sharp appreciation for the ambiguity and ambivalence of history. Wary of both shallow cultural optimism and facile theological sentimentality, he pursues an account of political judgment and civic life together that is at once honest and prophetic, hopeful and realistic. His diagnosis of the contemporary problem is Ramsey's diagnosis: "We have a hard time thinking about *politics* itself."[4] Mathewes's solution is also Ramsey's solution: he aims at what he calls "wise counsel," one of many allusions to core elements of Ramsey's work.[5]

Mathewes's commitment to the significance of the theological virtues is unwavering — in both form and content. He aims to show "how we might live our lives through the theological virtues," precisely because, as we learn from Augustine, they help us "to understand our life in its full ambivalence" (pp. 11-12). Here the connection between virtue and indeterminacy is perhaps even stronger than in the work of John Bowlin and Jennifer Herdt. As Mathewes observes, "We live in a time that is deeply intolerant, perhaps even fearful, of ambiguity and ambivalence" (p. 10). In the face of this fear, Christians must learn anew that "true 'moral clarity' doesn't make things clearer, but rather more vividly ambiguous and complicated" (p. 110).[6] We must acknowledge the ambiguity of history

3. "As the twentieth-century Augustinian Christian ethicist Paul Ramsey put it, 'the justice of sometimes resorting to armed conflict originated in the interior of the ethics of Christian love.' For Augustine, then, political action, held to account by God and the neighbor, can authentically explain itself in terms of love — even unto the use of force" (Charles Mathewes, *The Republic of Grace* [Grand Rapids: Eerdmans, 2010], p. 148). Here Ramsey doesn't speak for himself, but instead operates as a mouthpiece for deeper, enduring Augustinian truths.

4. Mathewes, *Republic of Grace,* p. 41. Politics "itself" — its *esse* and its *bene esse* — was precisely what occupied Ramsey. See Paul Ramsey, "The Uses of Power," in *The Just War: Force and Political Responsibility* (New York: Charles Scribner's Sons, 1968; reprint, Lanham, MD: Rowman and Littlefield, 1983), pp. 3-18.

5. Mathewes, *Republic of Grace,* p. 6. Hereafter, page references to this work appear in parentheses within the text.

6. He continues: "What Christianity as Augustine sees it offers is *moral obscurity,* moral difficulty" (p. 111).

and the indeterminacy of our moral judgments, and we do so precisely by cultivating the theological virtues: faith, hope, and love.

Unlike Ramsey and Gregory, who place strongest emphasis on the work of love in political life, Mathewes prioritizes hope. Cultivating hope "is the central political task of today — of every day, in fact" (p. 2). Of course, the challenge of hope is one of seeing rightly, which means avoiding illusions of empire. The symbols and promises of empire lure us into a false sense of moral clarity, by tempting us either to condemn everything "political" or to baptize the particular political order that commands our allegiance. Both temptations prevent us from resisting "the apprehension of ambiguity" (p. 103). In contrast, "[h]ope is the true realism" (p. 220). Hope refuses the temptation "to assume we know already what is going on and what will be going on" (p. 39). True Augustinian realism — true cultivation of the theological virtues — can never surrender the "torment of hope's necessary indeterminacy" (p. 14).

The impact of these commitments on his description of civic life is nowhere more apparent than in his account of political agency. He inherits from Ramsey, as Oliver O'Dononvan does, the belief that "the fundamental task of government is judgment" (p. 149).[7] This requires determinate action from those who hold political authority in the form of political and moral judgments. For Mathewes, "politics is crucially about decisions, and those who make the decisions are the people we call authorities" (p. 150). In fact, no Christian can be spared the act of judging: "After all, when one refuses to make moral judgments about ways of life out of a hesitation to 'judge' others, one weakens one's ability to understand one's own life in moral terms" (p. 135). This mirrors Ramsey's claims about political judgment that we examined in the first section of this book: a proper human response to divine judgment includes making determinate moral judgments. (Recall his insistence that "vertical" judgments cannot "level" the necessity of "horizontal" judgments.)[8] In Mathewes's terms, judgment sustains our "ability" to understand our civic life together in moral terms.

Through Augustine, Mathewes presents an account of judgment as primarily responsive. This, he notes, "is an entirely different picture of

7. "The task of politics in general, for this tradition, is quintessentially one of *judgment* — of policing the community to secure the closely approximation of peace, the tranquility of order" (p. 178). See also Oliver O'Donovan, *Ways of Judgment* (Grand Rapids: Eerdmans, 2005), pp. 3-4.

8. Paul Ramsey, "Two Extremes: Ramsey Replies to His Critics," *Dialog* 6, no. 3 (1967): 218-19.

agency, one that highlights humans' capacities of participation, receptivity, and particularly love: aspects of agency that subvert a picture of the human as fundamentally active" (p. 138).[9] While in broad agreement with Ramsey on these matters, Mathewes locates his account of agency within a richer eschatological frame. He says: "For Augustine, the fullest picture of good human agency is human agency as it will be exercised in the eschaton. . . . For him, true, fully achieved human agency was not one where 'choice' played any role at all, but rather was a kind of full voluntary exercise of one's being" (p. 138). This reflects the Augustinian sense that virtues are "not achievements but sufferings — not ways of accomplishing something but ways of being vulnerable, of being susceptible to God's efficacious work in one's soul" (p. 33). Mathewes's account does not violate the insights on habituation in virtue gained from both Augustine and Aquinas in the previous chapter. Instead, he directly connects the responsive and authoritative aspects of human agency: "Responsibility and authority are implicated in one another, and unintelligible, at least formally, without recourse to one another" (p. 152).[10]

Mathewes and Ramsey share this emphasis on the significance of moral agency, as well as the ineradicable role of agency in political life. Recall that (in chapter 4) I discussed what Ramsey calls "the problem of choice itself."[11] He combats "atomistic individualism" by suggesting that choice can only be rightly understood within a theological framework, namely, an "interpretation of the covenants of life with life." Doctrines of creation, Christology, and eschatology are central to this effort, and he locates creaturely agency in a movement "toward *steadfast* covenant, toward the image of Christ." Ramsey later turns his attention to prudence

9. In *Evil and the Augustinian Tradition,* Mathewes attempts to move away from "foundational subjectivist assumptions" of Reinhold Niebuhr and Hannah Arendt and toward "an account of the human as *responding*" (Charles Mathewes, *Evil and the Augustinian Tradition* [Cambridge, UK: Cambridge University Press, 2001], p. 17). As he says elsewhere, "We must learn to see our lives, and the actions that constitute them, as reducible, without remainder, to response" (Charles Mathewes, "Book One: The Presumptuousness of Autobiography and the Paradoxes of Beginning," in Kim Paffenroth and Robert Kennedy, eds., *A Reader's Companion to Augustine's* Confessions [Louisville: Westminster John Knox Press, 2003], p. 9).

10. Later he adds: "For to talk about agency at all, you must have some account of responsibility, some account, that is, of why we say this person is responsible for that act, and why the person did it — what were the person's reasons for so acting" (p. 162).

11. Paul Ramsey, *Deeds and Rules in Christian Ethics* (New York: Charles Scribner's Sons, 1965; Lanham, MD: University Press of America, 1967), pp. 91, 163, 164.

as a regulating virtue for the proper work of covenant love and, thereafter, endeavors to supply a richer account of eschatology for his understanding of political judgment in *Speak Up for Just War or Pacifism.*

In chapter 4, I also attempted to show why readers of Ramsey must learn to hear "judgment" when he says "choice." Reading Mathewes requires no such effort. This is because he has thoroughly embraced H. Richard Niebuhr's Augustinian theology articulated in *The Responsible Self.*[12] The responsive nature of agency means that political judgment is also primarily responsive. As I mentioned earlier, "political judgment is part of the larger judgment of God," which means that, "for Augustine, the point of political judgment is found in crucial part in its salvific benefits, its ability to serve the redemptive purposes of God" (Mathewes, p. 164). Thus, "the first act of 'judgment' must be an inner act for Augustine — a constant self-lacerating assessment of the reasons for one's continued acceptance of this terrible burden" (p. 165).

Of course, it was precisely his sensitivity to these issues that led Ramsey to attempt a theology of repentance in *War and the Christian Conscience* and several early essays. Mathewes, in one of his rare citations of Ramsey's work, credits Ramsey with the observation that war "done out of the compulsion of love" can only emerge "from the recognition of prior relation and responsibility, recognition of our implication in the violence of the world" (p. 172). Ramsey knows that the first act of judgment must be an inner act, but he also knows that an inner act of judgment must find its true end elsewhere.[13] It is precisely for this reason that he so often says, "The Christian soldier does not blubber over his gunpowder."[14] The challenge before Mathewes is the same one that we encountered in chapter 2. We require an account of human agency as responsive, even contrite, that does not eradicate the role of judgment at the heart of political authority. Mathewes helps us see the extent to which Ramsey's early struggle is a distinctly Augustinian effort.

It is all the more significant, then, that Ramsey returns to Augustine and the concept of responsibility in *Speak Up for Just War or Pacifism.* This late effort goes unnoticed by Mathewes and Gregory, and I believe it marks

12. H. Richard Niebuhr, *The Responsible Self* (New York: Harper and Row, 1963).

13. As Oliver O'Donovan says, "Judgment *establishes a public context,* a practical context, that is, in which succeeding acts, private or public, may be performed" (O'Donovan, *Ways of Judgment,* p. 8).

14. Paul Ramsey, *Basic Christian Ethics* (New York: Charles Scribner's Sons, 1950), p. 188.

a significant contribution to contemporary discussions of Augustinianism. I will say more about these later developments in Ramsey's work shortly. First, however, we need to examine one additional contemporary thinker with considerable debts to Ramsey: Princeton theologian Eric Gregory.

Eric Gregory and the Politics of Love

In *Politics and the Order of Love,* Gregory aims to illuminate a variety of contemporary Augustinianisms, as well as to offer his own "rational reconstruction" of Augustinian political liberalism.[15] He shares with Mathewes (and Ramsey) an appreciation for Augustinianism's ability "to deflate moral and political pretension." However, he wants to avoid apathy and to push the tradition "in a new direction in order to reconstruct a kind of *Augustinian civic virtue* that might in turn encourage a more ambitious political practice" (p. 8). Martin Luther King Jr. is the hero of Gregory's project, given how rooted his political efforts were in an Augustinian theology of love. Gregory observes: "Indeed, one conclusion of this book is that Martin Luther King Jr, not Reinhold Niebuhr, is the great Augustinian liberal of modernity" (pp. 18-19). Still, Ramsey serves as something of an intellectual hero for Gregory, even if he occupies a relatively minor role in the broader scholarly debates over Augustinianism. In short, Ramsey's optimism about the possibilities of political life — or, better, his refusal to abandon politics as a potential site of God's redemptive work — makes him the intellectual figure who offers the closest approximation of Gregory's Augustinian civic virtue.[16] As with Mathewes, allusions to core elements of Ramsey's work are frequent in Gregory's text, even if direct citations are more rare. For instance, his very concept of civic liberalism reflects the essence of Ramsey's project: "Civic liberalism is a virtue-oriented liberalism that aims to avoid individualistic or rationalistic assumptions about human nature as well as romantic or totalitarian conceptions of political community" (p. 10).

Gregory seeks a robust account of love as a virtue of civic life, but he

15. Eric Gregory, *Politics and the Order of Love* (Chicago: University of Chicago Press, 2008), p. 2. Hereafter, page references to this work appear in parentheses within the text.

16. Gregory refuses a simple link between civic virtue and state action, as Ramsey did, though he envisions a more robust role for Christian action beyond the realm of government than does Ramsey. "This practice need not be statist, though the state is necessary given the practical challenges of securing the shared goods of actual 'peoples'" (p. 8).

refuses to make a stark choice between rules and virtues. He notes: "I think it is misleading to set moral evaluation of persons over against judgments about actions, and so will argue against those proposals of Christian love that rely exclusively on deontological or consequentialist accounts of act-specification. But for my purpose, any inquiry into the virtues of a citizen is an important part of the ethics of citizenship, whatever brand of ethical theory one happens to accept" (p. 70). This reflects the influence of Ramsey's moral theory, which I have examined in chapters 4 and 6. Gregory recognizes, as Ramsey does, that "the faithfulness of other-regarding love includes consideration of consequences in a world of complex injustices, especially in terms of practical knowledge of nonmoral facts about empirical economic, social, and political conditions" (p. 69). Still, love is of highest significance for Christian moral reasoning.

Unlike most other contemporary thinkers, Gregory actively wrestles with Ramsey's arguments. He admires the stringency of love in Ramsey's political writings, and he credits Ramsey with his belief that "*Christology* and *neighbor-love* rather than *theism and self-love* are the central conceptual terms for any Augustinian liberalism that wants to be theological" (p. 379).[17] Crucial to his work as an interpreter of Ramsey is his ability to highlight several aspects of Ramsey's project that are frequently overlooked by others, e.g., that he is a virtue thinker, that he seeks to correct a Niebuhrian account of love, and that he sees intuitionism as an insufficient ground of moral theory (see pp. 179-180, 184). I have focused on many of these themes throughout the preceding chapters.

Perhaps most important for this project, Gregory rightly grasps Ramsey's qualified inheritance of Reinhold Niebuhr's legacy: "Unlike Niebuhr, Ramsey does not speak about sacrificial love and powerlessness as ideals that find only ambivalent echo in the rational calculations of political morality. He does not speak in consistent refrains about love's transcendence that calls justice to be something other than justice." Instead, "Ramsey's account of the diversity of love's work can be distinguished from Niebuhr's dualistic tendency to restrict love to the interpersonal relations and give political communities over to utilitarian calculations." Even as Gregory affirms this shift, he suggests that Ramsey wrongly distances himself from Augustine in the process of distancing himself from Niebuhr

17. Gregory links this insight to Ramsey, saying, "Ramsey . . . claimed that his approach to ethics stands in decisive relation to Jesus Christ" and is "less merely theocentric" in its religious and ethical outlook "than was Jesus himself" (p. 378).

(pp. 182-83).[18] Gregory thus pursues his own position by offering an "ethic of citizenship" that alienates neither those committed to Augustine nor those committed to liberal democracy (p. 2).

It is noteworthy that Gregory focuses largely on *Basic Christian Ethics* and its inadequate account of Christian virtue. He makes no effort to trace a trajectory of Ramsey's thought, and this is most evident in his neglect of *Christian Ethics and the Sit-In* and *Speak Up for Just War or Pacifism.* To say it more directly, Gregory's reading of Ramsey on virtue fails to connect his early agapism with his later developments in covenant theology and, more significantly, his return to doctrines of creation and eschatology in later writings. (It is telling that Mathewes, too, turns to covenant language at the end of *The Republic of Grace,* but without reference to Ramsey's work.[19] Both Gregory and Mathewes miss the Augustinian themes in *Speak Up.*) I have said much about covenant already in this book, and I have argued at length for the importance of *Christian Ethics and the Sit-In* for Ramsey's development as a theologian. I will also trace his changing views on certain parts of *Basic Christian Ethics* in the following chapter. For now, I want to explore Ramsey's contributions to these contemporary debates by examining his use of responsibility as a central political theme in *Speak Up for Just War or Pacifism.* This is a theme he inherited directly from the one who taught him to read Augustine at Yale University, H. Richard Niebuhr.

Ramsey's Late Augustinianism: Strategy, Judgment, and Responsibility

In the early 1970s, "strategy" was the word on Ramsey's mind when it came to political ethics. He, like many, was troubled by the U.S. government's

18. Gregory rightly suggests that Ramsey "corrects Niebuhr's account of love and yet mistakenly condemns Augustinianism in the process" (p. 179). Gregory attends directly to the Augustinian influence on *Basic Christian Ethics,* but he underemphasizes Ramsey's writings on Augustine in *War and the Christian Conscience: How Shall Modern War Be Conducted Justly?* (Durham: Duke University Press, 1961) and misses entirely his later turn to Augustine in *Speak Up for Just War or Pacifism* (University Park: Pennsylvania State University Press, 1988).

19. "Yet hope's civic face is not simply negative, not simply a scolding frown, angry at the nations for being imperfect. It is also affirmative, joyously proclaiming liberation, calling politics beyond itself. Most immediately, it persistently presses beyond the contractual language of the state toward a deeper, covenantal language" (Mathewes, *Republic of Grace,* p. 239).

expanding stockpile of nuclear weapons and policy of Mutual Assured Destruction. It is remarkable that such a calculated thinker described it as "the most politically immoral nuclear policy imaginable." His response was to call for "maximum concern [for] strategic, moral and political reasoning."[20]

This interest in strategic thinking motivated a number of his political writings from this period. The most significant (and substantial) of these is "A Political Ethics Context for Strategic Thinking," which originally appeared in a volume entitled *Strategic Thinking and Its Moral Implications.*[21] In the first half of the essay he accepts the assignment of saying "something theological" about strategic thinking. In the second half he presents a number of conclusions from his life's work on "the morality of war and deterrence."[22]

In chapter 2, I examined Ramsey's reading of the covenant of Noah in the aforementioned essay as an example of his scriptural reasoning. Perhaps even more significant is his reintroduction of Augustine's *City of God* as a reference point for his political theology. He does this by way of a reading of H. Richard Niebuhr's *The Responsible Self.*[23] Ramsey had been fond of Niebuhr's ethic of responsibility since his days as a graduate student at Yale, and he strongly encouraged James Gustafson to publish *The Responsible Self* shortly after Niebuhr's death in 1962.[24] I believe his return to concepts of responsibility in his later work marks an important rethinking of several key aspects of his political theology.

Ramsey initiates the discussion by pointing to two different ways of interpreting "the international system."[25] The first of these is the secular strategic approach represented by Thomas Schelling's *The Strategy of Conflict,* which was a significant contribution to political science in the 1960s.[26] It interprets political action according to the "law of move and

20. Paul Ramsey, "The MAD Nuclear Policy," *Worldview* 15, no. 11 (1972): 16.

21. Paul Ramsey, "A Political Ethics Context for Strategic Thinking," in Morton A. Kaplan, ed., *Strategic Thinking and Its Moral Implications* (Chicago: University of Chicago Center for Policy Study, 1973), pp. 101-47.

22. Ramsey, *Speak Up for Just War or Pacifism,* pp. 183, 195.

23. Niebuhr, *The Responsible Self;* see also H. Richard Niebuhr, "The Idea of Covenant and American Democracy," *Church History* 23, no. 2 (1954): 126-35.

24. Ramsey wrote to James Gustafson: "I am very glad that you are to set forward that manuscript of Richard Niebuhr's so that it will secure the greatest possible understanding and impact" (Paul Ramsey to James Gustafson, January 14, 1963, Box 10, Ramsey Papers).

25. Ramsey, *Speak Up,* p. 187.

26. Thomas Schelling, *The Strategy of Conflict* (Cambridge, MA: Harvard University Press, 1960).

countermove" or by "the action-reaction syndrome." Because there are a variety of interests and agents in the political realm, strategic thinking must be constantly responsive. Ramsey demonstrates the complexity of political action this way:

> All action in the action-reaction syndrome is fitted to reciprocal action. The anticipated response affects the action put forth, even if not altogether determining it. The actor takes into account how he is expected to act and, as well, how he expects the other to act. . . . Interaction is, therefore, always based on *interpretation* of the actions coming upon the agents from one another. Without *some* interpretation of the action calling for response, a system of interacting actors would be a field of forces. The interplay would be automatic. We could not call it "action," unless the interacting actors were engaged in reciprocated self-involving interpretations of one another's moves and countermoves.[27]

Political action is always anticipatory, reactive, and responsive to the changing landscape of international relations. He calls this, uncontroversially, the "common *interpretation* of action coming upon us." Niebuhr represents the second approach, which Ramsey calls the "large pattern of interpretation." This position "defines the attitude and action of the 'church' in contrast to the 'state'" (p. 188).[28] It interprets political action according to "something more ultimate than the opposed international system" (p. 189). While the secular strategy is a closed system of response (i.e., only between actors in the same political sphere), the large pattern of interpretation is responsive and reactive to the transcendent action of God (or, in Niebuhr's language, radical monotheism).

Ramsey has three purposes in describing this division between the strategic "opposed-system" and the theological "trust-system" (p. 191). The first is to demonstrate to his secular audience that Niebuhr's understanding of response shares "remarkable similarities" with the strategic viewpoint, even as they are "contrapuntal" (pp. 189, 188). He suggests the possibility of common ground between the political scientists and the theologians by observing that both strategic and theological systems prioritize sensi-

27. Ramsey, *Speak Up,* pp. 186-87. Hereafter, page references to this work appear in parentheses within the text.

28. He also says, "This generalized interpretation of the meaning of interaction, response and responsibility, was the one espoused by the prophets of Israel" (p. 188).

tivity to the responsive and reactive character of human moral existence. This makes "the subtle analyses" of both systems "mirror images of one another" (p. 189). He exhibits this point by calling attention to similar interpretations of responsive action in Schelling's *The Strategy of Conflict* and Niebuhr's *The Responsible Self.*

But Ramsey also suspects that secular theorists will not buy into the Niebuhrian suggestion that the trust system is a comprehensive guide for political action. He suspects that his effort to stake out common ground will be rejected. Therefore, his second point concedes some inadequacies in the theological account by noting Niebuhr's inattention to the role of strategic political analysis. Because Niebuhr is "first and foremost a theologian, not an analyst of the international system," he sees that "there is good in whatever is happening" (p. 191). His account of human agency as responsive is "activated and given content by an interpretation of God's action as the context in which all finite actors live and move" (p. 190). This relativizes and subjects judgments of justice and injustice in the international system under the divine judgment of God. It also may give a wrong impression, Ramsey worries, by implying that a theological perspective is sufficient to "erode or displace" the significance of strategic insights in the secular perspective (p. 190).

To his secular audience, Ramsey acknowledges that the theological view alone will not suffice for the determination of right political action. There are important considerations that, "simply by omission, [Niebuhr] may seem to deny or underrate, namely, the need for independent analysis of action in the opposed international system" (pp. 191-92). He adds later that Niebuhr "can perhaps be faulted for *not* having analyzed the peculiar nature of various other action-systems" (p. 192).[29] Given his audience, Ramsey is eager to distance himself from this interpretation of strategic thinking; he seeks to affirm earlier commitments to the inherent obscurity of political calculation. His criticism of Niebuhr's viewpoint is a gesture of sympathy for the essential role of strategic analysis in international politics.

Shaun Casey interprets Ramsey's protest against Niebuhr as "a major theological break with his teacher."[30] But that judgment overlooks his cru-

29. He continues on the same page: Niebuhr "can probably be faulted for failure to analyze the relation between a Christian's trust and the wariness required by his office, or between 'the church' as a trust-system and 'the state' as an actor in an opposed-system."

30. Shaun Casey, "Eschatology and Statecraft," *Studies in Christian Ethics* 21, no. 2

cial third point: rescuing the interpretation of Niebuhr by demonstrating that a proper theological perspective on political action allocates a significant role for strategic thinking. In other words, those embracing the eternal truth of Niebuhr's "trust-system" need not neglect the inescapable reality of the "opposed system" of international politics. Instead of breaking with his teacher, Ramsey points to their shared theological inheritance: Augustine's two-cities doctrine.

Because the *civitas Dei* and the *civitas terrena* are "inextricably *intermingled* to the end of time," the Christian "lives by trust and he also lives in a system of distrust" (*Speak Up*, p. 192). This truth means that it would "not be a mistake to attribute to Niebuhr the view of the great Augustine." By looking to Augustine's account of responsive and responsible action, Ramsey is able to capture the necessary role for both strategic and theological reasoning. On one hand, the moral agent responds "in all action coming upon him, *also* to the action of God; he moves with confidence among the living." On the other hand, the agent responds "in all action coming upon him, *also* to the action and the anticipated action of a companion in an opposed-system; he . . . moves with wariness among the living" (p. 192). Ramsey's redundant use of the word "also" highlights the overlapping and intermingled cities in which political authorities find themselves.

The balance of moving jointly with confidence and wariness reflects a common theme in both Ramsey's work on covenant and repentance and the recent Augustinianism from Mathewes and Gregory. It is, as James Turner Johnson describes it, "an Augustinian appeal to charity in a world where until the end of time there exists an ambiguous mixture of the City of God and the City of Earth."[31] The two-cities language has the effect of rejecting the false assumption that the political realm is "wholly inimical" and radically opposite to the trust-system. It also rejects the assumption that "kingdoms of the world can *in time* become the kingdom of God and his Christ" (pp. 192-93).[32] Both views mistakenly elide the intermingled

---

(2008): 174. Ramsey says, "As a theologian, I believe the truth Niebuhr affirms" (*Speak Up*, p. 191).

31. James Turner Johnson, "Morality and Force in Statecraft: Paul Ramsey and the Just War Tradition," in David H. Smith and James Turner Johnson, eds., *Love and Society: Essays in the Ethics of Paul Ramsey* (Missoula, MT: Scholars Press, 1974), p. 109.

32. This assumption is based on a theological mistake. Earlier in *Speak Up*, Ramsey says: "It is when the 'already' and the 'not yet' of the presence of the kingdom are spread out, as it were, over historical time in which we live toward the incoming kingdom that longing for the peace of God tends to blur with longing for world peace. The density and depth of

character of historical time and avoid the delicate balance of working for good simultaneously with confidence and wariness.

Politics as a Realm of Responsibility

Ramsey's insistence that a theological perspective is essential for, but not identical to, the strategic approach to political action goes all the way back to his discussion of Augustine in *War and the Christian Conscience.* There he criticizes Ernest Barker's account of absolute justice for so radically transcending earthly determinations of justice that the heavenly city "did not fundamentally challenge the earthly one." Ramsey insists that Barker "did not take seriously into account Augustine's belief that there can be no justice, or rendering man his due, unless God is given his due."[33] In other words, the pursuit of justice in the time of two cities, which may well include some strategic thinking, is dependent on divine action. It is a response to God's justice. In *Speak Up,* Ramsey links this reading of Augustine directly to Niebuhr, and he suggests that the language of response and responsibility is wide enough to honor both the significance of strategic thinking in the pursuit of earthly justice and the overarching theological reality that makes any such pursuits possible. For this reason, Scott Davis claims, "Ramsey sees in H. R. Niebuhr the contemporary theologian who most fully embodies Augustine's insights into the transforming nature of Christ's advent into the human world."[34]

Casey suggests that Ramsey's later writings indicate a "break" from his teacher, but if Ramsey is attempting to distance himself from anything in his reading of *The Responsible Self,* it can only be his earlier embrace of a theological distinction between public and private.[35] In chapter 2, I observed that *War and the Christian Conscience* includes a rejection of "the modern period," where "a complete distinction between personal and

---

Christology and Christian eschatology are stretched so thin, into the wish that peace among the world's powers might be so. Only not yet. Not quite yet — ever" (*Speak Up,* p. 44).

33. Ramsey, *War and the Christian Conscience,* p. 19.

34. Scott Davis, "Et Quod Vis Fac: Paul Ramsey and Augustinian Ethics," *The Journal of Religious Ethics* 19, no. 2 (1991): 47.

35. To put it differently, Ramsey's role as "both successor and rival to [Reinhold] Niebuhr's Augustinian realism is nowhere more apparent than in his preference for H. Richard Niebuhr's Augustinianism in *Speak Up for Just War or Pacifism*" (Gregory, *Politics and the Order of Love,* p. 181).

political morality . . . [has] only exhibited or accomplished a return of mankind to significant citizenship in one city only."[36] Ramsey sees the public/private divide as a tempting distortion of the two-cities doctrine, but his allegiance to Reinhold Niebuhr keeps him from avoiding it altogether. In spite of his own warnings, he pushes a foreign public/private divide onto Augustine in *War and the Christian Conscience.* That division is nowhere to be found in *Speak Up.* He uses H. Richard Niebuhr's concepts of response and responsibility, as well as Augustine's two-cities doctrine, in a way that no longer juxtaposes demands on an individual in private capacity and demands on the office of the magistrate in the political community. Instead, Ramsey speaks of strategy and responsibility as reflective of the tension inherent in the ambiguous political life of two intermingled cities.[37] This is politics as a realm of strategy, responsibility, and judgment.

These developments in *Speak Up for Just War or Pacifism* move two central aspects of Ramsey's political theology onto firmer ground. First, as we have seen throughout this study, he aims to highlight the "ambiguity that characterizes much of our moral experience and many moral judgments."[38] In later writings he links the indeterminacy and ambiguity of political endeavors directly to the inherent limitations of the *civitas terrena.* He says: "Statesmen are called to action in the midst of the *unpredictabilities* of other collectives and their leaders. The nation-state is surrounded by arbitrariness on all sides." Note that being surrounded by arbitrariness is not the same as being surrounded by hostility. Even the strategic theorists can see that "animosity and conflict are not, unqualifiedly, the characteristics of the system or its interactions" (*Speak Up,* p. 195). Rather, the unpredictability of the political realm "requires, *among other things,*

36. Ramsey, *War and the Christian Conscience,* p. xxii.

37. This is not to say that his work in *War and the Christian Conscience* did not draw on Augustine's two-cities doctrine. It did. My point is simply that politics as deferred repentance drew heavily on the public/private distinction, and in the shift from repentance to responsibility that emphasis disappeared. Further, my examination of Ramsey's scriptural reasoning in chapter 3 makes clear that he never bought into what Charles Mathewes calls Niebuhr's "subjectivism": "The term 'subjectivism' refers to that set of understandings of human existence that assume that human subjects have priority over against what is 'outside' them — that human subjects make the first move in acting in the 'outside' world, coming to understand the world, and in general all their 'relations' to that outside" (Mathewes, *Evil and the Augustinian Tradition,* p. 130).

38. Paul Ramsey, "Incommensurability and Indeterminacy in Moral Choice," in Richard A. McCormick and Paul Ramsey, eds., *Doing Evil to Achieve Good: Moral Choice in Conflict Situations* (Chicago: Loyola University Press, 1978), p. 69.

preparedness, threat, and perhaps an actual use of force" (p. 196). This means that the politician must be at once responsible enough to prepare to encounter the worst of political threats and responsive enough to discern the real dangers facing the people from the false ones.

Of course, unpredictability rather than enmity as a hallmark of the political realm was Ramsey's point all along. He insisted to John Hick that deferred repentance was not sinister but rather merely doing what is right in a climate where the determination of right action depends on continuously changing circumstances.[39] The problem with his earlier account was that deferred repentance confusingly implied a suspension of moral norms in the political realm. The language of responsibility frees Ramsey to speak more clearly of the political system as "characterized by the unpredictability of autonomous actors and reactors." This allows him to maintain and define "the minimum morality of responsible action within the inter-state system" (p. 197). It also allows him to highlight the theological underpinnings of his observations on ambiguity and ambivalence, having long ago learned from Augustine that these are unavoidable aspects of living in the heavenly and the earthly cities. Thus he says: "While there exists no collectivity in which Cain, the fratricide who founded the earthly city, exists no longer, there exists no collectivity in which Abel, progenitor of the Founder of the heavenly city, does not also exist" (p. 195). When paired with the two-cities doctrine, the language of responsibility allows him to sidestep any indication of moral anarchy and emphasize the systemic unpredictability of political life alongside the certainty of God's eschatological promises.

The second aspect of Ramsey's political theology that finds surer footing in these later developments is an extension of the first. Ramsey had long insisted that, even amid the unpredictability of politics, political authorities are not permitted simply to do as they please. There are rules of practice governing political conduct. Because politics is a realm of response — in Ramsey's words, "since the actors are peoples (or their governments) who have purposes" — he rejects any attempt to analyze political interaction that refuses to come to terms with the systemic limitations and rules of practice. This is why the theory of justified war offers not merely "statements of the justifications needed for resorts to conflict," but, more widely, "an understanding of the strivings going on among interacting collectives by other political means" (p. 197).[40]

39. Paul Ramsey to John Hick, July 13, 1961, Box 11, Ramsey Papers.

40. The just-war theory is, for Ramsey, "a proposal concerning the very nature of the

To put it another way, Ramsey honors the importance of strategic thinking in the *civitas terrena,* but he consistently describes the rules of political practice — the moral criteria of political action — with reference to *civitas Dei.* He does allow that secular theorists are free to think of just-war criteria as "*systemic* requirements, and *not* as an external ethics vainly imposed" (p. 196). But his own Christian ethic never allows for the justification of war apart from the demands of love of neighbor and love of God. For Ramsey, the use of power has a "conditional value only" precisely because it is subject to higher purposes — "terminal goals" — related to love, order, and justice.[41] What we see in *Speak Up* is his effort to draw a straight line between a realist perspective on political life and the transforming work of love in the form of political justice. This requires a break from consequentialist tendencies in Reinhold Niebuhr's Augustinian realism and a fuller embrace of H. Richard Niebuhr's language of responsibility. As Gregory notes, "Unlike [Reinhold] Niebuhr, Ramsey does not speak about sacrificial love and powerlessness as ideals that find only ambivalent echo in the rational calculations of political morality."[42] Ramsey does not denigrate strategy here, but neither does he ground the norms of justified war in secular political reasoning. Instead, he reasserts his basic convictions about the work of love in justified (and therein also limited) political action from within a more directly theological frame.

As with other central aspects of Ramsey's political theology, we should not be surprised that his later work strengthens claims he had been making all along. Prominent in his reading of Luke 14 (which I examined in chapter 3) is the observation that Jesus' parable points the way toward limitations on justifiable war. He also consistently rejects the consequentialist notion that Christians could participate in morally atrocious behavior to achieve desirable political outcomes. As Eric Gregory notes, Ramsey "does not denigrate justice to elevate love, a denigration that often blinds Niebuhrians to injustices in the private realm and permits injustice through

---

international system." Mathewes puts the same point in more overtly Augustinian terms: "The *libido dominandi* is a knife that cuts both ways, for the lust to dominate all too easily becomes the dominating lust, and the mournful warrior all too easily becomes one who really enjoys his day job, who cannot imagine another way of life — and so becomes subject to the logic of subjugation in a way more profound than those he subjugates" (Mathewes, *Republic of Grace,* p. 107).

41. Ramsey, *The Just War,* pp. 11, 29.

42. Gregory, *Politics and the Order of Love,* p. 183.

the 'dirty hands' of the public realm."[43] We have already seen some of the more determinative fruits of this shift in an earlier chapter on tragedy and the limits of political authority so central to the concept of "moral anguish" in *Speak Up*. What passes away here is any effort to use language of deferred repentance. Gone, too, is reference to Reinhold Niebuhr and, as mentioned earlier, the public/private distinction. Instead, Ramsey relies on Augustine to highlight the transforming and regulating work of love in political judgment and the pursuit of justice. Chief among the moral criteria generated from this account of love are, as Ramsey so frequently reiterated, commitments to distinguish combatants from noncombatants and to avoid disproportionate use of force in war.

Ramsey Among the Contemporary Augustinians

At this point similarities and differences with Mathewes and Gregory come into view more clearly. Each thinker endorses Mathewes's edict: "Christians affirm that politics turns out to be theology, a way of seeking God."[44] Each echoes the Augustinian commitment to moral ambiguity and perpetual irresolution in politics in the time of two cities. As Mathewes notes, "Far from absolving political agents of responsibility, this love-based account means to accentuate their sensitivity to the fraught character of their actions."[45] The significance of responsible and responsive political action is central to their interpretations of Augustine.

We encounter some difference with Mathewes on the matter of political action. In his version of Augustinianism, "proper political action is exercise of *authorized power.*"[46] As I described in chapter 2, Ramsey requires purpose to accompany authorized power in order for it to be properly political: "A polit-

43. Gregory, *Politics and the Order of Love,* p. 183. Gregory continues: "Unlike Niebuhr, Ramsey allowed room for the self within an ethics of love, and he did not reduce justice to contractual reciprocity" (p. 183). I hope I have made clear the significance of *Christian Ethics and the Sit-In,* and particularly Ramsey's appreciation of Karl Barth's covenant theology, to this aspect of his moral theology. When Gregory says, "Ramsey thinks Christians owe people love," he fails to indicate that Ramsey locates this debt precisely within doctrines of creation and eschatology through a theology of covenant (p. 183).

44. Charles Mathewes, *A Theology of Public Life* (Cambridge, UK: Cambridge University Press, 2007), p. 161.

45. Mathewes, *Republic of Grace,* p. 172.

46. Mathewes, *Republic of Grace,* p. 168.

ical action is always an exercise of power and an exercise of purpose. Power without purpose and purpose without power are both equally nonpolitical."[47] Ramsey insists that *purpose* is essential to action that is properly political precisely because the purpose of such action is subject to judgment. The proper ends of power — the *bene esse,* as he calls it — must always be in view. This stems from his rigid commitment to the inviolability of limitations of proportion and discrimination in war. Only political action within the justification and limitation of these norms can be considered "properly" political.

This may simply be a semantic difference, but I don't think it is. Mathewes certainly intends the word "authorized" in *authorized power* to communicate the subjugation of all human exercises of power under God's authority. He says: "The legitimation of this power comes at a cost to those who wield it: authority always stands under the eschatological judgment of God, and all of us in positions of authority must recognize implication in the violence and necessities of the world."[48] Still, it is difficult to locate the proper ends of power in the more generic word "authority," and Ramsey's insistence that blind exercise of power is "nonpolitical" is striking. As we shall see in the following chapter, Daniel M. Bell Jr. is closer to Ramsey on this matter than he is to Mathewes, saying that, for Christians, "the authority granted the head of state in matters of war is intrinsically related not simply to *power* but to the *responsibility* the governing authorities have for attending to the common good."[49]

It should also be quite clear at this point that Gregory and Mathewes surpass Ramsey as virtue thinkers. Of the two, Gregory develops a fuller account of habituation in virtue. He offers insight on agency and habituation similar to that obtained in the preceding chapter through Bowlin and Herdt. For instance, he observes: "Augustinians are usually nervous with the language of habituation given their strong doctrine of grace (there is no ascent without the prior descent) and their strong doctrine of sin (the perpetual ruptures of the will in obeying moral demands placed upon us in any given moment)." Yet "Augustinians need not make virtue an enemy of confession. . . . A reconstructed political Augustinianism needs to empha-

47. Ramsey, *The Just War,* p. 8.

48. Mathewes, *Republic of Grace,* p. 168. Mathewes inches closer to Ramsey's position when he says, "The exercise of political power — an exercise sometimes entailing the use of force and always relying tacitly on the threat of force — is something that should affect our souls" (p. 177).

49. Daniel M. Bell Jr., *Just War as Christian Discipleship* (Grand Rapids: Brazos, 2009), p. 108.

size the ways in which the practice of love is a virtue."[50] Where Mathewes displays the breadth of the theological virtues and their role in political life, Gregory shows the forms of habituation by which we put on virtue. But he applies these insights into habituation to only one virtue: love. If Mathewes needs a richer account of habituation more broadly, Gregory needs a fuller account of habituation in faith and hope. Both lack an account of the role of the cardinal virtues in political life, even as they speak of civic virtue.

Mathewes admits that "ultimately" faith, hope, and love "do not disable civic virtue; they properly *en*able it."[51] But we hear little of prudence as an important civic virtue, and he tends to treat prudence separate from political authority. In *A Theology of Public Life,* Mathewes draws a straight line between prudence and providence, describing prudence as "not just one more way of managing reality," but instead "the way we participate in the rhythms of God's providence."[52] Within a proper relationship of prudence and providence, "worldly action should be performed not just for its immanent value, but because it is exploration into God, a mode of inquiring into God."[53] How does this fit with his account of authority? In response to the question of what this looks like in "less abstract, more human terms," Mathewes describes a number of important forms of Christian action in the world, including work in soup kitchens, the formation of community alliances, and participation in political demonstrations. Absent from this list, however, is the task of political judgment.[54] If we want to know what the relationship between prudence and providence looks like in the world of political authority, we will have to turn to Ramsey for a better answer.

For his part, Gregory suggests that a theology of civic life will rely "on a virtue-oriented rather than merely sin-oriented Augustinian politics."[55]

50. Gregory, *Politics and the Order of Love,* pp. 68-69.

51. Mathewes, *Republic of Grace,* p. 83.

52. Mathewes, *A Theology of Public Life,* p. 94. Later he continues: "Prudence is the discernment of what is going on — what God is doing now — and in so being, it itself leads to the *imitatio Dei,* and the participation in the ongoing work of providence" (p. 102).

53. Mathewes, *A Theology of Public Life,* p.103. Here it is helpful to remember what Mathewes wrote elsewhere: "Love is a form of inquiry, and inquiry is a form of love" (Mathewes, *Evil and the Augustinian Tradition,* p. 206).

54. Mathewes, *A Theology of Public* Life, p. 103. Elsewhere he adds: "This is why just-reasoning always leaves space for 'prudential judgments' on the part of the enactors. . . . It means that the command of God cannot be captured in a neat algorithm, and that at any particular moment space must be given for those of proper discernment to discern what God is calling them to do" (Mathewes, *Republic of Grace,* p. 173).

55. Gregory, *Politics and the Order of Love,* p. 14.

Of course, virtue and sin are not mutually exclusive orientations, as he is well aware. Rather, Gregory is working to respond to the challenge he sees at the heart of contemporary Augustinianism. He says: "We can . . . identify two flawed possibilities for the political implications of an Augustinianism: one primarily oriented to love, the other primarily oriented to sin. The challenge for Augustinian liberalism is to work out a version of this relationship that avoids both arrogant forms of perfectionism and essentially negative forms of liberalism."[56] This brings us back to the theme of the preceding chapter — moral psychology. Gregory seeks a "virtue-oriented" account of Augustinian politics precisely because he sees civic virtue as the most proper form of response to the ambiguity of political life in the intermingled cities.

It is noteworthy, then, that when Gregory says of Reinhold Niebuhr that "too much fascination with sin and ambivalence can render a rather fantastical moral psychology of hope," he does not subject Ramsey's work to the same judgment.[57] Rightly so. Ramsey consistently resists a fantastical moral psychology, even as he seeks to maintain the relevance of the theological virtues for political judgment. This commitment to a realist moral psychology, while maintaining an uncompromised theological commitment to God's eschatological care of creation, leads Ramsey to a sharp focus on prudence and practical reasoning. His emphasis on the role of judgment in political authority anchors his political theology in a "deflationary" moral psychology, to use Herdt's term. This is nowhere clearer than in his admission of the unavoidable role strategy must play alongside response and responsibility for those who would be faithful in the ambivalent time of the two cities.

As I suggested earlier, Ramsey clearly lacks Mathewes's sweeping structural allegiance to the theological virtues and the deliberate emphasis on civic life in Gregory's work. His indebtedness to Reinhold Niebuhr's account of sin is well known. But I hope that the scope of this book has made clear the extent to which Ramsey's Augustinian politics are, in Gregory's words, "virtue-oriented" rather than "sin-oriented." Further, it should be clear that prudence holds a significant place among the virtues necessary for political authority. As Ramsey writes in 1961, prudence "is not a de-

56. Gregory, *Politics and the Order of Love,* p. 20.

57. Gregory, *Politics and the Order of Love,* p. 94. This comment refers to the "realist hope" in both Reinhold Niebuhr and Robert Markus. For additional comments on Markus, see Gregory, *Politics and the Order of Love,* pp. 83-95.

rogatory word. . . . It is 'practical wisdom' in applying ethical principles to actual cases. Without prudence there would be no morality at all put forth into actual practice and decision-making."[58] Without prudence there is no faithful political judgment.

Recall the discussion of "moral anguish" from chapter 5. As Ramsey reiterates there, Christian political action must fall within a matrix of obligation (to the neighbor and to God), justification (the course of action adheres to the norms that regulate and authorize militant action), and limitation (in short, the course of action does not violate the principles of proportion and discrimination). Love of God and neighbor generates the obligation to act: as Gregory says, "Ramsey thinks Christians owe people love."[59] But love alone is not enough for Ramsey, especially when we operate in a realm of war, where a desire to "help" can have devastating consequences. He explains the significance of prudence for Christian political action most clearly in this context:

> We who are not pacifists are put at war with ourselves, as I pointed out, by the requirement that *all* the just-war norms be fulfilled in any use of any force. . . . Any *generous* understanding of "just cause" will generate these claims; a realistic political understanding will limit them. In the previous chapter I called this *moral anguish* — the anguish of being bonded to rescue the perishing in a fallen world, where justice and peace do not (yet) lie down together and the wretched of the earth are trodden upon daily. To do justly and love mercy cannot *in principle* be limited to responding to aggressive attack upon our own nation or our allies. Prudence or proportionality sets that limit; and if so, such proscriptions are not to be breached even for just cause. Prudence also determines whether nonviolence or violence is opportune or not.[60]

Prudence offers vital assistance to the work of love in political action. If we lived in a world with determinate choices — Ramsey spoke of this as a choice between right and wrong "per se" — then we would have no need

58. Paul Ramsey to Byron Johnson, February 17, 1961, Box 12, Ramsey Papers.

59. Gregory, *Politics and the Order of Love,* p. 183.

60. Ramsey, *Speak Up,* p. 89. Ramsey sometimes writes "rational calculation" or "reason" in place of prudence, though his intention is surely not to prioritize consequentialism by doing so. For example, "What can be better than rational calculation discriminating between justice and injustice in answering the questions, Whether to war? and, If to war, how?" (Ramsey, *Speak Up,* p. 55).

of prudence.[61] But Ramsey is an Augustinian, and the business of politics is obscure, ambiguous, and indeterminate. Politics involves actions with intended (but not guaranteed) consequences, purposive (but not unassailable) judgments, and desired (but nonetheless contingent) outcomes. Alongside faith, hope, and love, Ramsey insists that Christians must cultivate prudence if they are to do justice, love mercy, and walk humbly with God. This is, I believe, where his distinctive contributions to the contemporary Augustinians appear.

There can be no doubt that his work lacks the overarching theological structure (and consistency) of Mathewes's *The Republic of Grace.* It also lacks the nuanced reading of Augustine in Gregory's *Politics and the Order of Love.* He is simply more content to provide a theological frame of reference (e.g., covenant as internal basis of our created life together) before belaboring the technical details of property rights and common law in the debates of the 1960s. This tendency has, to put it mildly, decreased the "readability" of his work in the decades since its publication. But Ramsey never shies away from the technical details of the knotty moral issues of his day, and he insists that practical reasoning and cultivation of prudence will be essential to any Christian response to such issues. Both Mathewes and Gregory display a profound sense of appreciation for civic virtue, and they labor to clear the conceptual and theological ground for its possibility. Ramsey puts prudence to work and shows what practical reasoning, governed by love, looks like in public.

If Ramsey was, as Gregory says, "ahead of his time" in recognizing the importance of the virtues for moral theory, then he is now behind the times in the articulation of the role the virtues play in theological ethics.[62] This is where Mathewes and Gregory so clearly surpass Ramsey's efforts. It also brings into view Ramsey's differences with the contemporary author who has worked hardest to connect discipleship and justified war within the Christian tradition, Daniel M. Bell Jr. I conclude this discussion of Ramsey's place in contemporary Christian political theology by examining the relationship of his writings with Bell's *Just War as Christian Discipleship* in the following chapter.

61. Ramsey, *Speak Up,* p. 52. But, as Ramsey says, "*The future is radically unpredictable,* for pacifist and just warrior alike" (p. 123).

62. Gregory, *Politics and the Order of Love,* p. 180.

CHAPTER NINE

Discipleship, Christology, and Justified War: Engaging Daniel M. Bell Jr.

In 1951, John Rawls had recently completed his Ph.D. and was a young instructor in the department of philosophy at Princeton University. In May of that year he published a review of Ramsey's *Basic Christian Ethics* in *Perspective: A Princeton Journal of Christian Opinion.*[1] The review extends a few scripted compliments and summaries, but it moves quickly to criticisms that Rawls sharply directs at the issue of transcendent principles in Christian ethics. Rawls asks how "Christian criterion of right action" can intelligibly be said to transcend "all concepts of natural law, all ways of ordinary reasoning, and all dictates of conscience."[2] In his view, Ramsey's description of agape simply disregards "what seems to me is our best authority on matters of right and wrong in daily affairs: namely, the free and uncoerced agreement of competent persons wherever it exists."[3]

Although his equation of collective agreement, common reason, and natural law may lack theological nuance, Rawls raises an important question. He wants to know whether Ramsey's ethics can honor any wisdom

1. John Rawls, "Paul Ramsey's *Basic Christian Ethics,*" *Perspective: A Princeton Journal of Christian Opinion* 3, no. 7 (May 1951): 8-12, Box 32, Ramsey Papers.

2. Rawls, "Ramsey's *Basic Christian Ethics,*" p. 10. Several critics called for Ramsey to develop a more prominent doctrine of creation. For instance, Charles Curran observed that "nowhere in *Basic Christian Ethics* does Ramsey give sufficient development of the role of creation in Christian theological ethics" (Curran, "Paul Ramsey and Traditional Roman Catholic Natural Law Theory," in James T. Johnson and David H. Smith, eds., *Love and Society: Essays in the Ethics of Paul Ramsey* [Missoula, MT: Scholars Press, 1974], p. 56). Meanwhile, Ramsey continued to admit into the mid-1970s, "I may be faulted for never having developed my own theory of natural justice or doctrine of creation" (Ramsey, "Some Rejoinders," *Journal of Religious Ethics* 4, no. 2 [1976]: 190).

3. Rawls, "Ramsey's *Basic Christian Ethics,*" p. 9.

in the reasoning of those who are not Christian. Or, more pointedly, he worries that Ramsey's account of agape strictly denies the validity of rationalist calculations of justice. Rawls challenges Ramsey to demonstrate precisely what obedient love adds to moral deliberation that cannot be found in basic moral systems such as utilitarianism by asking, "What does Christian love tell us that these cannot tell us . . . ?"[4] He also suggests that if it is merely impulse or motivation that distinguishes Christian ethics from philosophical ethics, then no compelling reason exists for demanding allegiance to the former.

Besides confirming that Rawls, even at a young age, showed evidence of the rationalist and contractarian impulses that would characterize his later work, the review of *Basic Christian Ethics* provides an interesting point of contrast to criticisms of Ramsey's later work. Ramsey never claims that Christians have a monopoly on truth and virtue. As early as *Nine Modern Moralists,* he acknowledges that there might be "some virtue in man's ordinary moral decisions."[5] But as his work progresses, Ramsey finds himself more and more frequently in the position of defending the *Christian* foundations of his political ethics. He does so often enough that he occasionally becomes testy, on one occasion writing to Joseph Fletcher: "But mostly what I'm about, if anyone is interested, is the careful articulation of the requirements of agape, not so much those of natural justice. My treatment of warfare does NOT rest upon a natural law basis; it rests rather on a prior demonstration that non-combatant immunity was and is a rule and work of charity — Christ illuminating the meaning of justice."[6]

Rawls's curiosity about Ramsey's ability to honor secular reasoning is replaced, over time, by the repeated suggestion that Ramsey's ethics are, ultimately, secular. (Or, at least, that they do not adequately indicate theological content.) John Howard Yoder reflects this approach in his critique of just-war theory, which locates the "fundamental rights of other parties" as the foundation of the tradition.[7] As Ramsey says, Yoder takes "universal and minimalist natural justice" as "the morality on which just war *bottoms.*"[8]

4. Rawls, "Ramsey's *Basic Christian Ethics,*" p. 12.

5. Paul Ramsey, *Nine Modern Moralists* (Englewood Cliffs, NJ: Prentice-Hall, 1962), p. 4. He quickly adds that "no moral judgment is sufficient by nature alone" (p. 4).

6. Paul Ramsey to Joseph Fletcher, June 29, 1965, Box 8, Ramsey Papers.

7. John Howard Yoder, *When War is Unjust* (Minneapolis: Augsburg, 1984), p. 58.

8. Paul Ramsey, *Speak Up for Just War or Pacifism* (University Park: Pennsylvania State University Press, 1988), p. 101.

By the time of *Speak Up for Just War or Pacifism,* Ramsey seeks to locate his insistence on the distinctiveness of his Christian ethics on surer theological footing.[9] This leads him to restate some of his earliest claims with direct reference to revised doctrines of creation, Christology, and eschatology. He also seeks — again — to clarify the theological foundations of his reasoning on justified war. For instance, he responds directly to Yoder:

> Unless his understanding is corrected or supplemented elsewhere, Yoder believes that just-war appeals are only and simply to *natural justice*. . . . If that were sufficient, then the state's function in the use of armed force and citizen participation are based entirely on *another morality* than that of the Gospel; there is then a "double morality" needed to warrant Christian participation in the resistance of evil, . . . it would require a doubling of loyalties to couple *that* or natural justice or universal human rights with Christian charity.[10]

This is a swift rejection of the suggestion that his political ethics lack christological foundations. He does not denounce "natural justice or universal human rights," but he does make a significant distinction between those and the work of Christian love. Whatever the pitfalls of his emphasis on the transcendence of agape, Ramsey establishes an upper limit for the usefulness of strictly "natural" or "independent" considerations in Christian ethics. Rawls is put off by this; Yoder misunderstands Ramsey's just-war ethic by failing to account for it. But as Ramsey matures, we see that the doctrine of creation informs — rather than distracts from — the primacy of Christian love. (I will return to the dispute with Yoder later in this chapter.)

Still, we would do well not to ignore Rawls's concern about the "transcendence" of Christian ethics; in fact, Ramsey shares similar concerns. Recall that he warns readers of "The Case of the Curious Exception" that his approach is "bifocal": on occasion he will side with the philosophers against the theologians, and at other times he will use theological insights

9. For instance, the doctrine of creation is a driving force behind Ramsey's chapter on "Biblical and Theological Foundations" in *Speak Up.*

10. Ramsey, *Speak Up,* p. 100. There is, unquestionably, a disconnect in *Basic Christian Ethics* between the work of agape and the doctrine of creation, but Ramsey refuses to compromise his allegiance to the primacy of "the Gospel" for moral theology. *Speak Up* is rooted in an emphasis on the centrality of doctrines of creation, eschatology, and Christology for ethics (*Basic Christian Ethics* defended the primacy of agape almost entirely in reference to the latter two).

to challenge and clarify philosophical arguments.[11] He does not think this approach violates the fact that all justice depends, first, on God's justice. Rather, concerning "abstract values, standards of justice, or natural rights," he says in *Basic Christian Ethics* that, "while justice may seldom arise *with* these, it does not arise *from* them. It arises from conformity to covenant conditions demanded by the God of truth and righteousness, by which measurement alone human consent and intelligence become right."[12]

Ramsey's consistently "bifocal" approach raises questions about how Christians are to engage secular political reasoning, of which Rawls's question is only one example. For instance, if "universal human rights" is a different morality from "the Gospel," does this mean Christians should oppose efforts to secure those rights? Or — perhaps more to the point of this discussion — can Christians learn from political theorists who advocate for them? This is both a moral and an ecclesiological question. To what extent should Christians expect to encounter truth and justice beyond the walls of the church? In the time of two intermingled cities, is the church the only community of true virtue? This takes us to the heart of Daniel M. Bell Jr.'s work and his claims in *Just War as Christian Discipleship.*

Daniel Bell, Ramsey, and the Character of Justified War

Bell is a student of Stanley Hauerwas, and he aims to resuscitate the just-war theory from within a commitment to the primacy of ecclesiology. Hauerwas aims, in his work, "to call into question abstract accounts of justice often associated with liberal political theory, which assumes a just social order is possible without the people who constitute that order being just."[13] Bell internalizes this critique and points it toward those who would provide a list of moral rules restricting participation in war without linking those rules to a particular people who are accountable for upholding them. In other words, the problem with "fundamentally secular" accounts of justice is the circumscribed identity they require of the church: "This

11. Paul Ramsey, "The Case of the Curious Exception," in Gene H. Outka and Paul Ramsey, eds., *Norm and Context in Christian Ethics* (New York: Charles Scribner's Sons, 1968), p. 70.

12. Paul Ramsey, *Basic Christian Ethics* (New York: Charles Scribner's Sons, 1950), p. 388.

13. Stanley Hauerwas, *War and the American Difference: Theological Reflections on War and National Identity* (Grand Rapids: Baker Academic, 2011), p. 100.

is a vision that reinforces the politics of modernity, where the church is consigned to the role of cultural custodian of values tightly cordoned off from political practice, which finds its highest expression and guarantor in the nation-state."[14]

Given his anxiety about secular accounts of justice, Bell writes for Christians who "want to live faithfully in a time of war."[15] He aims to provide an introduction to the just-war tradition and, more importantly, an account of "concrete practices that might contribute to the church's ability to make faithful moral judgments regarding justice in war and then live out those judgments" (p. 15). This leads him away from the debate between just war and pacifism; instead, he seeks to distinguish Christian reflection and practice from secular reasoning on war, even as Christians author much of what falls under the "fundamentally secular" heading. Given his effort to distinguish the traditional moral criteria of just-war theory (read: rules) from the broader communal habits necessary to wage justified war (read: virtues), Bell echoes Ramsey's insight that it is more helpful to speak of the just-war *tradition* than of the *doctrine* or *theory* (p. 71).

Bell organizes his reflection around a distinction between "Just War as Public Policy Checklist," or "Just War (PPC)," and "Just War Christian Discipleship," or "Just War (CD)" (p. 72). Just War Christian Discipleship is "an expression of the character of the Christian community; an outgrowth of its fundamental confessions, convictions, practices, and an extension of its consistent, day-to-day life and work on behalf of justice and love of neighbor (even enemies) in the time and realm of war" (p. 74). Just War Public Policy Checklist, on the other hand, "thinks primarily in terms of the laws and rules that do and/or should regulate the behavior of modern nation-states in war. . . . Just War (PPC) is cast not as an aid to discipleship but as an instrument of public policy, a checklist of criteria that aspires to guide politicians, rulers, and military leadership in times of war. Moreover, as a checklist of criteria, this vision of just war does not concern itself with daily life outside of war" (p. 74).

We might say that the difference between Just War (CD) and Just War (PPC) lies in their respective communities: church and state. After all, "war is a communal practice," and Just War (CD) is "an explicitly church-centered

14. Daniel M. Bell Jr., "Jesus, the Jews, and the Politics of God's Justice," *Ex Auditu* 22 (2006): 90. See also Hauerwas, *War and the American Difference,* p. 101.

15. Daniel M. Bell Jr., *Just War as Christian Discipleship* (Grand Rapids: Brazos, 2009), pp. 14-15. Hereafter, page references to this work appear in parentheses within the text.

instead of state-centered approach" (pp. 75, 77).[16] To the question of which community the tradition serves, he writes: "The prevailing answer is that the just war tradition first and foremost serves the state."[17] Given this distinction, Bell suggests that faithful disciples must abandon any notion that "the nation-state is either the primary anchor of Christians' identity or the most important ensemble of institutions in a time of war" (p. 77). But Bell doesn't quite deny, altogether, the function of the state. He denies secular theories of governance. Just War (CD) is "a practice of the Christian community," whereas the "sources" of Just War (PPC) are "either secular or thoroughly secularized" (pp. 75-76). In other words, Christians must choose, exclusively, between just war as a form of Christian discipleship and just war as a "theory of statecraft," even as Just War (CD) "remains an account of governance — which is the kernel of truth in the arguments of proponents of just war as 'statecraft.'"[18] I will return to this point in a moment.

Initially, Bell also draws a sharp line in the sands of moral theory. Just War (PPC) is "law or rule centered," where Just War (CD) is "by way of contrast . . . character- or virtue-based" (pp. 78-79). Immediately after drawing this distinction, however, he rolls it back for Just War (CD): "That is not to say that rules, law, commands, and the virtue of obedience are unimportant, only that focusing narrowly on them is insufficient" (p. 80). In fact, he allocates a significant place for moral rules within Just War (CD): "A person or a community of character is one that has internalized what rules and laws, in their irreplaceable if incomplete ways, point to" (p. 82). His treatment of virtues/rules is similar to that of church/state; the dichotomies that plague secular reasoning find their true ordering within his account of Christian discipleship.

I dispute neither Bell's prioritization of the ecclesial community for the moral formation of those who would be Christian, nor his preference for a virtue-oriented account of the Christian community's life together. Ramsey's work does not offer disagreement on those points either.[19] I do,

16. Bell writes elsewhere: "The difficulty facing the tradition stems from how one answers the question, 'what is the just war tradition for?' . . . What end, what community, does it serve?" (Daniel M. Bell Jr., "Can a War against Terror Be Just? Or, What Is Just War Good For?" *Crosscurrents* [Spring 2006]: 36-37).

17. Bell, "Can a War against Terror Be Just?" p. 37.

18. Bell, "Can a War against Terror Be Just?" p. 39.

19. That means neither that Ramsey's ecclesiology is equivalent to Bell's nor that it is sufficient on its own terms. It simply means that, to use Bell's language, the church is *primary* for both of them.

however, have concerns that his characterization of "secular" public policy tempts Christians into thinking that they have a monopoly on the moral formation necessary for justified war and little to learn from those who reflect on just war from beyond the walls of the church. To express it another way, I worry that Bell's typology overemphasizes the church/world distinction and underemphasizes the ambivalence and ambiguity of living in the City of God and the City of Earth. Given the church's history with war, as well as the fact that "public policy" cannot be a simple stand-in for the moral formation that military service in the United States requires, I am wary of any system that implies that Christians have nothing to learn from institutions not named "church." Bell is not unaware of this danger. He repeats the word "primary" in several claims as a shield against an overwrought church/world distinction: "Just War (CD) is a practice of the Christian community. Therefore, the Christian faith is the *primary* source of moral guidance for what constitutes justice and injustice in waging war" (p. 75). "The *primary* purpose of the just war discipline is not to guide princes, presidents, and politicians who stand at the helm of nations and states" (p. 77). "The first function of Just War (CD) is not to guide modern states through the turbulent waters of international politics; rather, its *primary* function is to guide Christians (including Christian politicians) in loving God and serving their neighbors faithfully in the midst of wars and rumors of wars" (p. 77). Just War (CD) "does not assume that the nation state is either the *primary* anchor of Christians' identity or the most important ensemble of institutions in times of war" (p. 77).

In each of these examples, Bell attempts to prioritize the church without assuming that it is sufficient to assume the functions of the state entirely. But how much weight can the word "primary" bear, given its place alongside such a rigid division between discipleship and policy? (It is noteworthy that the word "primary" appears nowhere on the concise chart identifying the differences between Just War [CD] and Just War [PPC] in the book's appendix.) Further, what is gained and lost by pinning the attributes of Just War (CD) so closely to the inadequacies of Just War (PPC)?

Perhaps I can make the point more clearly by referring to an insight from the conclusion of Jennifer A. Herdt's *Putting on Virtue* (which I addressed in chapter 7). There she notes that the contemporary Protestant revival of virtue ethics involves a strong emphasis on the ecclesiological formation and location of virtue. She says that, within this revival, contamination of the community "is now to be avoided not through the individual's ceding moral agency to God but by locating each person's formation in Christian virtue within an emphatically defined social and institutional context." When thinking of Bell, we might underscore "emphatically defined social and institutional context." However, this trend worries Herdt, and she suggests that "once we concede that distinctively Christian virtues, like the virtues of non-Christians, develop through habituation, we should also recognize that this means that Christian identity is porous. What attending to habituation allows us to articulate is a *chastened* account of Christian distinctiveness, which can serve finally to free us from anxiety over the splendid vices and the threat of contamination."[20]

"Chastening," of course, was one of Ramsey's favorite terms, and it is noteworthy that he does not fit neatly into Bell's categories. This is perhaps because he has less anxiety about the threat of contamination than he does about habituation in the virtues, including moral limitations, necessary to wage justified war. Bell, it seems, recognizes this, since he wrote elsewhere of Ramsey's work: "War is disciplined as it is brought within the fold of the just war doctrine, itself a form of ordered love, which Ramsey understood to be about not simply a checklist of criteria but a configuration of institutions that would make war morally possible."[21] But to say that Ramsey views just-war doctrine as a "configuration of institutions" is not quite correct. After all, he understands that war is a practice. Indeed, all political endeavors are "a kind of doing."[22] For this reason he writes: "Statecraft is not primarily a matter of social engineering, of building institutions; it is rather a system of interacting *doings*."[23] Ramsey offers a definitively Christian proposal for moral formation, and it is one that prioritizes ecclesiology without denigrating the proper role of strategic thinking and institutional

20. Jennifer A. Herdt, *Putting on Virtue: The Legacy of the Splendid Vices* (Chicago: University of Chicago Press, 2008), p. 351.

21. Daniel M. Bell Jr., "The Way of God with the World: Hauerwas on War," in Charles R. Pinches, Kelly S. Johnson, and Charles M. Collier, eds., *Unsettling Arguments: A Festschrift on the Occasion of Stanley Hauerwas's 70th Birthday* (Eugene, OR: Wipf and Stock, 2010), p. 117.

22. Paul Ramsey, *The Just War: Force and Political Responsibility* (New York: Charles Scribner's Sons, 1968; reprint, Lanham, MD: Rowman and Littlefield, 1983), p. 525. It is also limiting to say that "Ramsey's effort to distance just war from the lesser evil logic is commendable and important" (Bell, "The Way of God with the World," p. 117). This is to read his work as a subtle but ultimately insignificant improvement on that of Reinhold Niebuhr.

23. Paul Ramsey, "Force and Political Responsibility," in Ernest W. Lefever, ed., *Ethics and World Politics: Four Perspectives* (Baltimore: Johns Hopkins University Press, 1972), p. 50.

political authority. As we discussed in the preceding chapter, Ramsey seeks alliances with political theorists, and he sees their insights as an important part of serious Christian reflection on the possibilities and responsibilities of political authority.[24]

Bell's Just War (PPC)/Just War (CD) dichotomy assumes Christian superiority on a number of issues, and that was precisely the sort of thing that caused Ramsey such irritation with Christian thinkers in his day. For instance, when speaking of the criterion of just cause, Bell writes:

> As a matter of statecraft, the only just cause for war is national self-defense. . . . Such, however, is not the case with just war as a form of Christian discipleship. This is because the Christian community, constituted as it is by virtues such as charity and fortitude and practices like hospitality, is much more other-directed than modern nation states.[25]

This sounds good in theory, and it works well as a reminder of how Christians embody practices of hospitality. But Bell seems to be making an empirical claim: the Christian community "is much more other-directed," while the "only" just cause within a theory of statecraft is self-defense.[26] Just War (PPC) is "justice for me" (p. 132). Just War (CD) is "other regarding" (p. 134). This dichotomy overstates the integrity of the real-world Christian community and entirely overlooks important work in political theory on justified humanitarian intervention, to give but one example.[27] Bell is surely right to highlight the ways the nation-state can present an idolatrous challenge to the church. But why suggest that Christians have a monopoly on meaningful reflection and purposeful action about causes and practices of war? Why hold public policy theorists responsible for the blunders of "nations," while claiming a superiority for the "other-regarding

24. For instance, Ramsey's engagement with secular theorists in "A Political Ethics Context" lacks the animosity toward secular thinking that characterizes Bell's account.

25. Bell, "Can a War against Terror Be Just?" p. 40. See also Bell, *Just War as Christian Discipleship,* pp. 131-36.

26. Bell, "Can a War against Terror Be Just?" p. 40.

27. Even political theorists who embrace something as individualistic as "cosmopolitanism" are reflecting on the importance of humanitarian intervention. For Christians, a cosmopolitan challenge to the primacy of nation-states may not persuade us away from the centrality of the ecclesial community, but we at least ought to take their arguments seriously. See, for instance, Cecile Fabre, *Cosmopolitan War* (Oxford: Oxford University Press, 2012). I am grateful to William Feldman for bringing these discussions of humanitarian intervention to my attention.

manner" of Just War (CD) without reference to actual Christian practices of waging (or abstaining from) war?[28] Again, this assumption that the church in theory is better than the behavior of "nations" in reality is just the kind of thing that infuriated Ramsey.[29] Bell's call to discipleship is an important one, but it isn't clear, on his account, that Christians have anything to learn from those who are not Christian, and he issues a special warning to stay away from secular political theorists, who are assumed to be, by default, apologists for the nation-state.

To repeat an important point, I am not suggesting that we should displace Bell's emphasis on the primacy of the church for Christian reflection on and participation in war. There is much to appreciate in his work concerning the daily habits and practices that are necessary for a discipleship capable of waging just war. What I am suggesting is that his constructive proposal is simply not equivalent to the empirical claim that Christians are "much more other-directed than modern nation-states."[30] Reflecting on his own denomination, the United Methodist Church, Bell writes this in an essay on Hauerwas and war: "Unfortunately, there is very little that identifies contemporary United Methodism as a distinctive body of Christians, certainly not any kind of disciplined commitment to either just war or pacifism or to a process of discerning between them. After all, George Bush was a United Methodist in good standing with the church."[31] Surely recognition of this reality should chasten Bell's attempt to describe — neatly — a division between "Christian discipleship" and "public policy." Even more surely, it should make us hesitant to describe the church as superior to other communities on matters of war.

Bell offers an important word about discipleship and the significance of the church for Christians who would cultivate virtues capable of sustaining the pursuit of justice. This is a word Ramsey desperately needs to hear.

28. Bell says: "Particularly over the last decade of the last century but continuing to the present day, the difficulty that the modern just war vision has had dealing with humanitarian intervention has been painfully displayed as nations have ignored or belatedly and/or ineffectively intervened in a number of what are termed humanitarian crises" (*Just War,* p. 132).

29. As G. Scott Davis wrote of Ramsey's work: "Justice proper can be attributed only to the city of God, but the character of this city is ineradicably mixed in this life, and such justice as can be found reflects only the various agreements of men. The judgments available to those *in media res* will always have their own justifications, and outside our heavenly home, there is no privileged ground from which to ascribe justice to causes" (Davis, " 'Et Quod Vis Fac': Paul Ramsey and Augustinian Ethics," *Journal of Religious Ethics* 19, no. 2 [1991]: 51).

30. Bell, "Can a War against Terror Be Just?" p. 40.

31. Bell, "The Way of God with the World," pp. 130-31.

For instance, Bell's emphasis on discipleship as central to justice corrects Ramsey's susceptibility to Reinhold Niebuhr's public/private division. He is right to say, "As a form of Christian discipleship the just war tradition is an extension or expression of those virtues that consistently characterize the Christian life, in peacetime as well as war."[32] Ramsey does not speak adequately about the connection between justice in war and justice in everyday life. Indeed, one challenge of this book has been to show how some of his insights into the practical reasoning required for all moral decision-making is present in his account of political authority.

Still, Ramsey sets an example by refusing to grant priority to those who write within the Christian tradition. He says in "The Case of the Curious Exception": "It ought not to be surprising if there are philosophical analyses that are useful in repairing some of the worst aspects of theological ethics, and Christian ethical understanding that may improve some of the best philosophy."[33] We may disagree with his reading of Thomas Schelling or Thomas E. Murray, to give two examples, but he makes an important statement simply by engaging with their work.[34] His work displays an ecclesiology much closer to the one provided by David Fergusson, who says: "In proclaiming the truth of Jesus, the church is not thereby committed to possessing all truth. The validity of its witness is compatible with the assumption that there is much to learn from other sources, traditions, and faiths."[35]

As I mentioned at the beginning of this chapter, Ramsey outlines an upper limit for the usefulness of strictly "natural" or "independent" considerations in Christian ethics. He refuses to compromise the theological foundation of his just-war reasoning. But, for Ramsey, this does not lead him to reject any and all forms of secular reasoning. It does not lead him into a neat division between discipleship and public policy. Nevertheless, while he may lack confidence in the ability of the ecclesial community to bridge the divide between this world and the coming kingdom, he lacks

32. Bell, "Can a War against Terror Be Just?" pp. 40, 39.

33. Ramsey, "The Case of the Curious Exception," p. 70.

34. Perhaps I misunderstand Bell's ecclesiology. Perhaps I downplay his indication that there is a "kernel of truth" in secular political reasoning. Nevertheless, the problem with the rigid discipleship/policy division is that, while it works in theory, it tempts Christians into a platform of superiority that denies the need of the church to learn anything from those who are not Christian.

35. David Fergusson, *Church, State and Civil Society* (Cambridge, UK: Cambridge University Press, 2004), p. 114.

no confidence in Christ. This brings us to the issue of Christology, where, it turns out, Bell and Ramsey have much in common.

Jesus and the Justice of God

In "Jesus, the Jews, and the Politics of God's Justice," Bell advances the central theological claim of his political writings: Jesus is "the justice of God," and "the identification of justice with this one person wreaks havoc with what justice is commonly understood to mean and to entail."[36] What does it mean to speak of Jesus as the justice of God?

> To begin with, justice is not extrinsic to Christian confessions and practices; it is not extrinsic to Jesus. Justice is not something that happens to Jesus or to which he submits. Jesus does not point to justice nor motivate us to go out and do some version of secular justice. Rather, Jesus in his person *is* the justice of God. . . . Jesus in his person is the enactment of God's justice, God's righteousness, God's longsuffering fidelity to the promises of redemption. Jesus is justice. (p. 97)

According to this argument, any Christian vision of justice that fails to see Jesus as the justice of God makes three crucial errors: it "displaces the church," "displaces Jesus," and "displaces the Jews in the same manner" (pp. 90-91). Instead, by "rereading" Romans to correct these errors, Bell concludes: "Jesus is the justice of God as the embodiment of God's fidelity to the covenant to redeem humanity, even in the face of humanity's cruciform rejection and rebellion" (p. 96).

Bell insists on the liturgical (and therefore ecclesial) character of this justice and points to Augustine's *City of God* as evidence. He says: "Augustine lauds Christianity not because Christians are somehow able to do more than pagans are able to do but because Christians are liturgically incorporated into Christ, who renders the impossible possible, namely, our praise and worship of God" (p. 98). There is dissonance between this account and the claims in *Just War as Christian Discipleship* highlighted above.[37] Here Bell includes a section entitled "Learning from Outsiders,"

36. Bell, "Jesus, the Jews, and the Politics of God's Justice," p. 89. Hereafter, page references to this essay appear in parentheses within the text.

37. As I said above, Bell's neat dichotomy between Just War (PPC) and Just War (CD)

and he notes, "There is no reason Christians should not or cannot learn from others what justice entails" (p. 109).[38]

The dissonance generated between Bell's Christocentric account and "pagan" and "secular" accounts of justice is nowhere clearer than in "the reconnecting of justice with its Jewish roots."[39] This "begins to come into focus when we consider that in the [Old Testament] matters of justice are frequently associated with a word pair, *mispat* and *sedaqah,* usually translated justice and righteousness" (p. 90). This pairing indicates that true justice is "redemptive and restorative . . . it redeems or saves." Jesus as the justice of God is the embodied fulfillment of *mispat* and *sedaqah,* which are "preeminently manifestations of God's faithful activity to renew and uphold the covenant relation with humanity, even in the face of human rebellion" (p. 100).

If I may say it, Bell's Christocentric account of justice bears striking resemblance to the central claims of Ramsey's *Basic Christian Ethics.* Where, precisely, is the difference between "justice . . . is not extrinsic to Jesus" (Bell, p. 97) and "Christian ethics and Christian political theory must be decisively and entirely Christocentric" (Ramsey, pp. 16-17)? Or between "subsuming justice under the divine order of charity" (Bell, p. 99) and "love is always the primary notion, justice derivative" (Ramsey, p. 243)? Between "justice is no longer about a strict rendering of what is due . . . justice is now oriented toward redemption" (Bell, p. 99) and "We must wrench our minds around from supposing that all the poor and weak of the earth need is 'equality before the law' or justice in the sense of equal opportunity and the devil take the hindmost. . . . Instead, partiality for them lies at the heart of the biblical notion of justice; this shows the influence of the vocabulary of salvation" (Ramsey, p. 10).

Remember that Ramsey opens his first book with the language of *mispat* and *sedaqah,* insisting that "[t]he righteousness *(tsedeq)* of God, then, actually borders on the meaning of *chesed,* or God's keeping troth, his

---

fails to account for the ambiguity and ambivalence of life in the City of God and City of Man. Here he notes that the "superiority" Augustine claims for the Christian community is not in what Christians are "somehow able to do." Rather, "Augustine argued that true justice is to be found in the Christian community, which was superior to pagan Rome because it worshiped the triune God whereas Rome did not" (p. 98).

38. It is not entirely clear whether Bell means here that Christians can learn from all "others" or only from "the others who are called Jews" (p. 109).

39. Hereafter, page references to Ramsey, *Basic Christian Ethics,* appear in parentheses in the text.

unwavering faithfulness in keeping the covenant" (Ramsey, p. 5). "Justice *(mishpat)* means what we today call justice *permeated* by the character of God's righteousness *(tsedeq)*" (p. 10). He refuses, in Bell's words, to "displace the Jews" in Christian ethics.[40] As I outlined in chapter 1, this refusal to displace Jesus and the Jews from Christian ethics raises a specific challenge for Ramsey, namely, the one of moving from covenant as the foundation of the community of Israel to covenant as the ground of the "human community" (Ramsey, p. 388). Bell faces this same difficulty, noting that seeing Jesus as the justice of God "proffers an account of justice that is at once tied to a particular people and person — the Jews and Jesus — and of universal scope — justice as restorative of human communion" (Bell, p. 101). Both thinkers offer similar answers: "[Israel's] nationalistic promise is not given without other words: 'in thee shall all the families of the earth be blessed' ";[41] "justice is not sectarian, and the people of God are to be about the welfare, the peace, and the justice of all persons" (Bell, p. 101).

In light of these similarities, is it possible that Ramsey's work continues to offer resources for a Christocentric ethic that sees Jesus as the justice of God? Common interpretations of his work would surely suggest not. They classify Ramsey among the liberals who lack the theological foundations necessary to contribute to the contemporary discussion. I believe, in fact, that Ramsey shows more awareness on this front than first appears, in part because he does not always make clear the extent to which he revisits and revises the errors of *Basic Christian Ethics* in later writings. Here, as has been the case so frequently in this book, *Speak Up for Just War or Pacifism* emerges as the key to understanding Ramsey's lasting contributions.

The Coming Kingdom and Participation in Christ

In 1987, Ramsey exchanged regular letters with his friend Stanley Hauerwas in preparation for a joint volume to be published under the title *Speak Up for Just War or Pacifism.* The letters address a range of theological and logistical issues related to the preparation of the manuscript (eventually they decided that Hauerwas's contribution would be listed as an epilogue).

40. Bell, "Jesus, the Jews, and the Politics of God's Justice," p. 91. On the first page of his first book, Ramsey writes: "The ethics of Jesus . . . cannot be understood without some understanding of the God of Abraham, Isaac, and Jacob, Moses and the prophets, the God of the people of the covenant" (Ramsey, *Basic Christian Ethics,* p. 1).

41. Ramsey, Unpublished Notes, Box 42, Ramsey Papers.

In one of those letters, dated March 6, 1987, Ramsey says: "I'll take the time here to tell you what I would change in BCE about eschatology." What follows is a lengthy discussion in which Ramsey proposes that he now considers not eschatology but Christology to be the "real issue."[42] While he explains in the text of *Speak Up* that Christology, rather than eschatology, is the basis of disagreements between pacifists and advocates of just war, only in this private correspondence does he link that assertion to a transition in his thinking since the publication of *Basic Christian Ethics.*

That letter from Ramsey to Hauerwas is not his first admission that his perspective on eschatology shifts from that first book. In the final chapter of *Nine Modern Moralists,* he flags a discussion of eschatology with this observation: "The above paragraph significantly changes the emphasis, but not the substance, of my interpretation of the relation between eschatology and ethics in Jesus' teachings in *Basic Christian Ethics.*"[43] He rejects Albert Schweitzer's notion of an interim ethic (as he had also done in *Basic Christian Ethics*). As Schweitzer is a central figure in this discussion of Christology, a brief examination of *The Quest of the Historical Jesus* will illuminate the significance of Ramsey's later comments.[44]

Schweitzer argues against eighteenth- and nineteenth-century attempts to interpret Jesus' moral teachings independently of his vision of the coming apocalypse. Against this view he argues, first, that those teachings must be seen in the context of his apocalyptic vision, that they must be interpreted as an "interim ethic" because of his sense of the coming apocalypse (p. 485). Second, most modern individuals of Christian faith hold views of the apocalypse radically different from those of Jesus. He notes that they are "incapable of translating his world-view from its late-Jewish form into their own forms of understanding" (p. 482). These conclusions present him with the challenge of reconciling the indispensability of Jesus' eschatological vision with the modern inability to adopt that vision.

Schweitzer's response is to call for modern analogues to the radical apocalyptic perspective. He notes that "a period can have a real and living relationship with Jesus only to the extent to which it thinks ethically and eschatologically within its own categories, and can produce in its own

42. Paul Ramsey to Stanley Hauerwas, March 6, 1987, Box 1, Ramsey/Hauerwas Papers, Perkins-Bostock Library, Duke University. Hereafter Ramsey to Hauerwas.

43. Ramsey, *Nine Modern Moralists,* p. 248.

44. Albert Schweitzer, *The Quest of the Historical Jesus: First Complete Edition,* ed. John Bowden, trans. W. Montgomery, J. R. Coates, Susan Cupitt, and John Bowden (London: SCM, 2000). Hereafter, page references to this work appear in parentheses in the text.

world-view equivalents of those desires and expectations which hold such a prominent position in his" (p. 483). Later he adds: "All that is required is that we think of realizing the kingdom by moral effort with the same passion as that with which he expected it to be realized by divine intervention" (p. 485). This means that while we cannot genuinely replicate the interim ethic, it is our ability to mimic the intensity of the apocalyptic vision bearing down on Jesus that will enable us to realize the kingdom.

Ramsey inherits the belief that Jesus has a distinctive apocalyptic vision that cannot be separated from his moral teachings. He also agrees that modern society contains many individuals who "no longer in any vivid or significant sense share the primitive perspective of apocalypse." He is thus faced with a challenge similar to Schweitzer's, except that he plainly rejects the idea that Jesus offers only an "interim ethic." Instead, Ramsey charts an alternative course by proposing a distinction in Jesus' ethics between those teachings "in which the effect of Jesus' kingdom-expectation may be seen mainly in their greater urgency or stepped-up intensity, but whose essential meaning may be translated without great loss into more moderate statements," and those teachings "whose very *content* and *meaning*, not simply the urgency associated with them, show the effect of Jesus' kingdom-expectation."[45]

The suggestion that there is a division of apocalyptic-content teachings and apocalyptic-intensity teachings is heavily criticized in secondary literature for its illegitimacy as an exegetical strategy.[46] I wish neither to rehash those debates here nor to defend Ramsey's position on this point. For the purposes of this discussion it is sufficient to observe that both classes of moral teachings are principally defined by their relationship to Jesus' eschatological vision. Shaun Casey may be right to say that Jesus' eschatological perspective is, for Ramsey, "a problem to be dealt with," but I do not think this also means that it is "morally insignificant."[47] Rather, as David H. Smith observes, "the 'apocalyptic' element which appeared to be a liability in the teaching of Jesus turns out to be its strongest

45. Ramsey, *Basic Christian Ethics*, pp. 31, 32, 34.

46. See, e.g., Jeffrey S. Siker, *Scripture and Ethics: Twentieth-Century Portraits* (New York: Oxford University Press, 1997), pp. 95-96; Stanley Hauerwas, "How Christian Ethics Became Medical Ethics: The Case of Paul Ramsey," in *Wilderness Wanderings* (Boulder, CO: Westview Press, 1997), pp. 131-34; Shaun A. Casey, "Eschatology and Statecraft in Paul Ramsey," *Studies in Christian Ethics* 21, no. 2 (2008): 176-77; Scott Davis, "'Et Quod Vis Fac,'" p. 34.

47. Casey, "Eschatology and Statecraft," pp. 174, 176.

asset."[48] Schweitzer's influence leads Ramsey to underscore the indispensability of eschatology in Christian ethics.

Ramsey retains this approach in *Nine Modern Moralists,* saying that ethics are "not understandable apart from the presence of God's kingdom."[49] On this occasion, however, he shifts the accent away from eschatology as "urgency and intensity."[50] He says: "It was not, as Schweitzer supposed, the imminent *coming* of the kingdom which produced Jesus' teachings as an 'interim ethic.' It was rather the *presence* of the kingdom which produced this unlimited estimate of what one man owes another in prompt and radical service." Having been criticized for his interpretation of Schweitzer, Ramsey tries to change the "emphasis but not the substance" of his early work.[51]

In his letter to Hauerwas twenty years later, Ramsey links the presence of the kingdom not to apocalyptic eschatology but to Christology. He writes that, in *Basic Christian Ethics,* "I was too enamored with Schweitzer's 'consistent eschatology.' Not that I bought that view of interim ethics; exactly the opposite. But I used him — or came out of his analysis of the extremity of Jesus' teaching — for pedagogical purposes." What he revises in his later thought is the idea that eschatology is the theological doctrine on which the ethics of Jesus stand or fall. He says: "I would go back now and speak also of the Kingdom already present, of the words 'The Son of Man is Lord also of the Sabbath,' giving full credit in Christian faith to the Messianic claims in the Gospels and in the mouth of Jesus (with no worry about trying to prove out Jesus' self-consciousness)."[52] The ground of ethics lies primarily in Jesus as Messiah rather than Jesus as apocalyptic figure, just as the role of the kingdom in ethics lies largely in the possibilities opened by its inbreaking presence rather than intensity afforded by its expectation. He says of this shift, "The upshot is to say that not [eschatology] but Christology . . . is the real issue."[53]

48. David H. Smith, "Paul Ramsey, Love and Killing," in James T. Johnson and David H. Smith, eds., *Love and Society: Essays in the Ethics of Paul Ramsey* (Missoula, MT: Scholars Press, 1974), p. 5.

49. Ramsey, *Nine Modern Moralists,* p. 248.

50. Ramsey, *Basic Christian Ethics,* p. 32.

51. Ramsey, *Nine Modern Moralists,* p. 248.

52. Ramsey to Hauerwas.

53. Ramsey to Hauerwas. Of course, as noted above, Ramsey wrote in *Basic Christian Ethics:* "Christian ethics and Christian political theory must be decisively and entirely Christocentric"(pp. 16-17). This is precisely why he suggested, stubbornly, that he was simply clarifying his earlier arguments.

The most heavily criticized section of this discussion in *Basic Christian Ethics* falls under the heading "In What Way, Then, Are the Teachings of Jesus Valid?" Ramsey recognizes that he must reformulate its central claim about the need to translate Jesus' radical apocalyptic vision. He assumes that an emphasis on the presence of the kingdom absolves such a need, as he said to Hauerwas: "But the shift from eschatology to Christology (minimally, and of course I don't mean these themes are separable) renders silly the statement . . . about translating the teachings from their original eschatological setting and language without any loss of what this means for morality." In typical fashion, however, Ramsey does not think that the shift invalidates "the essential argument about preferential loves, protecting the innocent, etc." His political ethic remains intact, only "the ground is just more clearly in Christ, not in the times coming."[54]

Accordingly, Ramsey recognizes that the "burning intensity" of Jesus' moral teachings arises not strictly from the eschatological setting, but from the nature of the messianic claims about Jesus. It is crucial, however, to remember that those messianic claims are in turn productive of an eschatological viewpoint — that is, eschatology is not altogether dismissed. In other words, Ramsey reverses his claim in *Basic Christian Ethics* that "Jesus did not bring the kingdom; his sense of the kingdom brought Jesus."[55] Around the same time as his exchange with Hauerwas, Ramsey observes in a published letter to James Gustafson that "the distinguishing feature is the role Christology plays in moral analysis and in life."[56]

These insights into Ramsey's mindset during the preparation of *Speak Up* contribute both to scholarship on Ramsey and wider considerations of the relationship between pacifist and nonpacifist Christians. On the more narrow point, I refer to a recent article by Shaun Casey published in *Studies in Christian Ethics.* Casey builds on the work of Charles Curran in arguing that Ramsey's eschatology was eventually "trumped" by political realism.[57] The exchange with Hauerwas makes clear that *Speak Up* is Ramsey's attempt to situate his political realism *within* a richer account of eschatology (via its interconnectedness to doctrines of Christology and creation). Eschatology is one of the principal doctrines driving his political

54. Ramsey to Hauerwas.

55. Ramsey, *Basic Christian Ethics,* p. 40. Thus Ramsey's later work suggests that Christians do not look to the future for the kingdom of God, but to Christ. See Ramsey, *Speak Up,* p. 43.

56. Paul Ramsey, "A Letter to James Gustafson," *Journal of Religious Ethics* 13 (1985): 83.

57. Casey, "Eschatology and Statecraft," p. 192.

realism; it is not a case of having to choose between one and the other. If anything "trumps" eschatology in Ramsey's later work, his proposed revisions to *Basic Christian Ethics* reveal that it was a renewed emphasis on the importance of Christology for moral theology (and thus for political realism). In light of these developments in *Speak Up,* I find it difficult to accept Casey's claim that "Ramsey violated his own early commitments to the primacy of theology to policy in the search for the public implications of the Christian faith."[58] (As with Bell, we encounter here a forced contrast between "policy" and "theology.")

This, however, points us to the second contribution of these letters, and one that concerns a wider theological discussion on the foundations of just war and pacifism. Ramsey's revisions emphasize the indispensability of the lordship of Christ for his political realism. This is most obvious in his frustration with Yoder and Hauerwas over their attempt to monopolize the claim to an ethic unintelligible without Christ. To Hauerwas he says: "I do suggest that both pacifist and nonpacifist Christians take *the life and teachings of Jesus* with utmost seriousness. . . . Theological ethicists should simply cease charging one another with failure to take Jesus seriously."[59] To Yoder he says: "My point there, however, is simply to say that there is nothing to be gained from adherents, from one or another of these actual or possible accounts of the person and work of Christ[,] saying of the others 'We all participate in Jesus; you in your way, I in *his.*' "[60] Ramsey places Christology rather than eschatology at the heart of differences over the Christian understanding of war and violent resistance, and in so doing he invites his readers into a discussion about the theological components of political ethics. He advances the discussion by refusing to sit comfortably with a pacifist monopoly on the political significance of the life, teachings, death, and resurrection of Christ.

Given that Bell advocates for just war as a form of Christian discipleship, we might expect him to appreciate Ramsey's resistance to having his Christology dismissed by the pacifists. But Bell dismisses Ramsey as well, and he misses the scriptural and theological content of *Basic Christian Ethics,* as well

58. Casey, "Eschatology and Statecraft." Ramsey's more technical account of the basic features of his political realism, "A Political Ethics Context for Strategic Thinking," is reprinted at the *end* of *Speak Up* for a reason: he first establishes the primacy of Christology, eschatology, and creation for theological ethics before taking up the more particular reading of politics as a realm of response and responsibility.

59. Ramsey, *Speak Up,* p. 38.

60. Ramsey, *Speak Up,* p. 114.

as the shifts Ramsey made between *Basic Christian Ethics* and *Speak Up.* In an essay about Hauerwas "on war," he replays criticisms of Ramsey's work:

> Ramsey's Christology is problematically wedded to a liberal Protestant moral vision of Jesus as primarily pattern and example. In particular, Jesus taught and modeled a principle of disinterested and nonresistant love, which, Ramsey famously noted, we follow at a distance. Against this Hauerwas asserts, "Jesus is not the teacher of love, but rather he is the herald of the Kingdom whose life makes possible a new way of existence." In other words, discipleship is not merely a matter of following rules or principles Jesus disclosed but of ontological union, of participation in a new way of life, that Jesus effects as disciples are joined to Christ through the church.[61]

This downplays both the Christocentric claims of *Basic Christian Ethics* and the significant developments in Ramsey's Christology in his later work. It misses the extent to which Ramsey does present just war as a practice of Christian disciples made possible by the inbreaking presence of the kingdom. It does so precisely because Ramsey refuses to think that his abandonment of those mistaken christological claims in *Basic Christian Ethics* requires the *invalidation* of the rules and principles governing justified warfare that he illuminated in the years between his first and last books. As is most clear in his writings on moral theory, Ramsey never suggests that, as Bell reads him, discipleship is "merely a matter of following rules or principles." He *always* perceives that concept as a mistaken view of faithfulness to the obligations derived from our creation in covenant, and he *revises* his earlier Christology to insist that, ultimately, discipleship is participation in Christ. This does not resolve the continued need for thoughtful reflection on the form such faithfulness takes; Ramsey is certainly not the last word on these matters. But it does clarify a significant misreading of his work, and it should invalidate any suggestion that his work "remains hobbled by Niebuhrian realism's theological deficiencies."[62] It should also demonstrate his congruence with Bell on precisely this point: "Because justice is participatory, there can be no true justice that does not finally participate in the One who is justice."[63]

61. Bell, "The Way of God with the World," p. 118.

62. Bell, "The Way of God with the World," p. 118.

63. Bell, "Jesus, the Jews, and the Politics of God's Justice," p. 98.

Later in his essay on Hauerwas, Bell writes: "While Niebuhrian realism may suffer from an inadequate Christology, a broadly Augustinian account of just war is quite compatible with the sanctificationist vision of ontological participation in Christ that Hauerwas advocates." He credits Ramsey with the recognition that "advocates of the just war need not necessarily commit the eschatological errors of realism, effectively banishing Christ from history and binding upon humanity the heavy burden of ensuring that history come out right." Still, he denies Ramsey access to the club of adequately theological Augustinians. "Neither the medieval church," he says, "nor contemporary advocates of just war like John Milbank manifest the ecclesiological (and therefore also political) deficiencies that haunt the likes of Niebuhr and Ramsey."[64]

This dismissal of Ramsey's Christology, which is common among contemporary ethicists, calls to mind our continuing need to heed his dual admonition to Hauerwas and Yoder, this time in italics: *"Theological ethicists should simply cease charging one another with failure to take Jesus seriously"* and *"There is nothing to be gained from . . . saying of the others 'We all participate in Jesus; you in your way, I in his.'"*[65] Just as the opening chapters of *Speak Up* invite an epilogue from Hauerwas that must wrestle anew with the theological differences between pacifist and nonpacifist Christians, so also does Ramsey's work invite his readers into a wrestling with him for insight and clarity in the field of political theology.[66] This is not the same as saying that we have captured the last word on the subject. The claims in *Basic Christian Ethics,* as Ramsey rightly recognizes, are untenable in some places, enduring in others. Yet, by way of his later admissions and revisions, he directs our attention to the significance of the doctrines of Christology, eschatology, and creation — even for those who would wage justified war.

64. Bell, "The Way of God with the World," pp. 121-22.

65. Ramsey, *Speak Up,* pp. 38, 114.

66. Hauerwas acknowledges that "Ramsey is right when he says that the difference between advocates of just war and pacifists is Christological," but later he adds: "So the issue again comes back to eschatology" (Hauerwas, "Epilogue," in *Speak Up,* pp. 162, 178). Hauerwas prefers Yoder's description of two overlapping eons and the introduction of new possibilities for faithfulness made possible by the inbreaking of the kingdom. He feels that Ramsey remains too enamored of a vision of eschatology as (far off) final judgment (rooted in an account of the kingdom as already/not yet).

Conclusion

What can we say, then, of Ramsey's contributions to contemporary Christian thinking about political authority and justified war, of which Bell is the leading figure? Earlier I pointed to this quotation as evidence of Ramsey's insistence that all justice originates in God's justice: Of "abstract values, standards of justice, or natural rights" he says in *Basic Christian Ethics:* "[W]hile justice may seldom arise *with* these, it does not arise *from* them. It arises from conformity to covenant conditions demanded by the God of truth and righteousness by which measurement alone human consent and intelligence become right."[67] Of course, saying "conformity to covenant" is not the same as saying "Jesus," which Bell's argument makes abundantly clear. (In both *Basic Christian Ethics* and *Speak Up,* Ramsey acknowledges the centrality of Christology, but he does not always speak so directly about Jesus in the years in between.) Here Bell's insistence that Jesus is God's justice makes Ramsey's tendency to write in theological shorthand appear all the more inadequate. Nonetheless, Ramsey relies on the language of covenant precisely because he believes that it directs readers back to Christ. When accused of lifting "principles" from the biblical text without accounting for its narrative structure, he replied, "Now heretofore I had supposed that steadfast covenant love *(hesed, agape),* least of all biblical perspectives, is capable of being 'freed from the narratives of scripture.' "[68]

Covenant may be a place to return to, then, especially because, as Bell himself demonstrates, covenant is central to the understanding that Jesus is God's justice. Here Ramsey's insistence on the connection between justice and covenant operates in a softer key than does Bell's sharp antagonism between public policy and discipleship. Recall that in the transition from *Basic Christian Ethics* to *Christian Ethics and the Sit-In,* Ramsey seeks an account of the connection between God's covenant with Israel and the covenant foundation of all human community. He turns to Barth and the doctrine of creation in an effort to connect the reality of our collective life together in political society to the reality of our creation in and toward a covenant relationship with God. Thus Ramsey speaks of politics as "organized covenant" and suggests that "political decision . . . should be guided by the righteousness of the God we know through the covenant, especially

67. Ramsey, *Basic Christian Ethics,* p. 388.

68. Paul Ramsey, "A Question (or Two) for Stanley Hauerwas," Box 41, Ramsey Papers, 6.

through the restoration of the covenant in Jesus Christ."[69] Bell hopes that his "Just War as Christian Discipleship" model will displace, for Christians, just war as a theory of statecraft, even as it "remains a vision of political ends and the ordering of human community." But he is captivated by a church/world distinction that seems stuck in a posture of condemnation of that which is not the church.[70] This was most evident in the sleight of hand that held public policy theorists responsible for the behavior of nation-states, while the description of "Christian discipleship" operated above the fray of actual church communities.

Ramsey can be a helpful teacher in exploring how a theology of covenant can help Christians give an account of politics and collective political life without, by default, making villains of those who provide secular theories of governance. This does not mean forsaking the christological core of Christian ethics, and it does not violate the location of just war within the church. After all, it was Ramsey who wrote, "The just-war tests . . . those criteria are *of* the church."[71] However, it may mean engaging more charitably with those who are not Christian. As I demonstrated in the first chapter, Ramsey's covenant/contract analogy may fail to unearth anything particularly useful for Christians in Rousseau's social contract theory, but he is at least operating on the assumption that Christians might be able to make connections with political philosophy rather than simply condemning it.

More importantly, as I demonstrated in chapter 6, Ramsey sees that theological reflection on God's steadfast covenant faithfulness can animate us away from the temptations of consequentialism and exceptionalism. He flatly refuses "our contemporary penchant for escape-clauses" precisely because it is a perverted way "to introduce creativity and sensitivity into the moral life."[72] Instead, Christians should cultivate creativity and sensitivity in the face of rapidly changing contemporary challenges by exploring the bonds of faithfulness to covenant. In this way, theological reflection on the possibilities and demands of covenant faithfulness makes possible the cultivation of virtue.

69. Paul Ramsey, *Christian Ethics and the Sit-In* (New York: Association Press, 1961), p. 50; *Basic Christian Ethics,* p. 388.

70. Bell, "Can a War against Terror Be Just?" p. 40.

71. Ramsey, *Speak Up,* p. 129. He also writes, in words that might surprise those who critique his ecclesiology: "Witness to peace in the world unfolds and overflows from the *real presence* of the peace of Christ in Word and Sacrament, sealing together the 'already/not yet' " (p. 48).

72. Ramsey, "The Case of the Curious Exception," p. 92.

This is not different from Bell's claim that Christian discipleship involves both rules and virtues; but the presence of covenant theology offers something Bell's account does not. Ramsey uses the language of covenant to honor the place of moral rules, all the while promoting deepening moral commitments and the rejection of utilitarian exceptionalism. This includes a commitment to virtue, but Ramsey's emphasis on covenant means that his position extends beyond simple debates about rules and virtues. Ramsey's commitment rests not on a rigid church/world distinction, but, to borrow John Bowlin's phrase, on the "repository of wisdom" that is the shared memory of God's embodied faithfulness to covenant.[73] He calls Christians to explore the creative possibilities opened up by the covenant at the heart of creation. In fact, creativity and the cultivation of virtue are precisely the marks of discipleship that will enable Christians to resist the temptations of the nation-state that Bell describes so vividly.

Finally, Ramsey's concern with the integrity of the church, which I examined in chapter 4, also emerges as a helpful voice in contemporary discussions. In *Who Speaks for the Church?* he condemns ecumenical pronouncements on specific policy initiatives precisely because they blandly recycle the deficiencies of situation ethics. The "bag of specifics" issued by ecumenical councils cannot be "brought to bear upon the realities in the midst of which the statesman lives and must decide and act."[74] In this he speaks against the use of a secularized "checklist" as strongly as Bell does, and he shares the belief that the primary task of the church is decidedly "not the determination of policy."[75] But he does so by speaking directly to the church as it is rather than appealing to a stylized and idealized ecclesiology.

Ramsey suggests that the church should resist issuing specific decrees and focus instead on articulating the proper theological significance of the structures and ends of political action. This is not the eradication of moral judgment in the churches. (Ramsey does not eschew political action altogether in these claims; rather, his principal call is for witness to theological truth that is "made ready for action."[76]) He attempts to highlight the pitfalls of parachuting into particular situations without a broader and

73. John Bowlin, *Contingency and Fortune in Aquinas' Ethics* (Cambridge, UK: Cambridge University Press, 1999), p. 90.

74. Paul Ramsey, *Who Speaks for the Church? A Critique of the 1966 Geneva Conference on Church and Society* (Nashville: Abingdon, 1967), pp. 35-36.

75. Ramsey, *The Just War,* p. 190.

76. Ramsey, *Who Speaks for the Church?* p. 46.

deeper understanding of Christian commitments and obligations, without an appreciation for the structures and purposes of political authority. This is similar to Bell's insistence that the just-war tradition should be "a manifestation of the same faithful discipleship that is on display in our life in times and places of peace."[77] Certainly, some of Ramsey's language is misplaced (e.g., the role of "theoretician" is too circumscribed), and Bell's account of discipleship enables a richer ecclesiology. But Ramsey's work contains every bit of Bell's concern for the integrity of the church amid the various demands and constraints of the modern nation-state.[78] Ramsey is the same author who unsympathetically condemned narrow ecumenical pronouncements as "the most barefaced secular sectarianism and but a new form of culture-Christianity."[79]

Ramsey's work is compatible with the turn toward the virtues in Christian ethics, as became evident, I trust, in chapter 6. Still, Bell's emphasis on discipleship and virtue offers important resources for those seeking to articulate a theory of justified war within Christian ethics, and he does much to show the difference a robust ecclesiology must make for just war as a form of discipleship. Perhaps most interestingly, the challenges that Bell faces closely resemble those that Ramsey faces in *Basic Christian Ethics,* even as they both affirm the centrality of Christ for Christian accounts of justice. Ramsey does not always answer these challenges adequately, but he helps us see the significance of certain questions and issues that remain with us. Those challenges and questions linger in his legacy and leave a considerable amount of work for those who would be Christian ethicists.

77. Bell, *Just War as Christian Discipleship,* p. 74.

78. Again, Bell's mistake is to assume that Ramsey offers no improvement over Niebuhr: Ramsey's "political vision continues to be crippled by the deficient ecclesiology that marred Niebuhr's work. . . . [H]is vision remains one of politics as statecraft" (Bell, "The Way of God with the World," p. 118). Bell denies the possibility of locating, within Ramsey's work, an account of governance within broader Christian theological claims about the purposes and structures of our created existence, even as he claims this possibility in his own work.

79. Ramsey, *Who Speaks for the Church?* pp. 54-55.

Conclusion

It is time to draw together the various strands of this book and reflect on Paul Ramsey's intellectual legacy, including his contributions to contemporary Christian political theology. Central themes of his work should be familiar at this point: refusal to elide Christian responsibility in a world of conflict; recognition of the ambiguity and contingency of all purposive endeavors; anxiety about the connection between repentance and agency; and an appreciation for the significance of prudence and practical reasoning for political judgment. The theological and cardinal virtues are never far from his attention, even as his virtue theory leaves much to be desired. While it would be wrong to call his work theologically shallow, he frequently abbreviates the central doctrines of creation, Christology, and eschatology with the shorthand language of covenant, justice, and love.

As I have demonstrated over the preceding chapters, most emerging scholars in theological ethics have found no substantial need for Ramsey's work. The common assumption is that he is simply more useful (and persuasive) as a casuistical writer addressing specific problems in specialized ethics. However, I believe that his disappearance from Christian ethics is a great loss, and the aim of this study has been to show that we still have much to learn from Ramsey, even as we admit and seek to correct his deficiencies. It is for this reason that I have said that the lasting insights from his work lie not in his insight into particular moral issues of his day, but in his broader theological understanding of political authority, judgment, contingency, and virtue. As I hope I have made apparent throughout these pages, Ramsey leaves behind several important resources (and questions) for contemporary Christian political theology.

To begin, there are the central themes that occupied the early chapters of this study:

The absolute and eternal sovereignty of God is the ground of all political power and authority.

Ramsey's earliest writings on political authority concern Israel's proper response to Yahweh's sovereignty over the political community. Israel does not "consent" to God's sovereignty, for the very existence of its life in community presumes and displays that sovereignty. Instead, faithfulness to the covenant is the Israelites' proper response. Since the God who calls and makes covenant with Israel also calls and makes covenant with all of creation, all political communities find their true reference in God's sovereignty. Faithfulness to the covenant is also our proper response.[1] Political authority, indeed all human agency, is only intelligible in light of the Creator's unending commitment to be in covenant relationship with its creatures. That steadfast commitment is made flesh in Jesus, and thus we witness to the image of Christ by entering and upholding steadfast covenants with our neighbors.[2]

Similarly, political judgment finds its true reference in God's judgment.

Ramsey's efforts at a theology of repentance include a recurring interplay between what is human (limited judgments, ostensible justice, and so on) and what is divine (eternal judgment, absolute justice, and so on). He repeatedly insists on the significance of the distinction precisely because he wants both to avoid the presumption that human judgments neatly reflect divine judgment and to grant to those limited judgments their due regard in created existence. This is why he so frequently expresses anxiety about a theology of repentance that "levels" all political judgment, rendering it impotent or insignificant. He attributes great moral import to particular political judgments of justice and injustice while simultaneously contextualizing those judgments in a theological account of divine sovereignty.

1. For this reason, Ramsey says, "As long as God's covenant endures, human community cannot rightly be grounded in anything else" (Paul Ramsey, *Basic Christian Ethics* [New York: Charles Scribner's Sons, 1950], p. 388).

2. Ramsey notes that our creation is "toward *steadfast* covenant, toward the image of Christ" (Paul Ramsey, *Deeds and Rules in Christian Ethics* [New York: Charles Scribner's Sons, 1965; Lanham, MD: University Press of America, 1967], p. 164).

Eschatological hope seals the conviction that God's steadfast faithfulness sets the pattern for Christian behavior in the world.

Ramsey warns Christians against expecting that faithfulness will yield, programmatically, a better world. Eschatological hope is no such rational calculus. Christians can trust, however, that the "*ultimate* consequences cannot be such as to render [the] performance of fidelity obligations *wrong.*"[3] The community can "actively seek for a better-ordered, more just, and longer-lasting peace on earth," even as it awaits "the consummation of the peaceable kingdom of Christ."[4] If Christian witness is rooted fundamentally in the imitation of God's steadfast faithfulness, then its gaze must also be fixed on the eschatological hope of God's promised redemption of all creation in Christ.

Response and responsibility are key elements of hope. Ramsey rejects moral theories that lack "breadth," by which he means the ability to make sustained moral judgments over time.[5] This is due to a theological error, precisely because Christian ethics is a discipline that must sustain notions of obligation and responsibility to God and to our neighbors.[6] As Ramsey learned from H. Richard Niebuhr, hope in action is always a form of response to God's saving work.

Where there is justification for responsible action, there must also be the limitations and obligations of love.

Throughout his writings, Ramsey refuses any suggestion that Christian political responsibility can be functionally equivalent to power politics (i.e., might makes right) or technical performance of the kind that never demands prudence, only calculation. Even in politics, Christians must adhere to the "Pauline prohibition" never to do evil that good may come (Rom. 3:8).[7] Yet he believes in the possibility of faithful Christian obedi-

3. Paul Ramsey, "The Case of the Curious Exception," in Gene H. Outka and Paul Ramsey, eds., *Norm and Context in Christian Ethics* (New York: Charles Scribner's Sons, 1968), p. 133.

4. Paul Ramsey, *Speak Up for Just War or Pacifism* (University Park: Pennsylvania State University Press, 1988), p. 35.

5. Act-agapism and situation ethics fail because they "can find no sustaining moral bond between the present moment of action and a later moment of action" (Ramsey, *Deeds and Rules,* p. 45).

6. For Ramsey, the heart of all agency lies in "forms of steadfastness in responsibility and accountability one to another," and to God (Ramsey, *Deeds and Rules,* p. 164).

7. "And why not say (as some people slander us by saying that we say), 'Let us do evil so that good may come'? Their condemnation is deserved!" (Rom. 3:8; NRSV).

ence, even within the political realm, and this means that there will be *justifications* for faithful action. It also means there will be *limitations* on faithful action delimited by certain fixed moral concepts (e.g., "murder . . . means the same whether this is done by individuals or states"), as well as *obligations* to faithful action, as Christians go "deeper and deeper into the meaning of covenant obligations."[8] As he so frequently reiterates, justified political action must fall within a matrix of obligation (to the neighbor and to God), justification (the course of action adheres to the norms that regulate and authorize militant action), and limitation (in short, the course of action does not violate principles of proportion and discrimination).[9] This is what Ramsey describes as the "tension among just-war teachings, by the fact that we are obliged to observe *all* the norms."[10]

Politics is inescapably contingent and temporal. It is a "kind of doing." In his reading of Luke 14, Ramsey observes that the king takes counsel rather than counting costs because statecraft lacks the control and precision of tower-building: "In politics there are no completed towers."[11] No legislation, movement, or leader, can escape the contingencies of political life, and appreciation of this reality is central to a Christian political theology. The political realm is also inescapably temporal — that is, it is characterized and governed by its movement through time. There are continual flows of action and reaction surrounding every political initiative, as well as matters of timing, expediency, and patience. For this reason, "Statecraft is not primarily a matter of social engineering, of building institutions; it is rather a system of interacting *doings.*"[12]

Accompanying these themes are several knotty issues that linger unresolved. These are questions to which Ramsey does not so much provide the answers as he does alert us to their continuing significance for theological ethics:

8. Paul Ramsey, *War and the Christian Conscience: How Shall Modern War Be Conducted Justly?* (Durham: Duke University Press, 1961), p. 11; Ramsey, "Case of the Curious Exception," p. 125.

9. One cannot go to war justly without all three, and commitment to their rigidity may require inaction in the face of conflict or surrender amid it.

10. Ramsey, *Speak Up,* p. 73.

11. Ramsey, *Speak Up,* p. 194.

12. Paul Ramsey, "Force and Political Responsibility," in Ernest W. Lefever, ed., *Ethics and World Politics: Four Perspectives* (Baltimore: Johns Hopkins University Press, 1972), p. 50.

What is the relationship between repentance and political judgment?
Ramsey struggles to provide an interpretation of political agency that both honors the necessity of repentance and encourages a constructive sense of moral purpose. His account of "deferred repentance" fails to accomplish this, and in other writings he proves to be overly wary of extravagant emotional responses to sin. Jennifer Herdt provides indispensable resources for this discussion. She illuminates Augustine's work, showing that imitation of the humility of Christ is the proper response to God's gift of agency. She also presents a "deflationary" account of hypocrisy from Aquinas, showing that the work of divine grace on human agency need not be antagonistic.[13] Still, this issue requires more than adjudicating between Augustine and Aquinas on moral agency. We need to continue to unpack the relationship between repentance and political judgment, precisely because, as Ramsey suggests, there must be more to political judgment than a soldier blubbering over gunpowder. The concern at the heart of his writings on this subject remains with us, namely the realization that a theology of repentance must have profound implications for an account of political authority.

If cultivation of virtue is the most appropriate response to a contingent world, how can virtue animate Christian response and responsibility amid the contingencies of politics?
Ramsey pursues a genuinely theological account of political authority that includes a moral vision for faithful obedience and, at the same time, remains sensitive to the realities and limitations of all political endeavors. Virtue emerges as a significant component of this effort, even as his work lacks an adequate account of cardinal and theological virtues. Eric Gregory illuminates the role of love as a "civic virtue," but he says less about the role of faith and hope in public life. John Bowlin offers considerable help in showing how the cultivation of virtue is a form of faithful response to a contingent world, but he says little of the unique political implications of these claims. Daniel M. Bell Jr. describes the liturgical formation necessary for the church to live out its everyday faithful moral judgments in times of war and peace; but he sees little possibility of virtue in the determination of public policy. Ramsey's work does not supplant these accounts of virtue, but neither do they provide complete answers to the questions he raises. This leaves much work to be done in theological eth-

13. Jennifer A. Herdt, *Putting on Virtue: The Legacy of the Splendid Vices* (Chicago: University of Chicago Press, 2008), pp. 58, 82.

ics on the cultivation of virtue in the context of political authority and responsibility.

How does prudence assist faith, hope, and love in the task of political judgment?

As early as *Nine Modern Moralists,* Ramsey suggests that prudence is an indispensable virtue, but his account of prudence remains fragmented. Contemporary authors take a similar course. Charles Mathewes treats prudence in relationship to providence, but prudence remains largely absent in his reflections on political authority.[14] Prudence appears, briefly, as a virtue that enables faithful embrace of justified war in *Just War as Christian Discipleship,* but Bell does not connect it to the work of the theological virtues.[15] We would do well, then, to explore the political implications of Bowlin's suggestion that prudence is crucially important as a regulating virtue for faith, hope, and love. Recall his insight that I noted earlier: "The principal mark of the virtuous is their ability to consider an object good in one setting while silencing its goodness in another."[16] If all moral judgment is difficult, due to contingency, then political judgments are particularly difficult — due to the ambiguity and complexity of political "settings," configurations of power, and authority. This calls for a richer theological account of the work of prudence — alongside faith, hope, and love — in political judgment.

What role can covenant play in contemporary political theology?

Judging rightly requires putting on virtue through habits of constancy and the cultivation of character. Can reflection on the theme of covenant contribute to this work? Ramsey thinks that it can, and he warns us against neglecting its political and theological significance. God's steadfast faithfulness to the covenant at the heart of creation is a witness and a pattern for Christian faithfulness. In particular, it calls Christians to pursue "occasions of faithfulness" to covenant rather than "ex-

14. See Charles Mathewes, *A Theology of Public Life* (Cambridge, UK: Cambridge University Press, 2007), pp. 102-3.

15. Bell says: "Prudence is more than mere deliberation but also involves 'seeing' in the sense that prudence involves recognizing the morally important features of a situation in order to determine what acts are appropriate and what rules applicable" (Daniel M. Bell Jr., *Just War as Christian Discipleship* [Grand Rapids: Brazos, 2009], p. 85).

16. John Bowlin, *Contingency and Fortune in Aquinas' Ethics* (Cambridge, UK: Cambridge University Press, 1999), p. 64.

emptions" from covenant.[17] Just as the marks of God's steadfast love are not demonstrated through exceptions or escape clauses, but deeper and deeper commitments to the covenant bond that began with Abraham and Sarah and reached fulfillment in Christ, Christians, too, are called to probe the depths of our responsibilities and obligations to creation and those created in the image of God. This creative work is never done, Ramsey suggests, patterned as it is on the one who created the world with an everlasting "call into covenant."[18]

Conclusion

A few years after Ramsey's death, the *Journal of Religious Ethics* published an issue honoring him and his unique contributions to the field. At the opening of an article on Ramsey's role in debates surrounding the ethics of nuclear warfare, Jeffrey Stout recounts an unsettling and challenging encounter with Ramsey that he had as a young undergraduate at Brown University. He concludes: "Many readers of the journal can probably tell a story like mine. First comes a moral awakening, with its youthful attachments to great causes or charismatic heroes; next an initial encounter with Ramsey; and then an unending and ambivalent struggle with his arguments. . . . Ramsey did not win you over all the way; he just changed your life forever." Ramsey's work is certainly not the kind that "wins you over all the way." Few, if any, of his publications do. Yet, as Stout says, Ramsey's work has a keen ability to "define the conceptual space within which other thinkers [have] to move even when they have not been persuaded to accept his conclusions."[19]

As I have tried to show, this is true even for those contemporary writers who are unaware of the extent to which his work defines their own. Ramsey's work established and continues to establish several crucial conceptual spaces in which we discuss issues such as love of God and love of neighbor, power and its moral limitations, and the politics of Jesus and the coming kingdom of God.

I have tried throughout these pages neither to shield Ramsey from

17. Ramsey, "Case of the Curious Exception," p. 125.

18. Paul Ramsey to Deborah Streeter, July 7, 1978, Box 24, Ramsey Papers.

19. Jeffrey Stout, "Ramsey and Others on Nuclear Ethics," *Journal of Religious Ethics* 19, no. 2 (1991): 210.

criticism nor to cover up his missteps. To elevate his work to untouchable status would be to shortcut the (crucial) pedagogical exercise of wrestling with the truths, insights, deficiencies, overstatements, and questions that fill the pages of his books. It would attempt to come full circle on the matter of theological ethics, something Ramsey never thought we could do in the eon of life "amid earthly kingdoms and empires."[20]

I have tried, instead, to read Ramsey charitably. I have tried to take seriously his belief that theological ethics is an ongoing conversation. He wrote late in his career, ironically but nevertheless truthfully: "I regard publication as only another form of communication. One reaches a larger audience, but the printed word is only a little less perishable than good conversation."[21] His writings, including the many unpublished letters and exchanges in the Paul Ramsey Papers, attest to the fact that those who pushed Ramsey for good conversation about his work found a partner willing to rethink even some of his earliest and most fundamental commitments. As one author wrote, Ramsey was, at his best, "challenging but never dismissive, assured but never closed to correction."[22]

If Ramsey has disappeared from contemporary Christian ethics, this is nowhere a greater loss than in the classroom. He admitted this difficulty late in his career when he wrote to Stanley Hauerwas, "I wouldn't know how to teach myself if I tried."[23] I believe, however, that Ramsey's work has abiding pedagogical value for those who will put in the effort necessary to teach his work. My highest aim for this book is the hope that it might assist those teachers who will still teach Ramsey and those students who will still learn from him. Those who continue to wrestle with his work will find in Ramsey a teacher still capable of challenging their presumptions, refining their commitments, and sharpening their minds. They will find in him an unparalleled companion in the work of theological ethics on this side of the plowshares.

20. Ramsey, *Speak Up,* p. 49.

21. Paul Ramsey, *Ethics at the Edges of Life* (New Haven: Yale University Press, 1978), p. xvi.

22. William Werpehowski, *American Protestant Ethics and the Legacy of H. Richard Niebuhr* (Washington, DC: Georgetown University Press, 2002), p. 33.

23. Paul Ramsey to Stanley Hauerwas, November 25, 1987, Stanley Hauerwas private collection. Used by permission.

Sources Cited or Consulted

Works by Paul Ramsey

1935 "Christianity and War." *Christian Advocate* 110, no. 4: 202-3.

1943 "The Manger, the Cross, and the Resurrection." *Christianity and Crisis* 3, no. 4: 2-5.

1944 "Natural Law and the Nature of Man." *Christendom* 9, no. 3: 369-81.

1946 "The Idealistic View of Moral Evil: Josiah Royce and Bernard Bosanquet." *Philosophy and Phenomenological Research* 6, no. 4: 554-89.

1946 "A Theology of Social Action." *Social Action* 23, no. 2: 4-34.

1946 "A Theory of Democracy: Idealistic or Christian?" *Ethics* 56, no. 4: 251-66.

1947 "A Theory of Virtue According to the Principles of the Reformation." *Journal of Religion* 27, no. 3: 178-96.

1949 "Elements of a Biblical Political Theory." *Journal of Religion* 29, no. 4: 258-83.

1950 *Basic Christian Ethics.* New York: Charles Scribner's Sons.

1951 "God's Grace and Man's Guilt." *Journal of Religion* 31, no. 1: 21-37.

1956 "No Morality without Immortality: Dostoevsky and the Meaning of Atheism." *Journal of Religion* 36, no. 2: 90-108.

1959 "Religious Aspects of Marxism." *Canadian Journal of Theology* 5, no. 3: 143-55.

1960 "The Politics of Fear." *Worldview* 3, no. 3: 4-7.

1961 *Christian Ethics and the Sit-In.* New York: Association Press.

1961 *War and the Christian Conscience: How Shall Modern War Be Conducted Justly?* Durham, NC: Duke University Press.

1962 *Nine Modern Moralists.* Englewood Cliffs, NJ: Prentice-Hall.

1962 "Turn Toward Just War." *Worldview* 5, no. 7-8: 8-13.

1964 "The Status and Advancement of Theological Scholarship in America." *The Christian Scholar* 47, no. 1: 7-23.

1964 "The Uses of Power." *Perkins School of Theology Journal* 18, no. 1: 13-24.

1965, 1967 *Deeds and Rules in Christian Ethics.* Edinburgh and London: Oliver and Boyd; New York: Charles Scribner's Sons.

1965 "Lehmann's Contextual Ethics and the Problem of Truth-Telling." *Theology Today* 21, no. 4: 466-75.

1966 "Two Concepts of General Rules in Christian Ethics." *Ethics* 76, no. 3: 192-207.

1967 "Counting the Costs." In *The Vietnam War: Christian Perspectives,* ed. Michael B. Hamilton, 24-44. Grand Rapids: Eerdmans.

1967 "Is Vietnam a Just War?" *Dialog* 6, no. 1: 19-29.

1967 "Two Extremes: Ramsey Replies to His Critics." *Dialog* 6, no. 3: 218-19.

1967 *Who Speaks for the Church? A Critique of the 1966 Geneva Conference on Church and Society.* Nashville: Abingdon Press.

1968 "The Case of the Curious Exception." In *Norm and Context in Christian Ethics,* edited by Gene H. Outka and Paul Ramsey, 67-135. London: SCM.

1968, 1983 *The Just War: Force and Political Responsibility.* New York: Charles Scribner's Sons; Lanham, MD: Rowman & Littlefield.

1968 *Norm and Context in Christian Ethics* (ed. with Gene H. Outka). New York: Charles Scribner's Sons.

1968 "Political Repentance Now!" *Christianity and Crisis* 28, no. 18: 247-52.

1968 "Politics as Science, Not Prophecy." *Worldview* 11, no. 1: 18-21.

1970 *The Patient as Person.* New Haven and London: Yale University Press.

1972 "Force and Political Responsibility." In *Ethics and World Politics: Four Perspectives,* edited by Ernest W. Lefever, 43-73. Baltimore and London: The Johns Hopkins University Press.

1972 "The MAD Nuclear Policy." *Worldview* 15, no. 11: 16-20.

1973 "The Just Revolution." *Worldview* 16, no. 10: 37-40.

1973 "Military Service as a Moral System." *Military Chaplains' Review* 2, no. 1: 8-21.

1973 "A Political Ethics Context for Strategic Thinking." In *Strategic Thinking and Its Moral Implications,* edited by Morton A. Kaplan, 101-47. Chicago: University of Chicago Center for Policy Study.

1976 "Some Rejoinders." *Journal of Religious Ethics* 4, no. 2: 185-237.

1978 *Doing Evil to Achieve Good: Moral Choice in Conflict Situations* (ed. with Richard McCormick). Chicago: Loyola University Press.

1978 *Ethics at the Edges of Life.* New Haven: Yale University Press.

1978 "Incommensurability and Indeterminacy in Moral Choice." In *Doing Evil to Achieve Good,* edited by Richard A. McCormick and Paul Ramsey, 69-144. Chicago: Loyola University Press.

1979 "Liturgy and Ethics." *Journal of Religious Ethics* 7, no. 2: 139-71.

1981 "Kant's Moral Theology or Religious Ethics." In *The Roots of Ethics,* edited by Daniel Callahan and H. Tristam Engelhardt Jr., 139-69. New York: Plenum Press.

1982 "Tradition and Reflection in Christian Life." *Perkins Journal* 35, no. 2: 46-56.

1985 "A Letter to James Gustafson." *Journal of Religious Ethics* 13: 71-100.
1988 *Speak Up for Just War or Pacifism.* University Park, PA: The Pennsylvania State University Press.

Other Sources Cited or Consulted

Allen, Joseph L. "The Discriminating Realism of Paul Ramsey." *Worldview* 12, no. 12 (1969): 13-17.

Attwood, David. *Paul Ramsey's Political Ethics.* Lanham, MD: Rowman & Littlefield, 1992.

Bainton, Roland H. *Christian Attitudes toward War and Peace.* Nashville: Abingdon, 1960.

Barth, Karl. *Church Dogmatics* III/1: *The Doctrine of Creation,* edited by G. W. Bromiley and T. F. Torrance and translated by J. W. Edwards, O. Bussey, and Harold Knight. Edinburgh: T&T Clark, 1958.

———. *Church Dogmatics* III/4: *The Doctrine of Creation,* edited by G. W. Bromiley and T. F. Torrance and translated by A. T. Mackay, T. H. L. Parker, H. Knight, H. A. Kennedy, and J. Marks. Edinburgh: T&T Clark, 1961.

Bell, Daniel M., Jr. "Can a War against Terror Be Just? Or, What Is Just War Good For?" *Crosscurrents* (Spring 2006).

———. "Jesus, the Jews, and the Politics of God's Justice." *Ex Auditu* 22 (2006).

———. *Just War as Christian Discipleship: Recentering the Tradition in the Church rather than the State.* Grand Rapids: Brazos, 2009.

———. "The Way of God with the World: Hauerwas on War." In *Unsettling Arguments: A Festschrift on the Occasion of Stanley Hauerwas's 70th Birthday,* edited by Charles R. Pinches, Kelly S. Johnson, and Charles M. Collier, 112-31. Eugene, OR: Wipf and Stock, 2010.

Benne, Robert. "The Neo-Augustinian Temptation." *First Things* 81 (March 1998).

Biggar, Nigel. "The New Testament and Violence: Round Two." *Studies in Christian Ethics* 23, no. 1 (February 2010): 73-80.

———. "Specify and Distinguish! Interpreting the New Testament on 'Non-Violence.'" *Studies in Christian Ethics* 22, no. 2 (May 2009): 164-84.

Bowlin, John. *Contingency and Fortune in Aquinas' Ethics.* Cambridge, UK: Cambridge University Press, 1999.

Burk, John K. "Moral Law, Privative Evil, and Christian Realism: Reconsidering Milbank's 'The Poverty of Niebuhrianism.'" *Studies in Christian Ethics* 22, no. 2 (2009): 208-25.

Burrows, Millar. *An Outline of Biblical Theology.* Philadelphia: Westminster, 1946.

Camenisch, Paul F. "Paul Ramsey's Task: Some Methodological Clarifications and Questions." In *Love and Society: Essays in the Ethics of Paul Ramsey,* edited by David H. Smith and James T. Johnson, 67-89. Missoula, MT: Scholars Press, 1974.

Carnahan, Kevin. *Reinhold Niebuhr and Paul Ramsey: Idealist and Pragmatic Christians on Politics, Philosophy, Religion, and War.* Lanham, MD: Lexington Books, 2010.

Carville, John. "Love Transforming Justice in the Christian Ethics of Paul Ramsey." S.T.D. diss. Washington, DC: Catholic University of America, 1974.

Casey, Shaun A. "Eschatology and Statecraft in Paul Ramsey." *Studies in Christian Ethics* 21, no. 2 (2008): 173-93.

Childress, James F. *Civil Disobedience and Political Obligation.* New Haven: Yale University Press, 1971.

Clinton, Bill. Interview by Tim Russert. "Meet the Press." NBC. Web. 30 September 2007.

Curran, Charles E. "Paul Ramsey and Traditional Roman Catholic Natural Law Theory." In *Love and Society: Essays in the Ethics of Paul Ramsey,* edited by James T. Johnson and David H. Smith. Missoula, MT: Scholars Press, 1974.

———. *Politics, Medicine and Christian Ethics.* Philadelphia: Fortress, 1973.

Dahl, Gordon J. "Repentance Rather Than Rationalization." *Dialog* 6, no. 2 (1967): 144-45.

Davis, Scott. "'Et Quod Vis Fac': Paul Ramsey and Augustinian Ethics." *Journal of Religious Ethics* 19, no. 2 (1991): 31-70.

Dershowitz, Alan M. "Should the Ticking Time Bomb Terrorist Be Tortured?" In *Why Terrorism Works,* 131-63. New Haven: Yale University Press, 2003.

Eisen, Robert. *The Peace and Violence of Judaism.* Oxford: Oxford University Press, 2011.

Evans, Donald. "Paul Ramsey on Exceptionless Moral Rules." In *Love and Society: Essays in the Ethics of Paul Ramsey,* edited by David H. Smith and James T. Johnson, 19-46. Missoula, MT: Scholars Press, 1974.

Fabre, Cecile. *Cosmopolitan War.* Oxford: Oxford University Press, 2012.

Fergusson, David. *Church, State and Civil Society.* Cambridge, UK: Cambridge University Press, 2004.

Fletcher, Joseph. *Situation Ethics.* London: SCM, 1966.

Ford, David F. "An Interfaith Wisdom: Scriptural Reasoning between Jews, Christians and Muslims." In *The Promise of Scriptural Reasoning,* edited by David F. Ford and C. C. Pecknold, 1-22. Malden, MA: Blackwell Publishing, 2006.

Frankena, William K. "Love and Principle in Christian Ethics." In *Faith and Philosophy,* edited by Alvin Plantinga, 203-25. Grand Rapids: Eerdmans, 1964.

Green, Philip. *Deadly Logic: The Theory of Nuclear Deterrence.* Columbus: Ohio State University Press, 1966.

Gregory, Eric. "Before the Original Position: The Neo-Orthodox Theology of a Young John Rawls." *Journal of Religious Ethics* 35, no. 2 (2007): 179-206.

———. *Politics and the Order of Love: An Augustinian Ethic of Democratic Citizenship.* Chicago: University of Chicago Press, 2008.

Grotius, Hugo. *De jure belli ac pacis libri tres.* Translated by Francis W. Kelsey. Classics of International Law 3. Oxford: Clarendon Press, 1913-1925.

———. "The Right of War and Peace." In *From Irenaeus to Grotius: A Sourcebook in Christian Political Thought,* edited by Oliver O'Donovan and Joan Lockwood O'Donovan, 792-97. Grand Rapids: Eerdmans, 1999.

Gustafson, James M. "Context Versus Principle: A Misplaced Debate in Christian Ethics." *Harvard Theological Review* 58 (1965): 171-202.

———. *Ethics from a Theocentric Perspective.* Vol. 2. Chicago: University of Chicago Press, 1984.

———. "How Does Love Reign?" *The Christian Century* 83, no. 20 (1966): 654-55.

Harris, Charles E. "Love as the Basic Moral Principle in Paul Ramsey's Ethics." *Journal of Religious Ethics* 4, no. 2 (1976): 239-58.

Hauerwas, Stanley. "How Christian Ethics Became Medical Ethics: The Case of Paul Ramsey." In *Wilderness Wanderings,* 124-40. Boulder, CO: Westview Press, 1997.

———. "Situation Ethics, Moral Notions, and Moral Theology." In *Vision and Virtue.* Notre Dame, IN: University of Notre Dame Press, 1974.

———. *War and the American Difference: Theological Reflections on War and National Identity.* Grand Rapids: Baker Academic, 2011.

Hauerwas, Stanley, and Charles Pinches. *Christians among the Virtues.* Notre Dame, IN: University of Notre Dame Press, 1997.

Hays, Richard B. *The Moral Vision of the New Testament: A Contemporary Introduction to New Testament Ethics.* San Francisco: HarperSanFrancisco, 1996.

———. "Narrate and Embody: A Response to Nigel Biggar." *Studies in Christian Ethics* 22, no. 2 (May 2009): 185-98.

———. "The Thorny Task of Reconciliation: Another Response to Nigel Biggar." *Studies in Christian Ethics* 23, no. 1 (February 2010): 81-86.

Hendel, Charles W. "The Meaning of Obligation." In *Contemporary Idealism in America,* edited by Clifford Barrett, 237-96. New York: Macmillan, 1932.

Herdt, Jennifer A. *Putting on Virtue: The Legacy of the Splendid Vices.* Chicago: University of Chicago Press, 2008.

Hollowell, Adam E., and John K. Burk. "Paul Ramsey and Reinhold Niebuhr on a Public Theology of Tragedy and the Problem of Dirty Hands." *International Journal of Public Theology* 5, no. 4 (2011): 458-75.

Hoyer, Robert. "Sad Self-Justification." *Dialog* 6, no. 2 (1967): 142-44.

Jackson, Timothy P. *The Priority of Love: Christian Charity and Social Justice.* Princeton: Princeton University Press, 2003.

Johnson, James T. "Morality and Force in Statecraft: Paul Ramsey and the Just War Tradition." In *Love and Society: Essays in the Ethics of Paul Ramsey,* edited by David H. Smith and James T. Johnson, 93-114. Missoula, MT: Scholars Press, 1974.

Johnson, James T., and David H. Smith, eds. *Love and Society: Essays in the Ethics of Paul Ramsey.* Missoula, MT: Scholars Press, 1974.

Jones, W. T. "Rousseau's General Will and the Problem of Consent." *Journal of the History of Philosophy* 25, no. 1 (1987): 105-30.

Krauthammer, Charles. "The Truth about Torture: It's Time to Be Honest about Doing Terrible Things." *Weekly Standard,* 5 December 2005.

Lee, Gregory W. "Republics and Their Loves: Rereading *City of God* 19." *Modern Theology* 27, no. 4 (October 2011).

Lehmann, Paul. *Ethics in a Christian Context.* London: SCM, 1966.

Little, David. "The Structure of Justification in the Political Ethics of Paul Ramsey." In *Love and Society: Essays in the Ethics of Paul Ramsey,* edited by David H. Smith and James T. Johnson, 139-62. Missoula, MT: Scholars Press, 1974.

Long, D. Stephen. *Tragedy, Tradition, Transformism: The Ethics of Paul Ramsey.* Boulder, CO: Westview Press, 1993.

Long, D. Stephen, and Stanley Hauerwas. Foreword to Paul Ramsey, *Basic Christian Ethics.* Louisville: Westminster John Knox Press; reprint, 1993.

Lovin, Robin W. "Covenantal Relationships and Political Legitimacy." *The Journal of Religion* 60, no. 1 (1980): 1-16.

———. "Reinhold Niebuhr: Does His Legacy Have a Future?" *Speaking of Faith,* National Public Radio, http://speakingoffaith.publicradio.org/programs/niebuhr-rediscovered/lovin-hauerwas.shtml. Accessed 30 May 2010.

———. *Reinhold Niebuhr and Christian Realism.* Cambridge, UK: Cambridge University Press, 1995.

MacIntyre, Alasdair. *After Virtue: A Study in Moral Theory.* London: Gerald Duckworth, 1981; 2nd ed., Notre Dame, IN: University of Notre Dame Press, 1984.

Markus, Robert. *Saeculum: History and Society in the Theology of Saint Augustine.* Cambridge, UK: Cambridge University Press, 1970.

Masters, Robert D. *The Political Philosophy of Rousseau.* Princeton: Princeton University Press, 1968.

Mathewes, Charles. "Book One: The Presumptuousness of Autobiography and the Paradoxes of Beginning." In *A Reader's Companion to Augustine's* Confessions, edited by Kim Paffenroth and Robert Kennedy. Louisville: Westminster John Knox Press, 2003.

———. *Evil and the Augustinian Tradition.* Cambridge, UK: Cambridge University Press, 2001.

———. *The Republic of Grace.* Grand Rapids: Eerdmans, 2010.

———. *A Theology of Public Life.* Cambridge, UK: Cambridge University Press, 2007.

McKenzie, Michael C. *Paul Ramsey's Ethics: The Power of 'Agape' in a Postmodern World.* Westport, CT: Praeger, 2001.

Milbank, John. "The Poverty of Niebuhrianism." In *The Word Made Strange: Theology, Language, Culture.* Oxford: Blackwell, 1997.

Miller, Richard B. "H. Richard Niebuhr's War Articles: A Transvaluation of Value." *Journal of Religion* 68 (1988): 242-62.

———. *Interpretations of Conflict: Ethics, Pacifism, and the Just-War Tradition.* Chicago: University of Chicago Press, 1991.

Miller, Richard B., ed. *War in the Twentieth Century: Sources in Theological Ethics.* Library of Theological Ethics. Louisville: Westminster John Knox Press, 1992.

Neuhaus, Richard John. *Speaking to the World: Four Protestant Perspectives.* Washington, DC: Ethics and Public Policy Center, 1983.

Niebuhr, H. Richard. *Christ and Culture.* New York: Harper & Row, 1951.

———. "The Christian Church and the World's Crisis." *Christianity and Society* 6, no. 3 (1941): 11-17.

———. "A Christian Interpretation of War." In *Theology, History, and Culture: Major Unpublished Writings,* by H. Richard Niebuhr, edited by William Stacy Johnson, 159-73. New Haven and London: Yale University Press, 1996.

———. "The Grace of Doing Nothing." *The Christian Century* 49 (1932): 378-80.

———. "The Idea of Covenant and American Democracy." *Church History* 23, no. 2 (1954): 126-35.

———. "Is God in the War?" *The Christian Century* 59 (1942): 953-55.

———. "The Only Way into the Kingdom of God." *The Christian Century* 49 (1932): 447.

———. *The Responsible Self.* New York: Harper & Row, 1963.
———. "Utilitarian Christianity." *Christianity and Crisis* 6, no. 12 (1946): 3-5.
———. "War as Crucifixion." *The Christian Century* 60 (1943): 513-15.
———. "War as the Judgment of God." *The Christian Century* 59 (1942): 630-33.
Niebuhr, Reinhold. "Augustine's Political Realism." In *Christian Realism and Political Problems,* 119-46. New York: Charles Scribner's Sons, 1956.
———. "Do the State and the Nation Belong to God or the Devil?" in *Faith and Politics,* edited by Ronald Stone. New York: George Braziller, 1968.
———. *An Interpretation of Christian Ethics.* New York: Harper & Brothers, 1935.
———. *The Irony of American History.* New York: Charles Scribner's Sons, 1952.
———. *Moral Man and Immoral Society.* New York: Charles Scribner's Sons, 1932.
———. *The Nature and Destiny of Man.* Vol. 1: *Human Nature.* Louisville: Westminster John Knox Press, 1996.
———. *The Nature and Destiny of Man.* Vol. 2: *Human Destiny.* Louisville: Westminster John Knox Press, 1996.
———. "Theology and Political Thought in the Western World." In *Faith and Politics,* edited by Ronald Stone. New York: George Braziller, 1968.
O'Brien, Edwin F. "The Origin and Development of Moral Principles in the Writings of Paul Ramsey." S.T.D. diss. Pontificate University of St. Thomas, 1976.
Odgers, W. Blake. "A Defence of Rousseau's Theory of the Social Contract." *Journal of the Society of Comparative Legislation* 16, no. 2 (1916): 322-32.
O'Donovan, Oliver. *The Just War Revisited.* Cambridge, UK: Cambridge University Press, 2003.
———. "Karl Barth and Paul Ramsey's 'Uses of Power.'" In *Bonds of Imperfection,* edited by Oliver O'Donovan and Joan Lockwood O'Donovan, 246-75. Grand Rapids: Eerdmans, 2004.
———. "Obituary: Paul Ramsey (1913-1988)." *Studies in Christian Ethics* 1, no. 1 (1988): 82-90.
———. *Resurrection and Moral Order: An Outline of Evangelical Ethics.* Grand Rapids: Eerdmans, 1994.
———. *Ways of Judgment.* Grand Rapids: Eerdmans, 2005.
Porter, Jean. *Moral Action and Christian Ethics.* Cambridge, UK: Cambridge University Press, 1995.
———. "Torture and the Christian Conscience: A Response to Jeremy Waldron." *Scottish Journal of Theology* 61, no. 3 (2008): 340-58.
Rousseau, Jean Jacques. *The Discourses and Other Early Political Writings.* Edited and translated by Victor Gourevitch. Cambridge Texts in the History of Political Thought. Cambridge, UK: Cambridge University Press, 1997.
———. *The Social Contract and Other Later Political Writings.* Edited and translated by Victor Gourevitch. Cambridge Texts in the History of Political Thought. Cambridge, UK: Cambridge University Press, 1997.
Schelling, Thomas. *The Strategy of Conflict.* Cambridge, MA: Harvard University Press, 1960.
Schweitzer, Albert. *The Quest of the Historical Jesus: First Complete Edition.* Edited by John Bowden and translated by W. Montgomery, J. R. Coates, Susan Cupitt, and John Bowden. London: SCM, 2000.

Sichol, Marcia. *The Making of a Nuclear Peace.* Washington, DC: Georgetown University Press, 1990.

Siker, Jeffrey S. *Scripture and Ethics: Twentieth-Century Portraits.* New York and Oxford: Oxford University Press, 1997.

Smith, David H. "Paul Ramsey, Love and Killing." In *Love and Society: Essays in the Ethics of Paul Ramsey,* edited by James T. Johnson and David H. Smith, 3-17. Missoula, MT: Scholars Press, 1974.

Stevenson, William R., Jr. *Christian Love and Just War: Moral Paradox and Political Life in St. Augustine and His Modern Interpreters.* Macon, GA: Mercer University Press, 1987.

Stout, Jeffrey. *Democracy and Tradition.* Princeton: Princeton University Press, 2004.

———. "Ramsey and Others on Nuclear Ethics." *Journal of Religious Ethics* 19, no. 2 (1991): 209-37.

Thielicke, Helmut. *Theological Ethics.* Vol. 2: *Politics,* edited by William H. Lazareth. London: Adam & Charles Black, 1969.

Torrance, T. F. "God and the Contingent World." *Zygon* 14, no. 4 (December 1979): 332-33.

Turner, Philip. "Social Advocacy as a Moral Issue in Itself." *Journal of Religious Ethics* 19, no. 2 (1991): 157-82.

Vaux, Kenneth L., Sara Vaux, and Mark Stenberg, eds. *Covenants of Life: Contemporary Medical Ethics in Light of the Thought of Paul Ramsey.* Dordrecht: Kluwer Academic Publishers, 2002.

Waldron, Jeremy. "Torture and Positive Law: Jurisprudence for the White House." *Columbia Law Review* 105 (2005): 1681-1750.

———. "What Can Christian Teaching Add to the Debate about Torture?" *Theology Today* 63 (2006): 333.

Walters, LeRoy. "Historical Applications of the Just War Theory: Four Case Studies in Normative Ethics." In *Love and Society: Essays in the Ethics of Paul Ramsey,* edited by David H. Smith and James T. Johnson, 115-38. Missoula, MT: Scholars Press, 1974.

Walzer, Michael. *Just and Unjust Wars.* New York: Basic Books, 1977.

———. "Political Action: The Problem of Dirty Hands." *Philosophy and Public Affairs* 2, no. 2 (Winter 1973): 160-80.

Wells, Samuel. *Transforming Fate into Destiny: The Theological Ethics of Stanley Hauerwas.* Eugene, OR: Cascade Books, 1998.

Werpehowski, William. *American Protestant Ethics and the Legacy of H. Richard Niebuhr.* Washington, DC: Georgetown University Press, 2002.

———. "Christian Love and Covenant Faithfulness." *Journal of Religious Ethics* 19, no. 2 (1991): 104-32.

Werpehowski, William, and Stephen D. Crocco. Introduction to *The Essential Paul Ramsey: A Collection,* edited by William Werpehowski and Stephen D. Crocco, vii-xxv. New Haven and London: Yale University Press, 1994.

Yoder, John H. *The Original Revolution.* Scottdale, PA: Herald Press, 1971.

———. *The Politics of Jesus.* Grand Rapids: Eerdmans, 1972.

———. *When War Is Unjust.* Minneapolis: Augsburg, 1984.

Index

Index